GREAT PREACHING ON

PRAYER

GREAT PREACHING ON

PRAYER

COMPILED BY
CURTIS HUTSON

SWORD of the LORD
PUBLISHERS
P. O. BOX 1099, MURFREESBORO, TN 37133

Printed and Bound in the United States of America

Preface

"Why another book on prayer!"

Our thought is not to add another volume to an already crowded field, but rather to include in one book outstanding messages on one theme from outstanding men of the past and present which would have an appeal to all—the best sermons on prayer from 2,600 issues of THE SWORD OF THE LORD.

I have never tried to count all the promises in the Bible. Someone who has professed to do so says there are more than thirty thousand. And among these exceeding great and precious promises, there is probably no one so frequently repeated as the promise to hear and answer prayer. The expression "a prayer-hearing and a prayer-answering God" is one of the most common among Christians.

There is absolutely no substitute for prayer. Great preaching will not take its place, nor will a D.D. or a Ph.D., nor a winsome personality, nor a well-planned and executed promotional program, nor anything else.

Call the roll of history's spiritual giants—all were men of much prayer.

Hudson Taylor called it, *"Transacting business with God."*

Jonathan Edwards spoke of *"storming Heaven by prayer."*

Charles Finney said, *"Be full of prayer whenever you attempt to preach. . . ."*

E. M. Bounds wrote: *". . . we can curtail our praying and not realize the peril until the foundations are gone. Hurried devotions make weak faith, feeble convictions, questionable piety. To be little with God is to do little for God."*

A. C. Dixon expressed the need of prayer thus: *"When we depend upon our money, our teaching, our education, our preaching, we get what these can do. . . But when we depend upon prayer, we get what God can do."*

Prayer has divided seas, rolled up flowing waters, made flinty rocks gush into foundations, quenched flames of fire, muzzled lions, disarmed vipers, marshaled the stars against the wicked, stopped the course of the moon, burst open iron gates, conquered devils, commanded legions of angels down from Heaven. Prayer brought one man from the bottom of the sea and carried another in a chariot of fire to Heaven. WHAT HAS PRAYER NOT DONE!

We are here to tell you that believing prayer reaches the ear of God!

Why did Charles G. Finney, who saw as many as fifty thousand conversions in a single week, carry men with him to various places for revivals just to pray? Simply because he was convinced they would accomplish more than a team of talented singers, organists, pianists, song leaders and what have you. He was thoroughly persuaded, as were the old-timers who lustily sang the words penned by George Atkins:

> **Brethren, we have met to worship,**
> **And adore the Lord our God;**
> **Will you pray with all your power**
> **While we try to preach the Word?**
> **All is vain unless the Spirit**
> **Of the Holy One comes down;**
> **Brethren, pray, and holy manna**
> **Will be showered all around.**

You will find in this volume a new appreciation of the mighty power of prayer, a new understanding of the place prayer should have in our lives. You will learn again that prayer is the key that unlocks God's treasure-house.

From God's choicest servants you can learn that through prayer, we can claim the world for Christ. Each sermon is packed with practical suggestions.

Oh, may He who said, "Men ought always to pray, and not to faint," teach us all to pray!

Sword of the Lord Publishers

Table of Contents

  I. JOE HENRY HANKINS
     "Men Ought Always to Pray".....................9

 II. JOE HENRY HANKINS
     The Place of Prayer in Revivals..................21

III. BILLY SUNDAY
     Effectual Prayer...............................31

 IV. BILLY SUNDAY
     We Have a God Who Answers Prayer...........41

  V. CHARLES H. SPURGEON
     The Golden Key of Prayer.....................47

 VI. CHARLES H. SPURGEON
     Ask and Have.................................65

VII. CURTIS HUTSON
     Conditions to Answered Prayer................81

VIII. TOM MALONE
     "Is Any Thing Too Hard for the Lord?"..........93

 IX. DWIGHT L. MOODY
     Prevailing Prayer Requires Faith...............109

  X. DWIGHT L. MOODY
     Prayers of the Bible..........................119

XI. JOHN R. RICE
   "Open Thy Mouth Wide" 127

XII. HARRY J. HAGER
   The Power to Prevail 149

XIII. JOHN LINTON
   Unanswered Prayer 161

XIV. JESSE HENDLEY
   The Greatest Sin in America Today 171

XV. R. A. TORREY
   The Importance of Prayer 189

XVI. ROSALIND GOFORTH
   How I Know God Answers Prayer 203

XVII. CHARLES A. BLANCHARD
   *"Confess Your Faults One to Another,
   and Pray . . ."* 213

XVIII. CHARLES A. BLANCHARD
   "Always to Pray, and Not to Faint" 223

XIX. S. D. GORDON
   The Finnish Gold Story 233

JOE HENRY HANKINS
1889-1967

ABOUT THE MAN:

"He was a weeping prophet" is the way Dr. Hankins was characterized by those who knew him best—one of the 20th century's great soul-winning preachers.

BUT—Hankins preached sharply, strongly against sin. Would to God we had more men of his mettle in a ministry today that has largely been given over to namby-pamby, mealymouthed silence when it comes to strong preaching against sin.

Dr. John R. Rice wrote of him: *"His method and manifest spiritual power would remind one of D. L. Moody. He has the keen, scholarly, analytical mind of an R. A. Torrey, and the love and compassion of souls of a Wilbur Chapman."*

Hankins was born in Arkansas and saved as a youth. He graduated from high school in Pine Bluff, then from Quachita Baptist College. He held pastorates in Pine Bluff, Arkansas; in Whitewright, Greenville and Childress, Texas. His last and most productive pastorate was the First Baptist Church, Little Rock, Arkansas. There, in less than five years, 1,799 additions by letter, 1,144 by baptism—an average of 227 baptisms a year—made a total of 2,943 members added to the church. Sunday school spiralled to nearly 1,400; membership mushroomed to 3,200 despite a deletion of 882 to revise the rolls.

In 1942, Hankins gave up the pastorate for full-time evangelism.

In 1967, Dr. Hankins passed on to the Heaven he loved to preach about. Be sure that he was greeted by a thronging host of redeemed souls—saved under his Spirit-filled ministry.

I.

"Men Ought Always to Pray"

JOE HENRY HANKINS

"And he spake a parable unto them to this end, that men ought always to pray, and not to faint; Saying, There was in a city a judge, which feared not God, neither regarded man: And there was a widow in that city; and she came unto him, saying, Avenge me of mine adversary. And he would not for a while: but afterward he said within himself, Though I fear not God, nor regard man; Yet because this widow troubleth me, I will avenge her, lest by her continual coming she weary me. And the Lord said, Hear what the unjust judge saith. And shall not God avenge his own elect, which cry day and night unto him, though he bear long with them? I tell you that he will avenge them speedily." — Luke 18:1-8.

My text is the first verse, "Men ought always to pray, and not to faint."

For a long time in my Christian life I thought of prayer only as a privilege, as so many others do—a privilege to be exercised when we choose or to be left when we choose. Most of us exercise the privilege only when we need something from God. When everything is going along nicely and smoothly and the sun is shining, we are happy, the family is all well, and all of our physical needs are supplied, we have a tendency to push prayer into the background and forget.

Now prayer is one of the greatest privileges ever accorded God's people. But prayer is more than just a privilege. Jesus said, "Men *ought* always to pray," and with the word "ought" comes a sense of obligation.

Why is there an obligation resting upon us in the matter of prayer? Because it is in the plan of God that the forces of righteousness prevail in the battle against the world, the flesh, and the Devil, against sin and the hosts of wickedness; that we prevail when we pray; that we have power as we pray; that the work of the kingdom progresses as we pray;

that our churches prosper as we pray; that the Gospel reaches souls on the wings of prayer; that the Holy Spirit endues the preacher and the people of God as they pray.

Souls are saved when God's people pray. Oh, may we never forget what the Lord has said! When Zion travailed, sons and daughters were born. It is a part of God's plan, and when God's people fail to pray, men's souls go to Hell, the work of God languishes, the power is removed from us, and we become stale. We are formal and cold, careless, indifferent and worldly when we fail to pray.

Now if God has made it a part of His plan and if souls are saved when God's people travail in prayer, if the power of the Holy Spirit comes only as God's people pray, if the work of the kingdom of God prospers and the forces of God prevail only as God's people pray, then one of the greatest sins of which God's people are guilty is that of prayerlessness.

Oh, hear me tonight! We are in terrible plight because we have quit praying. We have gotten so busy with this, that and the other, so absorbed in the affairs of life, in the hurry, in the headlong rush of the world after things, that we haven't time to pray.

When the people of Israel sinned, they came to Samuel saying, "Pray for us, for we have sinned against God." The answer of that old man of God was, 'God forbid that I should ever sin in ceasing to pray for you.' In other words, if the time ever came when he failed to pray for them, he would be sinning against God.

When God's people forget to pray or get too busy to pray, we sin against God, the church, and a lost world. Oh, may God forgive us for the sin of prayerlessness!

When you fail to pray, you lose your passion for souls as well as your power. The awfulness of Hell fades out. But when a child of God lives on his knees, Hell becomes a reality, the condition of lost souls becomes real, the passion for souls burns in his heart, and the fire of God burns on the altar. The wheels of Zion move when people pray.

May God forgive us for our sin of prayerlessness while a world is going to Hell, while the foundations are crumbling from under us, while we are standing on the very verge of losing everything dear to our hearts and for which our forefathers have bled and died.

If there was ever a time when we ought to be on our faces before God, crying to Him like Israel did in Egypt until a mighty cry would go up to Heaven and God would say, "I have heard their cry, and I am going to deliver them"; if there was ever a time when God's people ought to besiege the throne of grace day and night, it is now.

Pray for the Unsaved

We ought to pray for unsaved people much more than we do. I have heard Christians, even preachers, say that they didn't believe in praying for the unsaved. I grant you that when a person is saved, he himself must make that final decision. If he hardens his heart and stiffens his neck, all the praying in the world can't save him. The heartbreak of a mother can't save a boy from Hell if he stiffens his neck and hardens his heart and determines to go to Hell. But praying can bring the power of God to convict a soul, can bring the Holy Spirit upon a lost soul, can move the feet of a lost man toward the house of God and work wonders in his salvation.

Did you know that Christians are the only intercessors that God has appointed to stand between a lost world and Hell and plead for their souls? You and I, saved and washed in the blood of Christ, have the Holy Spirit within us here on earth, making "intercession for us with groanings which cannot be uttered." We have the risen, glorified, ascended Redeemer at the right hand of God making intercession for us.

Have you ever thought what would happen if the Holy Spirit ceased His intercession for you? Have you ever thought what is going to happen to a lost world when God's appointed intercessors forget to pray for them and nobody else is left to stand in the breach, nobody else left to stand between the living and the dead to intercede for a poor, lost, dying, Hell-bound world?

That is why the world is plunging into Hell like it is now. That is why iniquity abounds. Churches have grown cold and worldly because God's people have been too busy about other things. We have forgotten to pray. Oh, prayer makes a mighty difference in the salvation of souls!

I am thinking now of an old mother whom I knew personally, who had a 19-year-old boy. He had gone away from home three years earlier, and she hadn't heard a word from him. A revival meeting was going on in their little country church.

One evening after service she, her husband and the rest of the family drove home in a two-horse wagon, like country people used to do. When they got to the gate that opened in to the lot, the mother got out and opened it. As her husband drove the wagon through, she said, "Daddy, go on and put the team up. I don't know when I'll be in. I'm going to pray for our boy out yonder somewhere in the world and on the road to Hell."

That mother slipped out through the orchard and under one of the fruit trees to tarry on her knees before God.

The next morning she came in, got breakfast for the family, and announced, "Daddy, I can't go to church today. I want to stay here and pray because our boy is out yonder somewhere lost. We don't know what is taking place in his life." All day long she prayed.

That boy told me the experience himself.

> I was down in Southwest Texas on a cattle ranch below San Antonio. I knew I was going to Hell just about as fast as a boy ever went at nineteen years of age. Late that afternoon I was riding that cow pony in a long lope over those hills on that cattle ranch, going to the ranch house, when suddenly something grabbed hold of my heart. I didn't understand, didn't know what was happening. I reined that pony up, jumped off, and went down on my knees by the side of that pony and prayed, "Lord, have mercy on me. Let me go back home."
>
> I hardly realized what I was saying, but when I got on that pony and rode up to the corral and saw the boss, I said, "I am going home tonight." When the boss asked me what had happened, I said, "I don't know, but I've got to go home."

The boss gave him his pay, and he boarded the midnight train. Just about sunup the next morning he walked up to the front-yard gate. When his old mother saw him, she began to shout the praises of God. He said that very day he went with her to the revival meeting and was gloriously saved.

A mother can pray her boy from the far country to the foot of the cross. We will never know until we get to Heaven how many are there because somebody wouldn't give up!

How we ought to pray for the unsaved! It makes a mighty big difference if an unsaved soul knows somebody is praying for him. He may be as hard as nails, he may be unkind, he may say hard things to you, but those prayers touch the cords that nothing else will ever touch.

When I was pastor at Childress, Texas, God put an unsaved young man and his unsaved wife on my heart. They had a fine three-year-old boy. I went into their home to talk and pray with them. Finally I won the wife to the Lord, but her husband was an awful sinner, a gambler and a drunkard. He told his wife, "If you get baptized tonight, I will not be here when you come home." She asked me what she should do.

I said, "God says that if you love father, mother, husband or wife more than Him, you are not worthy of Him." I asked, "Do you love the Lord?"

"Yes, I do."

"Then there is but one path. Follow it, and we will trust the Lord for the rest."

She came that night and was baptized. Sure enough—when she went home, her husband was gone. He stayed away for three weeks. I told her, "Just hold onto the Lord."

Finally he came back. Again and again I went by that filling station where he worked to talk with him. He was kind now and seemed glad when I came by.

After awhile I got him to come to the services at the church. One day I became so anxious for his salvation that during the invitation I walked off the platform and back to him. He resented it. I saw that I had to follow some other course. I asked God for wisdom. "If any of you lack wisdom, let him ask of God, that giveth to all men liberally, and upbraideth not" (Jas. 1:5).

God showed me what to do. When he came to the services, I would be standing at the door afterwards shaking hands with the people as they went out. Taking him by the hand, I would say, "I'm praying for you, Boy." He would grip my hand right tight and say, "Thank you, Preacher."

That went on for several weeks. One Sunday morning as he came out, I took him by the hand and said, "I'm still praying for you, Boy, and will keep on until you are either saved or have gone to Hell. I'll not give you up."

He took me by the hand, folded his hand and squeezed mine real tight and, with tears trickling down his cheeks, said, "God bless you, Preacher; keep it up. The Lord knows I need it. You'll never know what it means to an old sinner to know that somebody is praying for him."

The next Sunday morning after I had brought my message and given the invitation, he was the first one down the aisle. I was so happy that I jumped off the platform and ran down to meet him! About halfway down the aisle we met, and he threw both arms around me, put his head over on my shoulder, and wept for joy.

As we walked down to the altar together, he whispered in my ear, "Brother Hankins, would you mind if I say something to the people?" Of course, I didn't.

After we had gotten to the front, he took me bodily, turned me around, and with his arm around me, said, "Folks, listen! I'm a saved man this morning because this preacher and my wife wouldn't quit praying for me. If you could know what it means to a poor lost sinner to know that somebody won't quit praying for him, you would pray more for unsaved people."

Oh, how we ought to pray for lost souls!

Pray for Ourselves

How we ought, at the throne of grace, pray in behalf of our own lives! When Christians are in a world that hates us, we are up against the Devil in all of his subtlety. And the Devil is going to do his utmost to paralyze us, to close our mouth of testimony, and do everything else he can to make us useless in the kingdom of God. He knows that when we get saved, he can never get one of us as his own, but he has gone a long way to accomplish his purpose when he can shut our mouths and cause us to pass by on the other side with no testimony from our lips, no witnessing to a lost world.

More than that—if he can make you and me a compromising, worldly Christian, if the Devil can lead us into compromise about the truth of God and close our lips of testimony, if he can make us stumblingblocks over which sinners stumble into Hell, he will get many other souls thereby.

Practically every lost soul here in Chicago is stumbling over somebody tonight. Oh, what a tragedy! How we ought to ask God to keep us true, keep our feet in the straight and narrow. The Lord Jesus said it would be better for us to be cast into the sea rather than become a stumblingblock.

I have heard people say, "I would like to be a Christian, but I couldn't live it in the place where I work." Friend, prayer can make it where you can live it anywhere! But if you were put in the Garden of Eden and if you were to quit praying, the Devil would get you.

Daniel was taken into captivity as a seventeen-year-old lad. A thousand miles or more away from home, he was put in the most wicked court on the face of the earth, Babylon; subjected to every temptation, scorn and ridicule that could be heaped upon him. But Daniel lived there for God. When he was about eighty-five years of age, his bitterest enemy could find nothing of which to accuse him but his religion.

How did Daniel do it? Three times a day, on his knees, with his windows opened toward Jerusalem, he prayed to his God.

When our prayer life is like that, there will be victory. Wherever we are and whatever the surroundings, we will have a testimony that will turn sinners to the Lord Jesus Christ.

Pray for Our Homes

How we need to pray for our homes! The Devil is doing everything he can to destroy the American home. And when he does, he has destroyed the bulwark of Christianity, the bulwark of American liberty and American civilization. He has already practically destroyed the Lord's day, turning it into a fun day, a commercial day. The three great institutions upon which American liberty, religion and civilization were founded are the church, the Lord's day, and the old-fashioned Christian home. If the Devil can destroy those three, then he will have destroyed the foundation. And God said, "If the foundations be destroyed, what can the righteous do?"

How we ought to pray that the Devil will not destroy the family altar. Most homes don't have time for the family altar anymore. And when the Devil gets us too busy to have family altar, he has gone a long way toward destroying Christianity. The spirituality of your church or any other church cannot rise any higher than the spirituality of your homes.

We pray for the spiritual church. We pray for the power of the Spirit upon our churches. But it must start in the homes where we live six days out of seven.

I was reared around an old-fashioned family altar. We lived on a poor country farm. Mother and Dad and all the children worked in the field together. But we never worked too hard nor too late and were never too tired, but when the chores were done and the evening meal was through and we were ready for bed, for Daddy to get the family Bible down, lay it on Mother's lap, and us read the Word of God together, then get on our knees and pray. Beginning at the oldest and on down, we knelt around Mother's lap. She put her hands on our heads, called our names to God, and talked to Him about every one of us. She told Him the desires of her heart as we sat by the fireside.

Many a time since that day, when the Devil has had me in a close place, those experiences around a family altar kept me true. I can still feel those old hands resting on my head.

I was a college boy, away from home the first time. I was graduating that year, twenty-two years old. I thank God that I had a mother and father who taught their boys to live a life as clean as their sisters' and a father who set the example before his boys; who taught us if we sowed our wild oats we would have to reap them.

But I will tell you what happened. When Dad hitched up the horse to the buggy and put my trunk in the back, Mother followed me to the gate of that old farm home. I saw that she had her hands behind her when she came to the front gate and stood there, the last to tell me good-by. She wanted a private word with her oldest boy.

She said, "Son, you are going off to college now. You will stand on your own now, Son. You will make your own decisions now. You will meet temptations you never met before." Then she brought her hands from behind her and handed me a Bible. "Son, this is a lamp to your feet and a light for your pathway. Son, will you promise Mother that you will read it every day? And will you promise me that you will talk to God some time during the day and ask Him to help you, to strengthen you, to guide you?" I promised I would.

Daddy was waiting. As I started to turn to go on out to the buggy, Mother said, "Wait a minute, Son. You know our family altar hour is 9:00 o'clock. Son, as long as you and I live, at 9:00 o'clock Mother will be on her knees praying for you."

Later this hour came—the hour of my greatest temptation. The last football game was over, the last I would ever play. We had won. That night in Little Rock, Arkansas, the coach said, "Boys, we have been a great team. I'm going to turn you loose tonight. Go wherever you want, and have a good time."

In the room of a hotel the squad began to plan. That planning included the red-light district. I had never been in a place like that. I said, "Boys, I can't go." They began crooking their fingers at me and calling me "sissy," "tied to Mama's apron string," like boys will do. Finally I said, "All right, I'll go."

They got some liquor, and we started out. Every step I took my feet felt like hunks of lead. They grew heavier and heavier with every step. My heart was just about to break. But not wanting to be called a sissy and not wanting the crowd to make fun of me, I tagged along.

But while we walked an old clock in the courthouse began to strike. I counted: one, two, three, four, five, six, seven, eight, nine! It was about family-altar time at our home! I saw that little mother, that family altar. I felt those hands upon my head. I heard her pray, "God bless Joe. Keep him clean. Make him a good boy."

I made my decision. I said, "Listen, fellows! Call me whatever you please, but I'm not going any farther with you!" I turned and walked back to the hotel room.

At twenty-five years of age, when I came to the marriage altar, I brought the same in morals and character to her that my precious, sweet wife brought to me. Yes, I had something in me which I couldn't get away from.

Oh, how my heart goes out to boys and girls who have a thousand temptations where I had one! Many do not have the background I had. Mothers and fathers have gotten too busy after the things of the world and, in the rush and hurry, have broken down the family altar.

Pray for the Church

Oh, the church of the Lord Jesus Christ! Look back yonder in early days when the mighty power of God came. Look at her as she prays prison doors open. Look at her when persecution starts. She goes down on her face and prays until the very place is shaken where they are assembled, and they are all filled with the Holy Ghost; and with great power gave the apostles witness to the resurrection of the Lord Jesus, and great grace was upon them all, and five thousand in one service were brought into the kingdom of God! (See Acts, chapter 4 and verse 4.)

Oh, to see the church of the Lord Jesus Christ once again on her face, confessing her sins, shaking loose from the world, with a passion for souls, searching her heart and praying until the power of God falls once again!

I believe somehow God is going to do that. I am praying and standing on tiptoes expecting it. God can do it and wants to.

John Wesley was standing in Aldersgate, in London, England, when the Holy Spirit came upon him, set him on fire, and sent him out to turn England to God. An old black preacher went and stood right on that bronze tablet that marks the spot where Wesley stood, lifted his face toward Heaven, raised his hands up toward God while tears streamed down his face, and out of his heart cried, "Lord God, do it again! Do it again!"

That is the prayer of my poor heart tonight. Lord God, do it again! And God will do it again when His people pray.

"Men ought always to pray, and not to faint."

II.

The Place of Prayer in Revivals

JOE HENRY HANKINS

(Preached at Conference on Evangelism, Winona Lake, Indiana, 1945)

I will read two or three passages of Scripture for the basis of this message. In chapter 24 of the Gospel of Luke and verse 49, Jesus speaks these words to His disciples:

"And, behold, I send the promise of my Father upon you: but tarry ye in the city of Jerusalem, until ye be endued with power from on high."

Then in chapter 1 of the book of Acts, verses 13 and 14, we have this statement after Jesus had been taken up into Heaven:

"And when they were come in, they went up into an upper room, where abode both Peter, and James, and John, and Andrew, Philip, and Thomas, Bartholomew, and Matthew, James the son of Alphaeus, and Simon Zelotes, and Judas the brother of James. These all continued with one accord in prayer and supplication, with the women, and Mary the mother of Jesus, and with his brethren."

Then I call your attention to some very striking words in chapter 4 of the book of Acts. When persecution broke out, the first case of persecution, Peter and John were arrested and taken before the Sanhedrin, threatened and turned loose and commanded not to preach any more in the name of Jesus. Then they went back to the church.

I have often wondered what would happen today if the pastor were arrested, taken into court, beaten and threatened with death if he preached any more in the name of Christ. Probably the first thing we would do would be to get up a petition to the mayor of the town to stop such foolishness or to send a petition to the governor of the state; but this crowd took their case to the Supreme Court of the universe. In verses 31 and 33 we read:

"And when they had prayed, the place was shaken where they were assembled together; and they were all filled with the Holy Ghost, and they spake the word of God with boldness. . . And with great power gave the apostles witness of the resurrection of the Lord Jesus: and great grace was upon them all."

Dr. R. A. Torrey used to say:

> I have a theory, and I believe it to be true, that there is not a church, chapel, or mission on earth where you cannot have a revival, provided a little nucleus of faithful people will hold onto God until it comes.

Four men brought the revival to all the North of Ireland in 1859. Two were farmers, one a blacksmith, and one a schoolteacher. These four held onto God week after week. Though at first there seemed to be no results, the fire came at last. Ireland, Scotland, and Wales were shaken by the power of God. That has always been the experience of God's people through the ages.

God not only wants His people to pray, but He also wants them to agonize in prayer. I have this conviction, a conviction as deep as my soul, that there never was and never will be a real Holy Ghost, Heaven-sent revival until God's people agonize in prayer. I just do not believe that one ever comes any other way. When there is a revival, somebody has paid the price on his knees, though it be just one man or one woman. One person who is willing to stay at the throne of grace until God opens the windows of Heaven, one person who prays in the spirit of the song, "I Would Not Be Denied," can bring a revival from Heaven.

I have heard preachers say that Pentecost would never have come had it not been for that prayer meeting. But God had spoken all through the Old Testament of this day of Pentecost. Jesus had promised it. Pentecost would have come had nobody prayed. But I think it would have been a day without conversions and without the results had God's people not prayed. Three thousand conversions on that day were caused directly by ten days and ten nights in the Upper Room.

If I could stand before Simon Peter and discuss Pentecost, I would not take one bit of the honor, the glory, the credit from that great preacher of God for those three thousand souls that day. But Peter would tell me that we had given him far too much credit for what happened. Peter would say that his preaching was only the climax of something else; just a capstone, if you please, of the praying that went on.

Ten days of prayer, the outpouring of the Spirit of God, then 120 people in the power of the Holy Ghost gave testimony in at least fifteen different languages of the mighty work of God in their own lives. And when that was finished, Peter got up and preached. Who couldn't preach at a time like that! Three thousand souls were saved!

I. BIBLE EXAMPLES OF REVIVALS IN
ANSWER TO PRAYER

Every revival recorded in the Word of God, as far as I have been able to ascertain, was preceded by prayer, came in on the wings of prayer.

The other night I sat down and read through the book of Judges. Again and again I ran across this statement: "Israel sinned against God," "Israel served the gods of the Amorites and the Canaanites," and so on. But when Israel cried to God, He raised up a deliverer. The revival came when the cry to God came from the heart of His people.

In chapter 7 of I Samuel is a record of a mighty revival in Israel. If you read that entire account, you will find that Israel was just about at rock bottom; the people had gone down to the depths. I mean, everything was gone. Twice the Philistines had come in like a flood and plundered and murdered and burned whatever they could. They had taken away all their weapons. They had reduced them to abject poverty.

But Samuel, the man of God, called a meeting of the elders of Israel. The first thing they did was to confess their sins. They brought water and poured it out before the Lord, which typified the pouring out of their souls before and the dedication of everything to God. Then Samuel killed the sucking lamb and took the blood of the atoning sacrifice, put it on the altar of God, and lifted his heart to God in prayer.

Just at that time the Philistines heard of the gathering of the leaders of Israel, and they figured, "Now is the time to fall on them and blot them out. We will be through with this crowd forever now. They have all their leaders together, and at one stroke we can be rid of them."

Then the Philistines came into view and, the record says, "But God. . . . " There was the turning point every time to the children of God—when God stepped in. But God thundered from Heaven upon the Philistines.

It is different now. God's people, who have been the helpless victims of these same enemies before, have now confessed their sin. They have now laid themselves on the altar for God. They now come back and put their sins once again under the blood. And they are praying, led by that great prophet, Samuel. God thundered from Heaven, and confusion took hold of the Philistines. They fell on one another and slew one another in full view of the people of God, in answer to prayer and a confession of sin by the people of God and dedication of life and a putting of themselves under the blood again.

Brother, that will do the job anywhere, anytime, with any people!

Read the revival under Nehemiah. When God's people had been carried away captive and Jerusalem had been destroyed and the Temple had been torn down, word came to Nehemiah in the palace of Shushan. This broke his heart even though he himself was well established. As far as material things were concerned, he would never want for anything. But there was something to Nehemiah that was greater than material security. He sat down and fasted and wept and prayed until God moved upon the heart of the heathen king.

God is still able to make the wicked praise Him. God is still able to turn the devices of men to praise Him.

When I was just a lad, I read the story of that Negro slave orator, Frederick Douglas. To my thinking he was one of the greatest black orators ever born in America.

One day Frederick Douglas was addressing a group of his people. He was very much discouraged, sounding a low note, feeling in his heart that there was no future for his people and that they would never again see the light of freedom's hour.

Right in the midst of his speech a dear old black woman who loved the Lord and knew Him in an experience of grace, rose in the back of the house, raised her hand and said, "Mr. Douglas, may I ask you one question?"

The orator said, "Yes, you may."

"Mr. Douglas, am God dead?"

The orator was dumbfounded. He stood speechless for a moment, then answered, "Why, no; surely God is not dead!"

"Then might I ask you one more question? Am you a child of God?"

The orator replied, "Yes, I am. Praise the Lord!"

"Then, Mr. Douglas, as long as God lives, no child of His need despair."

God is still on His throne. He is still able. "I am with you always," said my Lord. He didn't say, "You go, and I will go with you." He didn't say, "I will go with you." He said, "I **am** with you." That means a lot more than "I **will go** with you." It is that eternal presence, "I am."

When Nehemiah prayed, God moved upon the heart of a heathen king. God provided an open door. God provided not only permission to rebuild the city of Jerusalem, but through that heathen king He provided the resources for the task.

They went back and rebuilt for God. When Nehemiah finished the walls of Jerusalem, he called the people together. How interesting to read in chapter 9 of that book how the revival really came!

The first thing the people did was to humble themselves before God. They clothed themselves in sackcloth and ashes, which signified not only humility but the confession of their absolute helplessness before God and their absolute dependence upon Him.

Then they separated themselves from all strangers. How we need to learn a lesson here. Separation! Separation!

Then for a fourth part of the day they stood up and read out of the Book of God, and for a fourth part of the day they confessed their sins.

Wouldn't you like to be in one more real old-time confession meeting, not where people stand up and say, "If I have done so and so, I hope the Lord will forgive me," but where people stand face to face with their sins and come clean for God?

In chapter 4 of Acts is another example. In the jail of Philippi is another biblical example of the coming of the mighty power of God in answer to prayer.

Paul had not accomplished much by his preaching in Philippi. About all that he had accomplished was the conversion of a few women and getting himself put in jail. But at the midnight hour while Paul and Silas prayed and sang praises to God, an earthquake came. The doors of the prison were opened, and every man's bands were loosed. A revival started in the Philippi jail in answer to prayer.

II. THE BIBLE FULL OF PROMISES OF REVIVAL IN ANSWER TO PRAYER

The Bible is not only full of examples of revival in answer to prayer, but the Bible is full of promises of revival and the power of God in answer to prayer. I put the two together because they are absolutely inseparable and synonymous. A revival means the power of the Holy Spirit coming upon the people of God. We can organize, preach, sing, have enthusiasm, have tent meetings; but we can have no revival without God's power. So many times we go far afield. We substitute pep many times for power. But there is no revival until the power of God comes upon the meeting. The two are synonymous.

The only worry I ever have about a revival campaign is in waiting until the power of God comes. When it comes, then I don't worry about it anymore. When God opens the flood gates, opens the windows of Heaven; when people can feel the thrill and the grip of the power of the divine Spirit, the revival has broken through, the beachhead has been established, victory is in sight; but not until then.

In II Chronicles 7:14 is that blessed promise to "my people, which are called by my name." I stop here to say that you will find that **the people of God** have always held the key.

Do not blame the sinners around us for lack of revival. Do not blame anything on outsiders. The people of God hold the key.

"If my people, which are called by my name, shall humble themselves, and pray, and seek my face, and turn from their wicked ways; then will I hear from heaven, and will forgive their sin, and will heal their land."

The reason we have such sin and such a flood of ungodliness is that there is not enough salt. A great deal of that which we have has lost its savor.

When Abraham stood yonder with the angel of God on that hill overlooking Sodom and Gomorrah, he said to that angel of God, "Wilt thou also destroy and not spare the place for the fifty righteous that are therein?"

God's answer was, "If I find in Sodom fifty righteous, then I will spare all the place for their sakes."

No doubt Abraham was thinking about Lot and his family who had been in Sodom all these years. He must have thought, *Surely Lot has won fifty people to God down there in these years.*

But then Abraham's courage failed. After God had said He would spare it for fifty, Abraham remembered what a selfish fellow, what a materially-minded fellow Lot was, contentious, worldly-minded; and Abraham must have said to himself, *I am afraid Lot may not have won fifty. I had better cut it down to forty.* Then he asked the Lord if He would spare the city if forty righteous could be found.

The Lord answered, "I will not destroy it for forty's sake."

His heart failed him again, knowing what he did about Lot: how he had tried to cheat him, how he had tried to take advantage of him; so now he asked, "Lord, would You spare it for thirty?"

"I will not destroy it if I find thirty there."

"For twenty?"

"Yes, for twenty I will spare Sodom."

Then Abraham must have thought, *Surely Lot has won ten during all his years there. He has a family of his own, with five or six children. Surely he has won them and a few others.* So again he asked, "Lord, would You spare it for ten?"

"Yes, for ten."

But Lot had so completely failed God that he had not even won his own family. And Sodom and Gomorrah went down under the curse and judgment of God because a family had failed.

The key is in the hands of the people of God.

"If my people, which are called by my name, shall humble themselves, and pray, and seek my face, and turn from their wicked ways; then will I hear from heaven, and will forgive their sin, and will heal their land."

Again I call your attention to that promise in Luke 24:49, ". . . tarry ye in the city of Jerusalem, until ye be endued with power from on high."

I am not much of a theologian, but I believe the Bible, and the Lord made this promise in Luke 11:13: "If ye then, being evil, know how to give good gifts unto your children: how much more shall your heavenly Father give the Holy Spirit to them that ask him?"

I believe with all of my heart in asking God for that divine power. I believe that He will give it in answer to prayer. You can talk about the Holy Spirit indwelling the believer—I believe that: you can talk about the Holy Spirit's being here upon the earth in this age to guide the church—I believe that: but I believe that a special outpouring and a special filling of the Spirit of God is given in answer to prayer and without that we shall never have a revival.

III. HISTORY FULL OF EXAMPLES OF REVIVALS IN ANSWER TO PRAYER

Not only is the Bible full of the promises of this power and the promises of revival and the promises of victory in answer to prayer, but history is full of examples of the people of God from the day of Pentecost until now.

Let me read you one or two testimonies.

One testimony is taken from the autobiography of Charles G. Finney. A tract had fallen into his hands, deeply impressing him; and he was speaking of the need of a revival being rekindled that had already started and died down. He said,

> . . . this article set me into a flood of weeping. I was at that time boarding with Mr. Gale, and I took the article to him. I was so overcome with a sense of the divine goodness in hearing and answering prayer and with a felt assurance that he would hear and answer prayer for the revival of his work in Adams, that I went through the house weeping aloud like a child.
>
> . . . At the next meeting of the young people, I proposed that we should observe a closet concert of prayer for the revival of God's work, that we should pray at sunrise, at noon, and at sunset, in our closets and continue this for one week, when we should come together again and see what farther was to be done.
>
> No other means were used for the revival of God's work. But the spirit of prayer was immediately poured out wonderfully upon the young converts. Before the week was out I learned that some of them, when they would attempt to observe this season of prayer, would lose all their strength and be unable to rise to their feet, or even stand upon their knees in their closets; and that some would lie prostrate on the floor, and pray with unutterable groanings for the out-pouring of the Spirit of God.

Finney's next statement reads:

> The Spirit was poured out, and before the week ended, all the meetings were thronged; and there was as much interest in religion, I think, as there had been at any time during the revival.

Listen to this same man in another testimony, speaking of a time when he and another man went out and prayed for a special service. In that prayer out there in the woods God gave a definite assurance of victory.

> As the time came for meeting, we left the woods and went to the village. The people were already thronging to the place of worship and those who had not already gone, seeing us go through the village, turned out of their stores and places of business, or threw down their ball clubs where they were playing upon the green and packed the house to its utmost capacity.

Then when he arose to preach, he had this to say:

> The Spirit of God came upon me with such power that it was

like opening a battery upon them. For more than an hour, perhaps for an hour and a half, the Word of God came through me to them in such a manner that I could see it was carrying all before it. It was a fire and a hammer breaking the rock and as the sword that was piercing to the dividing asunder of soul and spirit. I saw that a general conviction was spreading over the whole congregation. Many of them could not hold up their heads.

Brother, that is what my poor heart is crying for today. If God would put His Spirit like that on Charles G. Finney, God can do it to Joe Hankins. He is no respector of persons. God can do it to John Rice. That is what we need—not only what we need, but what we must have!

In the revival of Wales in 1905 (that is not an ancient time—many of you were living at that time, as I was), G. Campbell Morgan, that great preacher in England who was on the scene at the time of that mighty Welsh revival, went into his pulpit and preached this sermon from which I read an extract or two.

Let us look at the Welsh revival more generally. Let me speak of some of the incidental peculiarities of the revival as I saw it, and gathered information concerning it on the ground. In connection with the awakening there is no preaching, no order, no hymnbooks, no choirs, no organs, no collection, and finally, no advertising.

Think of that for a moment! Think of all our work. I am not saying these things are wrong. I simply want you to see what God was doing. G. Campbell Morgan continues:

There were the organs, but silent; the ministers, but among the people, rejoicing and prophesying with the rest, only there was no preaching. Yet the Welsh revival is the revival of preaching in Wales. Everybody is preaching. No order, yet it moves from day to day, week to week, county to county, with matchless precision, with the order of an attacking force. No song books, but ah, me, I nearly wept tonight over the singing of our last hymn. When the Welsh sing they abandon themselves to their singing. We sing as though we thought it would not be respectable to be heard by the one next to us. No choir, did I say? It was all choir!

Whence has it come? All over Wales—I am giving you roughly the result of the questioning of fifty or more persons at random in the week—a praying remnant has been agonizing before God about the state of the beloved land, and it is through prayer the answer of fire has come.

What effect is this work producing upon men? First of all, it is turning Christians everywhere into evangelists. There is nothing more remarkable about it than that, I think. People you never expected to see doing this kind of thing are becoming personal workers. The revival is characterized by the most remarkable confessions of sin, confessions that must be costly. I heard some of them, men rising who had been members of the church and officers of the church, confessing hidden sin in their heart, impurity committed and condoned, and seeking prayer for its putting away.

Then he mentions things in the way of a revival:

The church needs first to set itself to get things out of the way for God. What things? I do not know. All the things that are in His way: your habit that you know is unholy; your method in business that will not bear the light of day; your unforgiving heart toward a church member.

Oh, God forgive me that I mention anything! You know, you know! They are in God's way, these things. They must be cleared out. That is the first thing. There may be other things in God's way. Any organization in church life that does not make for the salvation of men is a fungus growth, and the sooner we drop it off the better. . . .

Are we ready to put things out of the way for God? I think we are. Oh, if there is anything, we must be prepared to sweep everything out for God to have highway.

Then hear his last word and that impassioned plea:

O God, lay the world's needs on our hearts. There is nothing so important as the saving of men, and when the church says that, and is ready, God will come. We need then to wait upon Him in earnest, constant prayer. Oh brothers, sisters, **pray! Pray! Pray** alone! Pray in secret.

1862-1935
WILLIAM ASHLEY SUNDAY

ABOUT THE MAN:

William Ashley (Billy) Sunday was converted from pro baseball to Christ at twenty-three but carried his athletic ability into the pulpit.

Born in Ames, Iowa, he lost his father to the Civil War and lived with his grandparents until age nine when he was taken to live in an orphanage. A life of hard work paid off in athletic prowess that brought him a contract with the Chicago White Stockings in 1883. His early success in baseball was diluted by strong drink; however, in 1886 he was converted at the Pacific Garden Mission in Chicago and became actively involved in Christian work.

Sunday held some three hundred crusades in thirty-nine years. It is estimated that a hundred million heard him speak in great tabernacles, and more than a quarter million people made a profession of faith in Christ as Saviour under his preaching. His long-time associate, Dr. Homer Rodeheaver, called him "the greatest gospel preacher since the Apostle Paul."

Billy Sunday was one of the most unusual evangelists of his day. He walked, ran, or jumped across the platform as he preached, sometimes breaking chairs. His controversial style brought criticism but won the admiration of millions. He attacked public evils, particularly the liquor industry, and was considered the most influential person in bringing about the prohibition legislation after World War I.

Many long remembered his famous quote: "I'm against sin. I'll kick it as long as I've got a foot, and I'll fight it as long as I've got a fist. I'll butt it as long as I've got a head. I'll bite it as long as I've got a tooth. And when I'm old and fistless and footless and toothless, I'll gum it till I go home to Glory and it goes home to perdition!"

Those who heard him never forgot him or his blazing, barehanded evangelism.

The evangelist died November 6, 1935, at age 72. His funeral was held in Moody Church, Chicago, and the sermon was by H. A. Ironside.

III.

Effectual Prayer

BILLY SUNDAY

"The effectual fervent prayer of a righteous man availeth much." —
James 5:16.

When Mrs. Browning asked Charles Kingsley for the secret of his
beautiful and attractive life, he replied, "Why, I have a friend."

If you can stand on the street and say to all who pass by, "They are
my friends," you are to be congratulated. But if you can look into the
face of a man and say, "All the world is my friend," you have made
a great mistake.

The friendship of the world is nothing to be compared with the friendship of the Lord. The only law half the people of the world today
recognize is the law of their own desires. I care nothing about the friendship of the world if I know I am pleasing God and have His sign of
approval.

There are two ways in which blessing will come from a life of prayer.
First, self-reflex blessing; second, indirect blessing which comes as a result
of the life of prayer and in answer to prayer.

A Life of Prayer Grows Radiant, Happy Christians

Henry Drummond tells of a young lady who was prepossessing and
attractive. When asked for the secret, each time she refused to reveal
it, always replying, "Wait until I am dead, then pry open the locket which
hangs about my neck, and you will discover the secret." When at last
she died, they pried open the locket and found this verse of Scripture,
"Whom having not seen I love."

Such is the transforming power of prayer, and I am talking from
experience.

Prayer helps us to realize the presence of God better than in any other way. If you can do anything to make you realize the presence of God, then do it. "In the secret of His presence how my soul delights to hide!" In the busy marts of trade, behind the counter selling your wares, in the homes or wherever we are, praying will help us to realize the presence of God.

Prayer helps us realize our dependence upon God. Jesus Christ is not weak, so lean on Him.

Jesus spent whole nights in prayer; and as He would come down from His all-night vigils, multitudes pressed upon Him for healing power, and virtue went out from Him.

It was after one of these all-night vigils and as a result of prayer that He did three important things. First, He chose twelve men to be His disciples, who formed the nucleus of the church today; second, the people pressed upon Him for His healing, and He fed the 5,000 hungry souls in the desert; third, He sat and taught those matchless precepts that we call the Sermon on the Mount, the like of which the world has never heard and never will hear again.

Spend a night in prayer, people of Pittsburgh, and you'll see wonderful results. The trouble with people today is that we are not willing to make a sacrifice for God. We are trying to play with God. The biggest farce in the modern church is the prayer meeting. It was the biggest victory the Devil ever won when he got the church to give up prayer.

Pray! When you get up from your knees, you are not likely to look at the world as you would through the bottom of a beer glass. Who are the people whose souls are most open and responsive, my friends, to the Spirit now? The crowds who are upholding the hands of the preacher in the prayer meeting.

Prayer opens the soul and makes it responsive and receptive to the influence of God. Many a preacher wants to win souls to Jesus Christ but is handicapped and his hands are tied by a godless, card-playing crowd. No wonder some wither and are powerless in revivals!

They have a lot of people in the church that never darken the doors of a prayer meeting. It's an insult to God to pray, "Thy kingdom come," then when the collection plate is passed, drop a nickel and have a hundred thousand in the bank. That stuff doesn't go with God.

When We Pray for God's Power and Blessing, We Should Work to Do His Will

You can't pray, "Thy kingdom come," then do everything in your power to prevent it from coming. So that prayer is a lie if you don't mean it.

You pray for God to save people in Pittsburgh, then sit around and play poker.

It is so with your prayer list. You can't pray honestly for the salvation of your husband and friends and not turn every stone to lead them to Christ. Your prayers are worth no more than you are willing to redeem in work.

Prayers are costly. God will hold you to them.

Livingstone prayed; and God said, "You pack your grip and go to Africa and answer your own prayer."

John G. Paton prayed, and God sent him to the New Hebrides.

Carey prayed, and God told him to go to India.

David Brainerd prayed; and God said, "Go to the Indians. Answer your own prayers."

You pray; and God says, "Go out into the neighborhood and answer your own prayer."

I have more respect for a man who shoves a gun under my nose than one who writes an anonymous letter. God treats any prayer without an effort like I do an anonymous letter. When I see an unsigned letter, I rip it up.

Prayer leads to activity. You can't honestly pray, "Save my boy," then not do anything in your power to further that end.

Men and women now are looking in my face who are not trying to get your prayers answered.

I was holding a meeting in Iowa. Every time I asked for those who wished to be remembered, a woman rose and asked prayer for her son. Every night at the invitation a young man got up and left. One night I saw the woman get up and follow him to a little restaurant, the loafing place of the town. She asked him to come back to the meeting, but he refused. She repeated her question several times. Still he refused. Then she said, "My son, I am ashamed of you, that you should care more for these young men who never did anything for you than you do for your mother who suffered for you and cared for you these many years." She then knelt down and prayed for him. Then the boy said to her, "Mother, your prayer is answered. I'll go."

Mothers, hold on and pray. He'll come. God will send you out after the one you're praying for.

Prayer impresses men with the character and mind of God and produces a corresponding desire to be like God in holiness, to hate sin, and to live out and out for Jesus Christ.

Prayer impresses you with submission to the will of God.

The God Who Put in Us an Instinct
to Pray, Wants to Answer Prayer

How do I know that God will answer prayer? There is an argument from the standpoint of instinct.

Who tells the birds that fly South in the winter that the leaves will be stripped from the trees and the ground will be covered with snow? Who tells the birds to come back when the leaves have come out and blossoms have burst forth?

Who told the bee to fly three miles to the clover patch and fly back with unerring instinct to its hive? If the hive were moved 50 feet while it was gone, it would fly to the spot where he left, straight as an arrow, but would not know enough to go that 50 feet.

Who tells the squirrel to lay up nuts in the North, when if the same squirrel were taken to the South, would not do so?

If God won't disappoint a bird, bee or a squirrel, He will grant your request when you ask Him. If God is great and good and is disposed to bless, why should He require me to ask? Why doesn't He give? It is advantageous to you. Why do you require your child to ask for anything? To make the child realize its relationship to you. It is natural. God is my Father, and it is necessary that I ask to show my relationship to Him.

Prayer, a Means of Growth

We grow by expression. When I first started out to be a Christian, I couldn't stand up in a prayer meeting and use three sentences consecutively, but I made it a rule and so I overcame my natural diffidence. God blesses me because I am determined to do something for Him. I could have sat still and withered and mildewed like a lot of you. God wants to develop us according to nature.

Take for instance the parent and the child. The child is taught to ask the parent. When the child comes to the parent and asks for bread, does he give him a stone? Do you think you know more than God? God wants us to pray because it is natural. God wishes you to pray because it is necessary.

The Lord is jealous. You've got the right to demand that your husband love you and he has the right to demand your love. But God has a better right to that love. When you think you know more than God, you are heading for trouble.

We get by giving. That's why the farmer sows seed. That's why we have gymnasiums. Give a little strength and get much. I am descendant of a consumptive family. When I was a boy, every little cold affected my lungs. I went to Chicago to the best instructors in the gymnasiums. I have preached for seventeen years and developed a physique that enables me to stand the strain I'm under now.

The reason some of you get so little is that you give so little to God. All you amount to is to count one more when the preacher goes to conference or the synod or whatever it may be. Half the church members could die, and the world would not lose anything in spiritual force.

The more I give up to prayer and the study of the Word of God, the more I develop spiritually. Remember, you are blessed in proportion to your obedience and your capacity to receive. I believe it is experimental religion. Half of the people don't know what it is to be converted. All they know about prayer they have read in a book.

God Answers Believing, Persistent Prayer

Prayer is assurance. All things whatsoever ye desire, ask and ye shall receive them. There are immediate as well as deferred answers to prayer. Daniel's answer to prayer was deferred twenty-three days. When you start praying, the Devil sends somebody to delay the answer. He is working just as hard to damn old Pittsburgh as Jesus Christ is working to save her. The Devil never takes a vacation. While you pray for a brother, the Devil or his band is working just as hard to keep him away. All the devils Hell can spare are turned loose in Pittsburgh for the next week. I think they must have abandoned some towns and turned the whole shooting match loose here.

Some people don't get an answer to their prayer because they are always looking down. Others seem to be omnipotent because they are in touch with God.

We went to a town in Indiana. Men met us as we got off the train; and one said, "I am president of a praying band of fifty-five men and women who are pledged to pray three times a day during the meetings. We will die for the meetings if necessary. If you will call me up any hour of the day or night, we will come to your help, every one of us, and pray it through and pull through whatever the trouble may be."

We saw the power of God get hold of that old town like a cyclone would a straw stack. There is nothing too hard for God if the church will get on her face and pray.

Hannah prayed to become the mother of a child. And God heard, and she became the mother of Samuel.

When Peter was in prison, the disciples prayed, and he was delivered into freedom.

What paralysis the lack of prayer has brought on the church today!

There was the grasshopper siege in Minnesota when ex-Gov. Pillsbury appointed a day of fasting and prayer for relief. God answered their prayer.

There was the siege of Leyden when the fleet, taking provisions for their relief, could not get within three miles. They prayed to God for deliverance. God blew His breath against the North Sea and flooded up to the walls of the citadel with twenty feet of water. They stripped the ships and blew them back to the North Sea, and the water has never flooded that land since that day. It was God's answer.

I'm talking about the God of Moses, the God who destroyed Sodom and Gomorrah. You may change politics, the church, yourself. You may change the styles—but God is the same yesterday, today, and forever. Don't be limiting God and shoving Him back on a sidetrack. Prayer has power over devils and over weather.

People of Pittsburgh, you who profess Christianity, fall on your knees and pray. God will shake old Pittsburgh. God will do wonderful things.

Are you a *praying* Christian or a *playing* Christian? Some of you lie when you at church sing, "Jesus, Lover of My Soul." He is not a lover of your soul but a mere acquaintance you bow to when you enter the church door.

I ordinarily don't knock society, women's clubs, lodges, or anything else, but I do knock them when they push God into the background. And I've a right to. God isn't dead!

Are you a praying Christian, or do you think God is dead? You don't talk to Him anymore like you used to. There is no power like prayer. *"The effectual fervent prayer of a righteous man availeth much."*

IV.

We Have a God Who Answers Prayer

BILLY SUNDAY

"Jesus Christ the same yesterday, and to day, and for ever...."
—Heb. 13:8.

We live in a very practical age. People do things, not because the law compels them, but because they get something for their efforts.

The motto of today seems to be: Where do I come in on this? What do I get out of it?

We are willing to invest our money if we get good returns. That's right. We gladly try the doctor's treatment. We are a nation of tasters. Is the game worth the candle?

We do not have to comprehend the process in order to enjoy its results.

I do not understand electricity; but I turn the switch, and the room is flooded with light.

I do not understand the mechanism of the telephone; but I call the number, and I get my friends on the wire.

I do not understand the process of digestion, but I eat.

I do not understand the anatomy of the body, but I take the doctor's medicine.

I pray because of its proved helpfulness, but I cannot understand its mysteries.

If I never used an elevator until I understood how it worked, I would stay downstairs all my life.

If I never used an automobile until I understood its mechanism, I would have to walk.

If I never looked at my watch until I could make one, I would never know the time of day.

So if I never prayed until I understood all its mysteries, I would be a stranger to God all my days.

Nobody knows what takes place when we drop a lump of sugar in the coffee, whether the change is mechanical or chemical. All we know is that the sugar sweetens the coffee, and that's all we need to know.

There has never been a great moral or spiritual awakening in history that did not root itself in prayer. At Pentecost, where the Holy Spirit came down and where the church was born, they held a ten-day prayer meeting.

A prominent man told me he had visited scores of churches; yet he could not gather from what was preached whether the preacher was a follower of Confucius, Mohammed, Zoroaster, or Christ.

No wonder crime is rampant when they make individual opinion, instead of the Bible, the seat of authority. Rebellion is bound to follow.

No wonder that under this tidal wave of materialism, our churches have lost hundreds of thousands of members. They are trying to divert attention from their failure by attacking evangelism—the one force and power that has kept the spiritual flame alive.

Prayer is beginning to be looked upon as old-fashioned. People are not praying today. We are facing one of the greatest crises in our history. The one thing that will save our nation is a sweeping revival of religion.

Blackstone said that in his day you could not tell from what the preachers said whether they were heathen or Christian. Yet out of all this darkness came the revival under Wesley and Whitefield, which gave birth to the Methodist church with nine million adherents.

God Answers Prayer

Phillips Brooks said that prayer is not overcoming God's reluctance, but a laying hold of His willingness.

Abraham prayed for a son, and God gave him a posterity like the sands of the sea. He prayed for Ishmael; God spared the boy's life and made of him a great nation. He prayed for Sodom. God heard his prayer and postponed the day of doom.

Jacob prayed for a favorable reception by Esau.

Moses prayed for the forgiveness of the people.

Gideon prayed God to overthrow the Midianites.

Elijah prayed, and God heard and answered by fire.

Joshua prayed, and Achan was discovered.

Hannah prayed, and Samuel was born.

Hezekiah prayed, and 185,000 Assyrians died.

Daniel prayed, and the lions were muzzled.

The apostles prayed, and the Holy Spirit came down.

Not one of these would have happened without prayer.

Luther prayed, and the Reformation was the result.

Knox prayed, and Scotland trembled.

Brainerd prayed, and the Indians were subdued.

Wesley prayed, and millions were moved Godward.

Whitefield prayed, and thousands were converted.

Finney prayed, and mighty revivals resulted.

Taylor prayed, and the great China Inland Mission was born.

Mueller prayed, and more than seven million dollars were sent in to feed thousands of orphans.

Auntie Cook prayed; Moody was anointed, and the Moody Bible Institute was launched.

Men are always praying; God is always answering.

God has to make some of us wait on the side track while His through-trains rush by.

A plain seaman stood on watch on a U.S. battleship hundreds of miles out to sea on the Atlantic. A wireless message was handed to him, reading, "Little Donald died yesterday. Funeral Wednesday. Can you come?" It was signed "Mary." He forgot his duty and saw only the smiling face of his baby he had left three months before. He burst into tears. The captain asked, "What's the matter?" He handed the officer the message.

"Where do you live?" asked the captain.

"Cleveland, Ohio, Sir," replied the seaman.

The captain barked some orders to the engine room and then sent out a wireless message. It wasn't long before a cruiser was sighted; the sailor was put upon her, and she raced toward New York.

Another wireless, and a fast torpedo boat came over the horizon. He was lowered on to her. She made all speed to New York harbor, where the sailor was put in a cab and driven hurriedly to the Pennsylvania depot. He rushed up to the ticket office to inquire when the next train left for Cleveland. The agent told him it would leave in three minutes. He tore down the stairs and climbed aboard just as the train was pulling out of the station. He reached his home and Mary's arms just as the minister arose to deliver his sermon.

All the power of the United States Navy was placed at his disposal.

God Answers Prayer Through Human Cooperation

We need more prayer sense. It takes considerable planning before we get ready to pray, "O Lord, I want a house." Then say "Amen" with a hammer and saw. Or, "O Lord, I want to be a strong Christian." Then say "Amen" on your knees, with a membership in a church; otherwise your prayers will not create much commotion in Heaven.

We pray, "O Lord, save the world." That's an easy and cheap way. If we are in earnest we'll say "Amen" with our hands, our hearts, our money, and really get down on our knees and actually down to business.

Bishop Whipple was the Episcopal bishop of Minnesota. He tells of an Episcopal clergyman who was called to comfort a dying girl. The house in which she lay was kept by an incarnate fiend, who was offended that the clergyman should come to the home to pray. The woman met him with a butcher knife in hand and told him he could not pray in her house.

The clergyman had a cane. He said, "Madame, I came down here to commend this dying girl to Jesus. I want you to know that I can pray just as well with my eyes open as shut. If you stir one step while I pray, I will crack your head with this stick." The woman never budged. I like a fellow like that, don't you?

Too many Christians are slovenly in prayer. They are careless and thoughtless; they almost yawn in God's presence; they do not concentrate their thoughts.

"How" is one of the biggest words in our language. We are all curious. We are not satisfied to see a thing done, but we ask, "How?" That's why a child likes to take a watch apart.

Too many of us, when we take our problems to the Lord, drop our prayers before His throne and seem to say, "I wash my hands. Now it's up to You."

We must live and act in such a way that God can answer our prayers. Some think and teach that God has a mysterious wand to wave over the sick while the patient refuses to cooperate. If a man prays for health, he must use every means to keep himself well.

Moody was asked to pray for the recovery of a sick preacher. "No, I won't," he said. "He does ten days' work in five and eats everything in sight."

If a man prays for the ability to win souls, he will naturally do personal work.

If a man prays for a job, he will read the want ads.

If he prays for a wife, he will go out and meet women socially and not wait for some woman to come and say, "Good morning. I'm your wife. The Lord sent me to you."

Some try to make prayer a substitute for work. Real prayer is teamwork with the Lord. It's God at the front end leading us on. He wants us to be at the back end following.

Get rid of the idea that prayer is a one-power affair where God is the conductor and motorman.

A man was out in a boat with a black man. A storm arose. The man became frightened and said, "Moses, shall we pray *or* row?"

The black man replied, "Boss, let's mix 'em. Pray *and* row."

Dr. Norman McLeod, with a brother minister, was caught in a storm. Dr. McLeod was a big burly fellow. His friend was small. The latter said, "Dr. McLeod, let's pray." The Highland boatman said, "Na, na, Mon! Let the wee mon pray, and the big mon take an oar."

In all human history certain crises have arisen when the help of man was vain.

Dr. Jessup and Dr. Bliss of Syria sat together in Constantinople, both in tears over the edict of the Sultan ordering all American schools closed. Finally Dr. Bliss said, "Let's lay this before the Sultan of Heaven." They prayed all night. The next day the Sultan died and the edict was recalled.

Moody said that Jesus never taught His disciples how to preach, but how to pray; not how to run a church, or how to raise money, but how to pray.

Beecher said, "I pray on the principle that wine knocks the cork out of the bottle. Where there is inward fermentation there must be a vent."

We Do Not Put Enough Trust in Prayer

Henry Drummond tells of a little girl who was crossing the ocean. She dropped her doll overboard and, running to the captain, asked him to stop the ship and pick up her dolly. She had seen him do that to rescue a man, and she thought he was cruel when he refused. When the ship reached port, the captain bought her the finest doll he could find. He had refused her request, but he gave her something much better.

A little girl went to a hospital for an operation. The doctor said, "I must put you to sleep, and when you wake up you'll be better." She replied, "Oh, before I go to sleep, I always pray." She jumped down and prayed, "Now I lay me down to sleep." The doctors and nurses bowed their heads and waited. I believe that doctor received divine help in that special case.

During the first World's Fair in Chicago in 1893, Mr. Moody carried on numberless evangelistic meetings. He secured many speakers from abroad, rented halls and engaged theaters. It took a great deal of money to carry on such extensive work.

One day Mr. Moody invited a dozen men to luncheon at a downtown hotel. He said to them, "I didn't invite you here merely to eat. I invited you because I believe you have power in prayer. I need seven thousand dollars to keep this work going."

Before luncheon was served, they all definitely prayed for seven thousand dollars. Before lunch was finished, Moody was handed a telegram which read:

> We, your friends at Northfield, became impressed that you must have money to carry on your work in Chicago. We have taken an offering amounting to seven thousand dollars. I am mailing you a draft today for that amount, praying God's richest blessings upon you and His cause.

The prayers reached God, and He sent the answer via Northfield.

Charles M. Alexander went into a bank in England to see one of its officers. While waiting, he picked up a blotter and wrote on it, "Pray through." The officer was detained, and Mr. Alexander kept on writing until he had covered the blotter with the words, "Pray through."

After he left the room, a businessman was ushered into the same room to wait. He was discouraged and troubled. Picking up the blotter, he read it over and over again, and suddenly exclaimed, "Why, that's just the message I need. I've tried to worry it through; now I'll pray it through."

> Don't stop praying; the Lord is nigh.
> Don't stop praying; He'll hear your cry.
> God has promised; He is true!
> Don't stop praying; He'll answer you.

CHARLES HADDON SPURGEON
1835-1892

ABOUT THE MAN:

Many times it has been said that this was the greatest preacher this side of the Apostle Paul. He began preaching at the age of 16. At 25 he built London's famous Metropolitan Tabernacle, seating around 5,000. It was never large enough. Even when traveling he preached to 10,000 eager listeners a week. Crowds thronged to hear him as they came to hear John the Baptist by the River Jordan. The fire of God was on him as on the Prophet Elijah facing assembled Israel at Mount Carmel.

Royalty sat in his Tabernacle, as did washerwomen. Mr. Gladstone had him to dinner; and cabbies refused his fare, considering it an honor to drive for this "Prince of Preachers." To a housewife kneading bread, he would say, "Have you ever tried the Bread of life?" Many a carpenter was asked, "Have you ever tried to build a house on sand?"

He preached in all the principal cities of England, Scotland and Ireland. And although invited to the United States on several occasions, he was never able to visit this country.

HOW GREAT WAS HIS HEART: for preachers, so the Pastors' College was founded; for orphans, so the orphans' houses came to be; for people around the world, so his literature poured forth in an almost unmeasurable volume. He was a national voice; so every national issue affecting morals, religion or the poor had his interpretation, his counsel.

Oh, but his passion for souls! You can see it in every sermon.

Spurgeon published thousands of poems, tracts, sermons and songs.

HIS MESSAGE TO LOST SINNERS WILL LIVE AS LONG AS THE GOSPEL IS PREACHED.

V.

The Golden Key of Prayer

CHARLES H. SPURGEON

"Call unto me, and I will answer thee, and shew thee great and mighty things, which thou knowest not."—Jer. 33:3.

Some of the most learned works in the world smell of the midnight oil; but the most spiritual and most comforting books and sayings of men usually have a savor about them of prison-damp. I might quote many instances: John Bunyan's *Pilgrim* may suffice instead of a hundred others; and this good text of ours, all moldy and chill with the prison in which Jeremiah lay, hath nevertheless a brightness and a beauty about it which it might never have had if it had not come as a cheering word to the prisoner of the Lord, shut up in the court of the prison house.

God's people have always in their worst condition found out the best of their God. He is good at all times; but He seemeth to be at His best when they are at their worst.

Rutherford had a quaint saying that when he was cast into the cellars of affliction, he remembered that the great King always kept his wine there, and he began to seek at once for the wine bottles and to drink of the "wines on the lees well refined."

They who dive in the sea of affliction bring up rare pearls. You know, my companions in affliction, that it is so. You have proved that He is a faithful God, and that as your tribulations abound, so your consolations also abound by Christ Jesus.

My prayer is, in taking this text this morning, that some other prisoners of the Lord may have its joyous promise spoken home to them; that you who are straitly shut up and cannot come forth by reason of present heaviness of spirit, may hear Him say, as with a soft whisper in your ears and in your hearts, "Call unto me, and I will answer thee, and shew thee great and mighty things, which thou knowest not."

The text naturally splits itself up into three distinct particles of truth. Upon these let us speak as we are enabled by God the Holy Spirit. *First*, prayer commanded—"Call unto me"; *second*, an answer promised—"And I will answer thee"; *third*, faith encouraged—"And shew thee great and mighty things, which thou knowest not."

I. PRAYER COMMANDED

We are not merely counseled and recommended to pray, but bidden to pray. This is great condescension.

A hospital is built. It is considered sufficient that free admission shall be given to the sick when they seek it, but no order in council is made that a man *must* enter its gates.

A soup kitchen is well provided for in the depth of winter. Notice is promulgated that those who are poor may receive food on application; but no one thinks of passing an Act of Parliament compelling the poor to come and wait at the door to take the charity. It is thought to be enough to proffer it without issuing any sort of mandate that men *shall* accept it.

Yet so strange is *the infatuation of man* on the one hand, which makes him need a command to be merciful to his own soul, and so marvelous is the condescension of our gracious God on the other, that He issues a command of love without which not a man of Adam born would partake of the gospel feast, but would rather starve than come.

We Need the Command to Pray Because of Worldliness, Sin and Unbelief

In the matter of prayer, it is even so. God's own people need, or else they would not receive it, a command to pray. How is this? Because, dear friends, we are very subject to *fits of worldliness*, if indeed that be not our usual state.

We do not forget to eat; we do not forget to take the shop shutters down; we do not forget to be diligent in business; we do not forget to go to our beds to rest: but we often do forget to wrestle with God in prayer and to spend, as we ought to spend, long periods in consecrated fellowship with our Father and our God.

With too many professors the ledger is so bulky that you cannot move it; and the Bible, representing their devotion, is so small that you might almost put it in your waistcoat pocket. Hours for the world! Moments for Christ!

The world has the best, and our closet the parings of our time. We give our strength and freshness to the ways of mammon and our fatigue and languor to the ways of God. Hence it is that we need to be commanded to attend to that very act which ought to be our greatest happiness, as it is our highest privilege to perform, that is, to meet with our God. "Call unto me," saith He, for He knows that we are apt to forget to call upon God. "What meanest thou, O sleeper? arise, call upon thy God" (Jonah 1:16), is an exhortation which is needed by us as well as by Jonah in the storm.

He understands what *heavy hearts* we have sometimes, when under a sense of sin. Satan says to us, "Why should you pray? How can you hope to prevail? In vain, thou sayest, I will arise and go to my Father, for thou art not worthy to be one of his hired servants. How canst thou see the king's face after thou hast played the traitor against him? How wilt thou dare to approach unto the altar when thou hast thyself defiled it, and when the sacrifice which thou wouldst bring there is a poor, polluted one?"

O brethren, it is well for us that we are commanded to pray, or else in times of heaviness we might give it up. If God command me, unfit as I may be, I will creep to the footstool of grace. And since He says, "Pray without ceasing," though my words fail me and my heart itself will wander, yet I will still stammer out the wishes of my hungering soul and say, "O God, at least teach me to pray and help me to prevail with Thee."

Are we not commanded to pray also because of our *frequent unbelief?* Unbelief whispers, "What profit is there if thou shouldst seek the Lord upon such-and-such a matter? Either it is too trivial a matter, or it is too connected with temporals, or else it is a matter in which you have sinned too much, or else it is too high, too hard, too complicated a piece of business. You have no right to take that before God!"

So suggests the foul fiend of Hell. Therefore, there stands written as an everyday precept suitable to every case into which a Christian can be cast, "Call unto me; call unto me."

"Art thou sick? Wouldst thou be healed? Cry unto Me, for I am a Great Physician. Does providence trouble thee? Art thou fearful that thou shalt not provide things honest in the sight of man? Call unto Me! Do thy children vex thee? Dost thou feel that which is sharper than an adder's tooth—a thankless child? Call unto Me. Are thy griefs little, yet painful, like small points and pricks of thorns? Call unto Me! Is thy burden heavy as though it would make thy back break beneath its load? Call unto Me!"

"Cast thy burden upon the Lord, and he shall sustain thee: he shall never suffer the righteous to be moved."—Ps. 55:22.

We Are Commanded to Pray Both in God's Word and by His Spirit

We must not leave our first part till we have made another remark. We ought to be very glad that God hath given us this command *in His Word* that it may be sure and abiding.

It may be a sensible exercise for some of you to find out how often in Scripture you are told to pray. You will be surprised to find how many times such words as these are given:

"Call upon me in the day of trouble: I will deliver thee."—Ps. 50:15.

"Ye people, pour out your heart before him."—Ps. 62:8.

"Seek ye the Lord while he may be found, call ye upon him while he is near."—Isa. 55:6.

"Ask, and it shall be given you; seek, and ye shall find; knock, and it shall be opened unto you."—Matt. 7:7.

"Watch ye and pray, lest ye enter into temptation."—Mark 14:38.

"Pray without ceasing."—I Thess. 5:17.

"Let us therefore come boldly unto the throne of grace."—Heb. 4:16.

"Draw nigh to God, and he will draw nigh to you."—James 4:8.

"Continue in prayer."—Col. 4:2.

I need not multiply where I could not possibly exhaust. I pick two or three out of this great bag of pearls.

Come, Christian, you ought never to question whether you have a right to pray. You should never ask, "May I be permitted to come into His presence?" When you have so many commands (and God's commands are all promises and all enablings), you may come boldly unto the throne of heavenly grace by the new and living way through the rent veil.

But there are times when God not only commands His people to pray in the Bible, but He also commands them to pray directly *by the motions of His Holy Spirit.*

You who know the inner life comprehend me at once. You feel on a sudden, possibly in the midst of business, the pressing thought that you *must* retire to pray. It may be you do not at first take particular notice of the inclination, but it comes again and again and again—"Retire and pray!"

I find that in the matter of prayer, I am myself very much like a water wheel which runs well when there is plenty of water, but which turns with very little force when the brook is growing shallow; or, like the ship which flies over the waves, putting out all her canvas when the wind is favorable, but which has to tack about most laboriously when there is but little of the favoring breeze.

Now it strikes me that whenever our Lord gives you the special inclination to pray, that you should double your diligence. You ought always to pray and not to faint. Yet when He gives you the special longing after prayer and you feel a peculiar aptness and enjoyment in it, you have, over and above the command which is constantly binding, another command which should compel you to cheerful obedience.

At such times I think we may stand in the position of David, to whom the Lord said, "When thou hearest the sound of a going in the tops of the mulberry trees, that then thou shalt bestir thyself" (II Sam. 5:24). That going in the tops of the mulberry trees may have been the footfalls of angels hastening to the help of David, and then David was to smite the Philistines; and when God's mercies are coming, their footfalls are our desires to pray, and our desires to pray should be at once an indication that the set time to favor Zion is come.

Sow plentifully now, for thou canst sow in hope. Plow joyously now, for thy harvest is sure. Wrestle now, Jacob, for thou art about to be made a prevailing prince, and thy name shall be called Israel. Now is thy time, spiritual merchantmen. The market is high, trade much. Thy profit shall be large. See to it that thou usest right well the golden hour, and reap thy harvest whilst the sun shines.

II. AN ANSWER PROMISED

We ought not to tolerate for a minute the ghastly and grievous thought that God will not answer prayer.

God's Nature Demands He Answer Prayer

His nature, as manifested in Christ Jesus, demands it. He has revealed Himself in the Gospel as a God of love, full of grace and truth; and how can He refuse to help those of His creatures who humbly, in His own appointed way, seek His face and favor?

When the Athenian senate, upon one occasion, found it most convenient to meet together in the open air, as they were sitting in their deliberations, a sparrow, pursued by a hawk, flew in the direction of the senate. Being hard pressed by the bird of prey, it sought shelter in the bosom of one of the senators. He, being a man of rough and vulgar mold, took the bird from his bosom, dashed it on the ground and so killed it. Whereupon the whole senate rose in uproar, and without one single dissenting voice, condemned him to die, as being unworthy of a seat in the senate with them or to be called an Athenian, if he did not render succor to a creature that confided in him.

Can we suppose that the God of Heaven, whose nature is love, could tear out of His bosom the poor fluttering dove that flies from the eagle of justice into the bosom of His mercy? Will He give the invitation to us to seek His face; and when we, as He knows, with so much trepidation of fear, yet summon courage enough to fly into His bosom, will He then be unjust and ungracious enough to forget to hear our cry and to answer us? Let us not think so hardly of the God of Heaven.

God, Giving His Son, Proves Love
That Will Answer Prayer

Let us recollect next, *His past character* as well as His nature. I mean the character which He has won for Himself by His past deeds of grace.

Consider, my brethren, that one stupendous display of bounty—if I were to mention a thousand I could not give a better illustration of the character of God than that one deed— "He that spared not his own Son, but delivered him up for us all" —and it is not my inference only, but the inspired conclusion of an apostle—"how shall he not with him also freely give us all things?" (Rom. 8:32).

If the Lord did not refuse to listen to my voice when I was a guilty sinner and an enemy, how can He disregard my cry now that I am justified and saved! How is it that He heard the voice of my misery when my heart knew it not and would not seek relief, if after all He will not hear me now that I am His child, His friend? The streaming wounds of Jesus are the sure guarantee for answered prayer.

George Herbert represents in that quaint poem of his, "The Bag," the Saviour saying—

"If ye have anything to send or write
(I have no bag, but here is room)
Unto My Father's hands and sight,
(Believe Me) it shall safely come.
That I shall mind what you impart
Look, you may put it very near My heart,
Or if hereafter any of friends
Will use Me in this kind, the door
Shall still be open; what he sends
I will present and somewhat more
Not to his hurt."

Surely George Herbert's thought was that the atonement was in itself a guarantee that prayer must be heard, that the great gash made near the Saviour's heart, which let the light into the very depths of the heart of Deity, was a proof that He who sits in Heaven would hear the cry of His people. You misread Calvary if you think that prayer is useless.

But, beloved, we have *the Lord's own promise* for it, and He is a God that cannot lie. "Call upon me in the day of trouble, and I will answer thee." Has He not said, "Whatsoever ye shall ask in prayer, believe that ye receive it, and ye shall have it"? We cannot pray, indeed, unless we believe this doctrine; "for he that cometh to God must believe that he is, and that he is a rewarder of them that diligently seek him"; and if we have any question at all about whether our prayer will be heard, we are comparable to him that wavereth; "for he who wavereth is like a wave of the sea, driven with the wind and tossed; let not that man think that he shall receive any thing of the Lord."

Past Experience Shows That God Answers Prayer

Furthermore, it is not necessary, still it may strengthen the point, if we added that *our own experience* leads us to believe that God will answer prayer. I must not speak for you, but I may speak for myself. If there be anything I know, anything that I am quite assured of beyond all question, it is that praying breath is never spent in vain. If no other man here can say it, I dare to say it, and I know that I can prove it.

My own conversion is the result of prayer, long, affectionate, earnest, importunate. Parents prayed for me; God heard their cries, and here I am to preach the Gospel. Since then I have adventured upon some things that were far beyond my capacity as I thought; but I have never failed because I have cast myself upon the Lord.

You know as a church that I have not scrupled to indulge large ideas of what we might do for God. And we have accomplished all that we purposed. I have sought God's aid, assistance and help in all my manifold undertakings. And though I cannot tell here the story of my private life in God's work, yet if it were written it would be a standing proof that there is a God who answers prayer.

He has heard *my* prayers, not now and then, nor once nor twice, but so many times that it has grown into a habit with me to spread my case before God with the absolute certainty that whatsoever I ask of God, He will give to me. It is not now a "perhaps" or a possibility. I know that my Lord answers me, and I dare not doubt—it were indeed folly if I did.

As I am sure that a certain amount of leverage will lift a weight, so I know that a certain amount of prayer will get anything from God. As the rain cloud brings the shower, so prayer brings the blessing. As spring scatters flowers, so supplication ensures mercies.

In all labor there is profit, but most of all in the work of intercession. I am sure of this, for I have reaped it.

Still remember that prayer is always to be offered in submission to God's will; that when we say God heareth prayer, we do not intend by that, that He always gives us literally what we ask for. We do mean, however, this: He gives us what is best for us; and that if He does not give us the mercy we ask for in silver, He bestows it upon us in gold. If He doth not take away the thorn in the flesh, yet He saith, "My grace is sufficient for thee," and that comes to the same in the end.

Lord Bolingbroke said to the Countess of Huntingdon, "I cannot understand, your ladyship, how you can make out earnest prayer to be consistent with submission to the divine will."

"My lord," said she, "that is a matter of no difficulty. If I were a courtier of some generous king and he gave me permission to ask any favor I pleased of him, I should be sure to put it thus, 'Will your majesty be graciously pleased to grant me such-and-such a favor? But at the same time though I very much desire it, if it would in any way detract from your majesty's honor, or if in your majesty's judgment it should seem better that I did not have this favor, I shall be quite as content to go without it as to receive it.' So you see I might earnestly offer a petition, and yet I might submissively leave it in the king's hands."

So with God. We never offer up prayer without inserting that clause, either in spirit or in words, "Nevertheless, not as I will, but as thou wilt; not my will but thine be done." We can only pray without an "if" when we are quite sure that our will must be God's will because God's will is fully our will.

III. ENCOURAGEMENT TO FAITH

I come to our third point, which I think is full of encouragement to all those who exercise the hallowed art of prayer: encouragement to faith. "I will. . . shew thee great and mighty things, which thou knowest not."

God Opens Truth in Answer to Prayer

Let us just remark that this was originally spoken to a prophet in prison; therefore, it applies in the first place to *every teacher*; and, indeed, as every teacher must be a learner, it has a bearing upon *every learner* in divine truth. The best way by which a prophet and teacher and learner can know the reserved truths, the higher and more mysterious truths of God, is by waiting upon God in prayer.

I noticed very specially yesterday in reading the Book of the prophet Daniel, how Daniel found out Nebuchadnezzar's dream. The soothsayers, the magicians, the astrologers of the Chaldees brought out their curious books and their strange-looking instruments, and began to mutter their *abracadabra* and all sorts of mysterious incantations. But they all failed.

What did Daniel do? He set himself to prayer and, knowing that the prayer of a united body of men has more prevalence than the prayer of one, we find that Daniel called together his brethren and bade them unite with him in earnest prayer that God would be pleased of His infinite mercy to open up the vision.

And in the case of John, who was the Daniel of the New Testament, you remember he saw a book in the right hand of Him who sat on the throne—a book sealed with seven seals which none was found worthy to open or to look thereon.

What did John do? The book was by-and-by opened by the Lion of the tribe of Judah, who had prevailed to open the book; but it is written first before the book was opened, "I wept much." Yes, and the tears of John which were his liquid prayers were, as far as he was concerned, the sacred keys by which the folded book was opened.

Brethren in the ministry, you who are teachers in the Sunday school, and all of you who are learners in the college of Christ Jesus, I pray you remember that prayer is your best means of study. Like Daniel, you shall understand the dream and the interpretation thereof, when you have sought unto God; and, like John, you shall see the seven seals of precious truth unloosed, after that you have wept much.

"Yea, if thou criest after knowledge, and liftest up thy voice for understanding; If thou seekest her as silver, and searchest for her as for hid treasures; Then shalt thou understand the fear of the Lord, and find the knowledge of God."—Prov. 2:3-5.

Stones are not broken except by an earnest use of the hammer; and the stone-breaker usually goes down on his knees. Use the hammer of vengeance and let the knee of prayer be exercised, too; and there is not a stony doctrine in Revelation which is useful for you to understand, which will not fly into shivers under the exercise of prayer and faith.

"Bene orasse est bene studuisse" was a wise sentence of Luther, which has been so often quoted, that we hardly venture but to hint at it. "To have prayed well is to have studied well."

You may force your way through anything with the leverage of prayers. Thoughts and reasonings may be like the steel wedges which may open a way into truth; but prayer is the lever, the prise which forces open the iron chest of sacred mystery, that we may get the treasure that is hidden therein for those who can force their way to reach it.

The kingdom of Heaven still suffereth violence, and the violent taketh it by force. Take care that ye work away with the mighty implement of prayer, and nothing can stand against you.

Blessed Experience and Fellowship With God in Answer to Prayer

We must not, however, stop there. We have applied the text to only one case; it is applicable to a hundred. We single out another. *The saint may expect to discover deeper experience* and to know more of the higher spiritual life, by being much in prayer. There are different translations of my text. One version renders it, "I will shew thee great and fortified things which thou knowest not." Another reads it, "Great and reserved things which thou knowest not."

Now, all the developments of spiritual life are not alike easy of attainment. There are the common frames and feelings of repentance and faith and joy and hope which are enjoyed by the entire family; but there is an upper realm of rapture, of communion and conscious union with Christ which is far from being the common dwellingplace of believers.

All believers see Christ, but all believers do not put their fingers into the prints of the nails nor thrust their hand into His side. We have not all the high privilege of John to lean upon Jesus' bosom, nor of Paul, to be caught up into the third Heaven.

In the ark of salvation we find a lower, second and third story. All are in the ark, but all are not in the same story. Most Christians, as to the river of experience, are only up to the ankles; some others have waded till the stream is up to the knees; a few find it breast-high; and but a few—oh! how few!—find it a river to swim in, the bottom of which they cannot touch.

My brethren, there are heights in experimental knowledge of the things of God which the eagle's eye of acumen and philosophic thought have never seen; and there are secret paths which the lion's whelp of reason and judgment hath not as yet learned to travel. God alone can bear us there, but the chariot in which He takes us up and the fiery steeds with which that chariot is dragged are prevailing prayers.

Prevailing prayer is victorious over the God of mercy.

"Yea, he had power over the angel, and prevailed: he wept, and made supplication unto him: he found him in Bethel, and there he spake with us."—Hosea 12:4.

Prevailing prayer takes the Christian to Carmel and enables him to cover Heaven with clouds of blessing and earth with floods of mercy. Prevailing prayer bears the Christian aloft to Pisgah and shows him the inheritance reserved; ay, and it elevates him to Tabor and transfigures him, till in the likeness of his Lord, as He is, so are we also in this world.

If you would reach to something higher than ordinary groveling experience, look to the Rock that is higher than you, and look with the eye of faith through the windows of importunate prayer.

To grow in experience, then, there must be much prayer.

Here Is Comfort for Those Who Are Sorely Tried

You must have patience with me while I apply this text to two or three more cases. It is certainly true of *the sufferer under trial*. If he waits upon God in prayer much, he shall receive greater deliverances than he has ever dreamed of—"great and mighty things, which thou knowest not."

Here is Jeremiah's testimony: "Thou drewest near in the day that I called upon thee: thou saidst, Fear not. O Lord, thou hast pleaded the causes of my soul; thou hast redeemed my life" (Lam. 3:57, 58).

And David's is the same: "I called upon the Lord in distress: the Lord answered me, and set me in a large place" (Ps. 118:5). "I will praise thee: for thou hast heard me, and art become my salvation" (vs. 21).

Yet again: "Then they cried unto the Lord in their trouble, and he delivered them out of their distresses. And he led them forth by the right way, that they might go to a city of habitation" (Ps. 107:7).

"My husband is dead," said the poor woman, "and my creditor is come to take my two sons as bondsmen." She hoped that Elijah would possibly say, "What are your debts? I will pay them." Instead of that, he multiplies her oil till it is written, "Go thou and pay thy debts, and" —what was the "and"?—"live thou and thy children upon the rest." So often it will happen that God will not only help His people through the miry places of the way, so that they may just stand on the other side of the slough, but He will bring them safely far on the journey.

That was a remarkable miracle, when in the midst of the storm, Jesus Christ came walking upon the sea, the disciples received Him into the ship, and not only was the sea calm, but it is recorded, "Immediately the ship was at the land whither they went." That was a mercy over and above what they asked. I sometimes hear you pray and make use of a quotation which is not in the Bible: "He is able to do exceeding abundantly above what we *can* ask or even think." It is not so written in the Bible. I do not know what we can ask or what we can think. But it is said, 'He is able to do exceeding abundantly above what we ask or even think.' Let us, then, dear friends, when we are in great trial, only say, "Now I am in prison like Jeremiah; I will pray as he did, for I have God's command to do it; and I will look out as he did, expecting that He will show me reserved mercies which I know nothing of at present."

He will not merely bring His people through the battle, covering their heads in it, but He will bring them forth with banners waving, to divide the spoil with the mighty, and to claim their portion with the strong.

Expect great things of a God who gives such great promises as these.

Encouragement for Christian Workers

Again, *here is encouragement for the worker.* My dear friends, wait upon God much in prayer, and you have the promise that He will do greater things for you than you know of. We know not how much capacity for usefulness there may be in us. That ass's jawbone lying there upon the earth, what can it do? Nobody knows what it can do. It gets into Samson's hands, what can it *not* do? No one knows what it cannot do now that a Samson wields it.

And you, friend, have often thought yourself to be as contemptible as that bone, and you have said, "What can I do?" Ay, but when Christ by His Spirit grips you, what can you not do? Truly you may adopt Paul's language and say, "I can do all things through Christ which strengtheneth me" (Phil. 4:13).

However, do not depend upon prayer without effort.

In a certain school there was one girl who knew the Lord, a very gracious, simple-hearted, trustful child. As usual, grace developed itself in the child according to the child's position. Her lessons were always best said of any in the class.

Another girl said to her, "How is it that your lessons are always so well said?"

"I pray God to help me," she said, "to learn my lesson."

Thought the other, *Well, then, I will do the same.*

The next morning when she stood up in the class, she knew nothing; and when she was in disgrace she complained to the other, "Why, I prayed God to help me learn my lesson, and I do not know anything of it. What is the use of prayer?"

"But did you sit down and try to learn it?"

"Oh, no," she said, "I never looked at the book."

"Ah," then said the other, "I asked God to help me to learn my lesson; but I then sat down to it studiously, and I kept at it till I knew it well, and I learned it easily because my earnest desire, which I had expressed to God, was, 'Help me to be diligent in endeavoring to do my duty.'"

So is it with some who come up to prayer meetings and pray and then they fold their arms and go away hoping that God's work will go on. Like the Negro woman singing, "Fly abroad, thou mighty Gospel," but not putting a penny in the plate; so that her friend touched her and said, "But how can it fly if you don't give it wings to fly with?"

There be many who appear to be very mighty in prayer, wondrous in supplications; but then they require God to do what they can do themselves; and, therefore, God does nothing at all for them. "I shall leave my camel untied," said an Arab once to Mahomet, "and trust to providence." "Tie it up tight," said Mahomet, "and then trust to providence."

So you who say, "I shall pray and trust my church, or my class, or my work to God's goodness," may rather hear the voice of experience and wisdom which says, "Do thy best; work as if all rested upon thy toil; as if thy own arm would bring thy salvation"; "and when thou hast done all, cast thyself on Him without whom it is in vain to rise up early and to sit up late, and to eat the bread of carefulness; and if He speed thee, give Him the praise."

Here Is Comfort for Intercessors

I shall not detain you many minutes longer, but I want you to notice that this promise ought to prove useful for the comforting of those who are intercessors for others. You who are calling upon God to save your children, to bless your neighbors, to remember your husbands or your wives in mercy, may take comfort from this, "I will . . . shew thee great and mighty things, which thou knowest not."

A celebrated minister in the last century, one Mr. Bailey, was the child of a godly mother. This mother had almost ceased to pray for her husband, who was a man of a most ungodly stamp and a bitter persecutor. The mother prayed for her boy; and while he was yet eleven or twelve years of age, eternal mercy met with him. So sweetly instructed was the child in the things of the kingdom of God that the mother requested him—and for some time he always did so—to conduct family prayer in the house.

Morning and evening this little one laid open the Bible; and though the father would not deign to stop for the family prayer, yet on one occasion he was rather curious to know "what sort of an out the boy would make of it," so he stopped on the other side of the door. God blessed the prayer of his own child under thirteen years of age to his conversion.

The mother might well have read my text with streaming eyes, and said, "Yes, Lord, Thou hast shown me great and mighty things which I knew not. Thou hast not only saved my boy, but through my boy Thou hast brought my husband to the truth."

You cannot guess how greatly God will bless you. Only go and stand at His door—you cannot tell what is in reserve for you. If you do not beg at all, you will get nothing; but if you beg, He may not only give you, as it were, the bones and broken meat, but He may say to the servant at His table, "Take thou that dainty meat and set that before the poor man."

Ruth went to glean; she expected to get a few good ears. But Boaz said, "Let her glean even among the sheaves, and rebuke her not." He said moreover to her, "At mealtime come thou hither, and eat of the bread, and dip thy morsel in the vinegar." Nay, she found a husband where she only expected to find a handful of barley.

So in prayer for others, God may give us such mercies that we shall be astounded at them, since we expected but little. Hear what is said of Job and learn its lesson:

"And. . .the Lord said. . . my servant Job shall pray for you: for him will I accept: lest I deal with you after your folly, in that ye have not spoken of me the thing which is right, like my servant Job. . . . And the Lord turned the captivity of Job, when he prayed for his friends: also the Lord gave Job twice as much as he had before."—Job 42:7, 8, 10.

Now, this word to close with. Some of you are seekers for your own conversion. God has quickened you to solemn prayer about your own souls. You are not content to go to Hell. You want Heaven. You want washing in the precious blood. You want eternal life. Dear friends, I pray take you this text—God Himself speaks it to you—"Call unto me, and I will answer thee, and shew thee great and mighty things, which thou knowest not." At once take God at His word. Get home, go into your chamber, shut the door and try Him.

Young man, I say, try the Lord. Young woman, prove Him, see whether He be true or not. If God be true, you cannot seek mercy at His hands through Jesus Christ and get a negative reply. He must, for His own promise and character, bind Him to it, open mercy's gate to you who knock with all your heart.

God help you, believing in Christ Jesus, to cry aloud unto God, and His answer of peace is already on the way to meet you. You shall hear Him say, "Your sins which are many are all forgiven."

The Lord bless you for His love's sake. Amen.

VI.

Ask and Have

CHARLES H. SPURGEON

"Ye lust, and have not: ye kill, and desire to have, and cannot obtain: ye fight and war, yet ye have not, because ye ask not. Ye ask, and receive not, because ye ask amiss, that ye may consume it upon your lusts." —James 4:2,3.

May these striking words be made profitable to us by the teaching of the Holy Spirit.

Man is a creature abounding in wants. He is ever restless, and hence his heart is full of desires. I can hardly imagine a man existing who has not many desires of some kind or another. Man is comparable to the sea anemone with its multitude of tentacles which are always hunting in the water for food; or like certain plants which send out tendrils, seeking after the means of climbing.

The poet says, "Man never is, but always to be, blest." He steers for which he thinks to be his port, but as yet he is tossed about on the waves. One of these days he hopes to find his heart's delight, and so he continues to desire with more or less expectancy.

This fact appertains both to the worst and best of men. In bad men desires corrupt into lusts: they long after that which is selfish, sensual, and consequently evil. The current of their desires is set strongly in a wrong direction. These lustings, in many cases, become extremely intense: they make the man their slave; they domineer his judgment; they stir him up to violence. He fights and wars; perhaps he literally kills. In God's sight, who counts anger murder, he does kill full often. Such is the strength of his desires that they are commonly called passions; and when these passions are fully excited, then the man himself struggles vehemently so that the kingdom of the Devil suffereth violence, and the violent take it by force.

Meanwhile, in gracious men there are desires also. To rob the saints of their desires would be to injure them greatly, for by these they rise out of their lower selves. The desires of the gracious are after the best things: things pure and peaceable, laudable and elevating. They desire God's glory, and hence their desires spring from higher motives than those which inflame the unrenewed mind. Such desires in Christian men are frequently very fervent and forcible. They ought always to be so; and those desires begotten of the Spirit of God stir the renewed nature, exciting and stimulating it, and making the man to groan and to be in anguish and in travail until he can attain that which God has taught him to long for.

The lusting of the wicked and the holy desiring of the righteous have their own way of seeking gratification. The lusting of the wicked develops itself in contention; it kills, and desires to have; it fights and it wars. On the other hand, the desire of the righteous, when rightly guided, betakes itself to a far better course for achieving its purpose, for it expresses itself in prayer, fervent and importunate. The godly man, when full of desire, asks and receives at the hand of God.

At this time I shall by God's help try to set forth from our text, first, the poverty of lusting—"Ye lust and have not"; secondly, I shall sadly show the poverty of many professing Christians in spiritual things, especially in their church capacity; they also long for and have not; thirdly, we shall speak in closing, upon the wealth wherewith holy desires will be rewarded if we will but use the right means. If we ask, we shall receive.

I. THE POVERTY OF LUSTING

"Ye lust, and have not." Carnal lustings, however strong they may be, do not in many cases obtain that which they seek after. Saith the text, "Ye desire to have, and cannot obtain." The man longs to be happy, but he is not. He pines to be great, but he grows meaner every day. He aspires after this and after that which he thinks will content him, but he is still unsatisfied. He is like the troubled sea which cannot rest. One way or another his life is disappointment. He labors as in the very fire, but the result is vanity and vexation of spirit.

How can it be otherwise? If we sow the wind, must we not reap the whirlwind, and nothing else? Or, if peradventure the strong lustings of an active, talented, persevering man do give him what he seeks after, yet how soon he loses it! He has it so that he has it not. The pursuit is toilsome, but the possession is a dream. He sits down to eat, and lo! the feast is snatched away; the cup vanishes when it is at his lip. He wins to lose. He builds, and his sandy foundation slips from under his tower, and it lies in ruins. He that conquered kingdoms died discontented on a lone rock in mid-ocean; and he who revived his empire fell never to rise again. As Jonah's gourd withered in a night, so have empires fallen on a sudden, and their lords have died in exile.

So that what men obtain by warring and fighting is an estate with a short lease; the obtaining is so temporary that it still stands true—"They lust, and have not."

Or if such men have gifts and power enough to retain that which they have won, yet in another sense they have it not while they have it, for the pleasure which they looked for in it is not there. They pluck the apple, and it turns out to be one of those Dead Sea apples which crumbles to ashes in the hand. The man is rich, but God takes away from him the power to enjoy his wealth. By his lustings and his warrings the licentious man at last obtains the object of his cravings, and after a moment's gratification, he loathes that which he so passionately lusted for. He longs for the tempting pleasure, seizes it, and crushes it by the eager grasp.

See the boy hunting the butterfly, which flits from flower to flower, while he pursues it ardently. At last it is within reach, and with his cap he knocks it down; but when he picks up the poor remains, he finds the painted fly spoiled by the act which won it. Thus may it be said of multitudes of the sons of men—"Ye lust, and have not."

Their poverty is set forth in a threefold manner. *"Ye kill, and desire to have, and cannot obtain";* "Ye have not, because ye ask not"; "Ye ask, and receive not, because ye ask amiss."

If the lusters fail, it is not because they did not set to work to gain their ends; for according to their nature they used the most practical means within their reach, and used them eagerly, too. According to the mind of the flesh, the only way to obtain a thing is to fight for it, and James sets this down as the reason of all fighting: "Whence come wars and fightings among you? Come they not hence, even of your lusts that war in your members?"

This is the form of effort of which we read, *"Ye fight and war, yet ye have not."* To this mode of operation men cling from age to age.

If a man is to get along in this world they tell me he must contend with his neighbors, and push them from their vantage ground; he must not be particular how *they* are to thrive, but he must mind the main chance on his own account, and take care to rise, no matter how many he may tread upon. He cannot expect to get on if he loves his neighbor as himself. It is a fair fight, and every man must look to himself.

Do you think I am satirical? I may be, but I have heard this sort of talk from men who meant it. So they take to fighting, and that fighting is often victorious, for according to the text, *"Ye kill"*—that is to say, they so fight that they overthrow their adversary, and there is an end of him.

Multitudes are living for themselves, competing here and warring there, fighting for their own hand with the utmost perseverance. They have little choice as to how they will do it. Conscience is not allowed to interfere in their transactions, but the old advice rings in their ears, *"Get money; get money honestly if you can, but by any means get money."* No matter though body and soul be ruined, and others be deluged with misery, fight on; for there is no discharge in this war. Well saith James, "Ye kill, and desire to have, and cannot obtain; ye fight and war, yet ye have not."

When men who are greatly set upon their selfish purposes do not succeed, they may possibly hear that the reason of their nonsuccess is *"because ye ask not."*

Is, then, success to be achieved by asking? So the text seems to hint, and so the righteous find it. Why doth not this man of intense desires take to asking?

The reason is, first, because it is unnatural to the natural man to pray; as well expect him to fly. He despises the idea of supplication. "Pray?" says he. "No, I want to be at work. I cannot waste time on devotions; prayers are not practical. I want to fight my way. While you are praying I shall have beaten my opponent. I go to my countinghouse and leave you to your Bibles and your prayers."

He hath no mind for asking of God. He is so proud that he reckons himself to be his own providence; his own right hand and his active arm shall get to him the victory. When he is very liberal in his views, he admits that, though he does not pray, yet there may be some good in it for it quiets people's minds, and makes them more comfortable, But as to any answer ever coming to prayer, he scouts the idea and talks both philosophically and theologically about the absurdity of supposing that God alters His course of conduct out of respect to the prayers of men and women. "Ridiculous," says he, "utterly ridiculous"; and, therefore, in his own great wisdom he returns to his fighting and his warring, for by such means he hopes to attain his end. Yet he obtains not.

The whole history of mankind shows the failure of evil lustings to obtain their object.

For awhile the carnal man goes on fighting and warring; but by and by he changes his mind, for he is ill or frightened. His purpose is the same; but if it cannot be achieved one way, he will try another. If he must ask, well, he will ask. He will become religious and do good to himself in that way. He finds that some religious people prosper in the world and that even sincere Christians are by no means fools in business; therefore, he will try their plan. And now he comes under the third censure of our text—*"Ye ask, and receive not."*

What is the reason why the man who is the slave of his lusts obtains not his desire, even when he takes to asking? The reason is that his asking is a mere matter of form. His heart is not in his worship. He buys a book containing what are called forms of prayer, and he repeats these, for repeating is easier than praying and demands no thought.

I have no objection to your using a form of prayer if you pray with it, but I know a great many who do not pray with it but only repeat the form.

Imagine what would come to our families if instead of our children speaking to us frankly when they have any need, they were always to think it requisite to go into the library and hunt up a form of prayer, and read it to us. Surely there would be an end to all home-feeling and love. Life would move in fetters. Our household would become a kind of boarding school or barracks, and all would be parade and formality instead of happy eyes looking up with loving trust into fond eyes that delight to respond.

Many spiritual men use a form, but carnal men are pretty sure to do so, for they end in the form.

If your desires are the longings of fallen nature, if your desires begin and end with your own self, and if the chief end for which you live is not to glorify God but to glorify yourself, then you may fight, but you shall not have. You may rise up early and sit up late, but nothing worth gaining shall come of it. Remember how the Lord hath spoken in the 37th Psalm:

"Cease from anger, and forsake wrath: fret not thyself in any wise to do evil. For yet a little while, and the wicked shall not be: yea, thou shalt diligently consider his place, and it shall not be. But the meek shall inherit the earth; and shall delight themselves in the abundance of peace."

So much upon the poverty of lusting.

II. CHRISTIAN CHURCHES MAY SUFFER SPIRITUAL POVERTY

Christian churches may too "desire to have, and cannot obtain." Of course, the Christian seeks higher things than the worldling, else were he not worthy of that name at all. At least professedly his object is to obtain the true riches and to glorify God in spirit and in truth.

Yes, but look, dear brethren, all churches do not get what they desire. We have to complain of churches that are nearly asleep and are gradually declining. Of course, they find excuses. The population is dwindling, or another place of worship is attracting the people—there is always an excuse handy when a man wants one. But still there stands the fact—public worship is almost deserted in some places; the ministry has no rallying power about it; and those who put in an appearance are discontented or indifferent.

In such churches there are no conversions. And what is the reason of it?

1. Even among professed Christians there may be the pursuit of desirable things in a wrong method.

"Ye fight and war, yet ye have not." Have not churches thought to prosper by competing with other churches? At such and such a place of worship they have a very clever man: we must get a clever man, too; in fact, he must be a little more clever than our neighbor's hero. That is the thing—a clever man!

Ah me! That we should live in an age in which we talk about clever men in preaching the Gospel of Jesus Christ! Alas, that this holy service should be thought to depend upon human cleverness!

Churches have competed with each other in architecture, in music, in apparel and in social status. In some cases there is a measure of bitterness in the rivalry. It is not pleasant to little minds to see other churches prospering more than their own. They may be more earnest than we are and be doing God's work better, but we are too apt to turn a jealous eye towards them, and we would rather they did not get on quite so well.

Do ye think that the Scripture saith in vain, "The spirit that dwelleth in us lusteth to envy"? If we could see a disturbance among them so that they would break up and be ecclesiastically killed, we would not rejoice. Of course not; but neither should we suffer any deadly sorrow. In some churches an evil spirit lingers. I bring no railing accusation and, therefore, say no more than this: God will never bless such means and such a spirit. Those who give way to them will desire to have but never obtain.

Meanwhile, what is the reason why they do not have a blessing? The text says, *"Because ye ask not."* I am afraid there are churches which do not ask. Prayer in all forms is too much neglected. Private prayer is allowed to decay.

I shall put it to the conscience of every man how far secret prayer is attended to and how much of fellowship with God there is in secret among the members of our churches. Certainly its healthy existence is vital to church prosperity. Of family prayer it is more easy to judge, for we can see it. I fear that in these days many have quite given up family prayer. I pray you do not imitate them.

I wish you were all of the same mind as the Scotch laborer who obtained a situation in the house of a wealthy farmer who was known to pay well. All his friends envied him that he had gone to live in such a service. In a short time he returned to his native village; and when they asked him why he had left his situation, he replied that he "could not live in a house which had no roof to it."

A house without prayer is a house without a roof. We cannot expect blessings on our churches if we have none on our families.

As to the congregational prayer, the gathering together in what we call our prayer meetings, is there not a falling off? In many cases the prayer meeting is despised and looked down upon as a sort of second-rate gathering. There are members of churches who are never present, and it does not prick their consciences that they stay away. Some congregations mix up the prayer meeting with a lecture so as to hold only one service in the week.

I read the other day an excuse for all this. It is said that people are better at home attending to family concerns. This is idle talk, for who among us wishes people to neglect their domestic concerns? It will be

found that those attend to their own concerns best who are diligent to
get everything in order so that they may go out to assemblies for worship. Negligence of the house of God is often an index of negligence
of their own houses. They are not bringing their children to Christ, I
am persuaded, or they would bring them up to the services.

Anyhow, the prayers of the church measure its prosperity. If we
restrain prayer, we restrain the blessing. Our true success as churches
can only be had by asking it of the Lord.

Are we not prepared to reform and amend in this matter? Oh, for
Zion's travailing hour to come, when an agony of prayer shall move
the whole body of the faithful!

2. "Ye have not because ye ask amiss."

But some reply, "There are prayer meetings, and we do ask for the
blessing, yet it comes not."

Is not the explanation to be found in the other part of the text, *"Ye
have not, because ye ask amiss"*? When prayer meetings become a
mere form, when brethren stand up and waste the time with their long
orations instead of speaking to God in earnest and burning words; when
there is no expectation of a blessing; when the prayer is cold and chill,
then nothing will come of it.

He who prays without *fervency* does not pray at all. *We cannot com-
mune with God, who is a consuming fire, if there is no fire in our prayers.*

Many prayers fail of their errand because there is no faith in them.
Prayers which are filled with doubt are requests for refusal.

Imagine that you wrote to a friend and said, "Dear friend: I am in
great trouble; I therefore tell you and ask for your help because it seems
right to do so. But though I thus write, I have no belief that you will
send me any help. Indeed, I should be mightily surprised if you did
and should speak of it as a great wonder."

Will you get the help, think you? I should say your friend would be
sensible enough to observe the little confidence you have in him and
he would reply that, as you did not expect anything, he would not
astonish you. Your opinion of his generosity is so low that he does not
feel called upon to put himself out of the way on your account. When
prayers are of that kind, you cannot wonder if we "have not, because
we ask amiss."

Moreover, if our praying, however earnest and believing, is a mere
asking that our church may prosper because we want to glory in its pros-

perity, if we want to see our own denomination largely increased and its respectability improved that we may share the honors thereof, then our desires are nothing but lustings after all. Can it be that the children of God manifest the same emulations, jealousies, and ambitions as men of the world? Shall religious work be a matter of rivalry and contest? Ah, then, the prayers which seek success will have no acceptance at the mercyseat. God will not hear us but bid us be gone, for He careth not for the petitions for His work of which self is the object. "Ye have not, because ye ask not," or because "ye ask amiss."

III. THE WEALTH WHICH AWAITS THE USE OF THE RIGHT MEANS OF ASKING OF GOD

I invite your most solemn attention to this matter, for it is vitally important. And my first observation is this:

1. How very small, after all, is this demand which God makes of us.

Ask! Why, it is the least thing He can possibly expect of us, and it is no more than we ordinarily require of those who need help from us. We expect a poor man to ask; and if he does not, we lay the blame of his lack upon himself. If God will give for the asking and we remain poor, who is to blame? Is not the blame most grievous? Does it not look as if we were out of order with God so that we will not even condescend to ask a favor of Him? Surely there must be in our hearts a lurking enmity to Him, or else instead of its being an unwelcome necessity it would be regarded as a great delight.

However, brethren, whether we like it or not, remember, *asking is the rule of the kingdom.* "Ask, and ye shall receive." It is a rule that never will be altered in anybody's case.

Our Lord Jesus Christ is the Elder Brother of the family, but God has not relaxed the rule for Him. Remember this text: Jehovah says to His own Son, "Ask of me, and I will give thee the heathen for thine inheritance, and the uttermost parts of the earth for thy possession."

If the royal and divine Son of God cannot be exempt from the rule of asking that He may have, you and I cannot expect the rule to be relaxed in our favor.

God will bless Elijah and send rain on Israel, but Elijah must pray for it.

If the chosen nation is to prosper, Samuel must plead for it.

If the Jews are to be delivered, Daniel must intercede.

God will bless Paul, and the nations shall be converted through him, but Paul must pray. Pray he did without ceasing; his epistles show that he expected nothing except by asking for it.

Moreover, it is clear to even the most shallow thinker that. . .

2. Some things necessary for the church of God we cannot get other than by prayer.

You can get that clever man I spoke about, that new church, the new organ, the choir, without prayer; but you cannot get the heavenly anointing. The gift of God is not to be purchased with money.

Some of the members of a church in a primitive village in America thought that they would raise a congregation by hanging up a very handsome chandelier in the meetinghouse. People talked about this chandelier, and some went to see it, but the light of it soon grew dim.

You can buy all sorts of ecclesiastical furniture, purchase any kind of paint, brass, muslin, blue, scarlet, and fine linen, together with flutes, harps, sackbuts, psalteries, and all kinds of music—you can get these without prayer; in fact, it could be an impertinence to pray about such prayer. "He bloweth where he listeth." He will not be brought near by any process or method at our command apart from asking. There are no mechanical means which will make up for His absence. Prayer is the great door of spiritual blessing, and if you close it, you shut out the favor.

3. This asking which God requires is a very great privilege.

Suppose there were an edict published that you must not pray: that would be a hardship indeed. If prayer rather interrupted than increased the stream of blessing, it would be a sad calamity.

Did you ever see a dumb man under a strong excitement or suffering great pain, anxious to speak? It is a terrible sight to see. The face is distorted, and the body is fearfully agitated. The mute writhes and labors in dire distress. Every limb is contorted with a desire to help the tongue, but it cannot break its bonds. Hollow sounds come from the breast, and stutterings of ineffectual speech awaken attention, though they cannot reach so far as expression. The poor creature is in pain unspeakable.

Suppose we were in our spiritual nature full of strong desires, yet dumb as to the tongue of prayer. Methinks it would be one of the direst afflictions that could possibly befall us. We should be terribly maimed and dismembered, and our agony would be overwhelming.

Blessed be His name; the Lord ordains a way of utterance and bids our heart speak out to Him!

4. To pray seems to be the first thing we ought think of doing when in need.

If men were right with God and loved Him truly, they would pray as naturally as they breathe. I hope some of us are right with God and do not need to be driven to prayer, for it has become an instinct of our nature.

I was told by a friend the story of a little German boy, a story which his pastor loved to tell. The dear little child believed his God and delighted in prayer. His schoolmaster had urged the scholars to be at school in time, and this child always tried to be so; but his father and mother were dilatory people.

One morning, through their fault alone, he had just left the door as the clock struck the hour for the school to open. A friend standing near heard the little one cry, "Dear God, do grant I may be in time for school." It struck the listener that for once prayer could not be heard, for the child had quite a little walk before him, and the hour was already come. He was curious to see the result.

Now it so happened this morning that the master, in trying to open the schoolhouse door, turned the key the wrong way and could not stir the bolt, so they had to send for a smith to open the door. Hence a delay. Just as the door opened, our little friend entered with the rest, all in good time!

God has many ways of granting right desires. It was most natural that, instead of crying and whining, a child who really loved God should speak to Him about his trouble. Should it not be natural to you and to me spontaneously and at once, to tell the Lord our sorrows and ask for help? Should not this be the first resort?

Alas, according to Scripture and observation, and I grieve to add, according to experience, *prayer is often the last thing.*

Look at the sick man in Psalm 107. Friends bring him various foods, but his soul abhorreth all manner of meat. The physicians do what they can to heal him, but he grows worse and worse and draws nigh to the gates of death. "Then they cry unto the Lord in their trouble." That was put last which should have been first. "Send for the doctor. Prepare him nourishment. Wrap him in flannels!" All very well, but when will you pray to God? God will be called upon when the case grows desperate.

Look at the mariners described in the same Psalm. The barque is well-nigh wrecked. 'They mount up to the heaven, they go down again to the depths: their soul is melted because of trouble.' Still they do all they can to ride out the storm; but when "they reel to and fro, and stagger like a drunken man, and are at their wit's end, then they cry unto the Lord in their trouble." Oh, yes, God is sought unto when we are driven into a corner and ready to perish.

And what a mercy it is that He hears such laggard prayers and delivers the suppliants out of their troubles! But ought it to be so with you and with me and with churches of Christ? Ought not the first impulse of a declining church be, "Let us pray day and night until the Lord appears for us. Let us meet together with one accord in one place and never separate until the blessing descends upon us"?

5. What great things are to be had for the asking!

Have you ever thought of it? Does it not stimulate you to pray fervently? All Heaven lies before the grasp of the asking man. All the promises of God are rich and inexhaustible, and their fulfillment is to be had by prayer.

Jesus saith, "All things are delivered unto me of my Father." And Paul says, "All things are yours, and ye are Christ's."

Who would not pray when all things are thus handed over to us? Ay, and promises that were first made to special individuals are all made to us if we know how to plead them in prayer.

Israel went through the Red Sea ages ago, yet we read in Psalm 66, "There did we rejoice in him."

Only Jacob was present at Peniel, yet Hosea says, "There he spake with us."

When Paul wants to give us a great promise for times of need, he quotes from the Old Testament: "For he hath said, I will never leave thee, nor forsake thee." Where did Paul get that? That is the assurance which the Lord gave to Joshua: *I will not fail thee, nor forsake thee.*" Surely the promise was for Joshua only. No, it is for us. 'No Scripture is of private interpretation'; all Scripture is ours.

See how God appears unto Solomon at night and says, *"Ask what I shall give thee."* Solomon asks for wisdom. "Oh, that is Solomon," say you. Listen. "If any man lack wisdom, let him ask of God." God gave Solomon wealth and fame into the bargain. Is not that peculiar to Solomon? No, for it is said of the true wisdom, "Length of days is in her right hand, and in her left hand riches and honour." And is not this much like our Saviour's word, "Seek ye first the kingdom of God and his righteousness, and all these things shall be added unto you"?

Thus you see the Lord's promises have many fulfillments, and they are waiting now to pour their treasures into the lap of prayer. Does not this lift prayer up to a high level, when God is willing to repeat the biographies of His saints in us; when He is waiting to be gracious and to load us with His benefits?

I will mention another truth which ought to make us pray:

6. If we ask, God will give to us much more than we ask.

Abraham asked of God that Ishmael might live before him. He thought, *Surely this is the promised seed. I cannot expect Sarah will bear a child in her old age. God has promised me a seed; surely it must be this child of Hagar. Oh, that Ishmael might live before thee!* God granted him that, but He gave him Isaac as well and all the blessings of the covenant.

There is Jacob. He kneels down to pray. He asks the Lord to give him bread to eat and raiment to put on. But what did his God give him? When he came back to Bethel he had two bands, thousands of sheep and camels, and much wealth. God had heard him and done exceeding abundantly above what he asked.

It is said of David, "The king asked life of thee, and thou gavest him length of days," yea, gave him not only length of days himself but a throne for his sons throughout all generations till David went in and sat before the Lord, overpowered with the Lord's goodness.

"Well," say you, "but is that true of New Testament prayers?" Yes, it is so with the New Testament pleaders, whether saints or sinners.

They brought a man to Christ sick of the palsy and asked Him to heal him, and He said, "Son, thy sins be forgiven thee." He had not asked that, had he? No, but God gives greater things than we ask for.

Hear that poor, dying thief's humble prayer, "Lord, remember me when thou comest into thy kingdom." Jesus replies, "To day shalt thou be with me in paradise." He had not dreamed of such an honor.

Even the story of the Prodigal teaches us this. He resolved to say, "I am not worthy to be called thy son; make me as one of thy hired servants." What is the answer? 'This my son was dead, and is alive again: bring forth the best robe and put it on him; put a ring on his hands, and shoes on his feet.'

Once get into the position of an asker, and you shall have what you never asked for and never thought to receive. The text is often misquoted: "God is able to do exceeding abundantly above all that we *can* ask, or even think." We *could* ask for the very greatest things if we were but more sensible and had more faith, but God is willing to give us infinitely more than we do ask.

At this moment I believe that God's church might have inconceivable blessings if she were but ready now to pray.

Did you ever notice that wonderful picture in the 8th chapter of the Revelation? It is worthy of careful notice. I shall not attempt to explain it in its connection, but merely point to the picture as it hangs on the wall by itself.

Read on—"When he had opened the seventh seal, there was silence in heaven about the space of half an hour." Silence in Heaven: there were no anthems, no hallelujahs; not an angel stirred a wing. Silence in Heaven! Can you imagine it! And look! You see seven angels standing before God, and to them are given seven trumpets. There they wait, trumpet in hand, but there is no sound. Not a single note of cheer or warning during an interval which was sufficiently long to provoke lively emotion but short enough to prevent impatience. Silence unbroken, profound, awful, reigned in Heaven.

Action is suspended in Heaven, the center of all activity. "And another angel came and stood at the altar, having a golden censer."

There he stands, but no offering is presented. Everything has come to a standstill. What can possibly set it in motion? "And there was given unto him much incense, that he should offer it with the prayers of all saints upon the golden altar which was before the throne." Prayer is presented together with the merit of the Lord Jesus.

Now, see what will happen. "And the smoke of the incense, which came with the prayers of the saints, ascended up before God out of the angel's hands." That is the key of the whole matter.

Now you will see the angel beginning to work. He takes the censer, fills it with the altar fire, and flings it down upon the earth, "and there were voices, and thunderings, and lightnings, and an earthquake . . . And the seven angels which had the seven trumpets prepared themselves to sound."

Everything is moving now. As soon as the prayers of the saints were mixed with the incense of Christ's eternal merit and had begun to smoke up from the altar, then prayer became effectual. Down fell the living coals among the sons of men while the angels of the divine providence who stood still before sound their thunderblasts and the will of the Lord is done. Such is the scene in Heaven in a certain measure even to this day.

Bring hither the incense. Bring hither the prayers of the saints. Set them on fire with Christ's merits, and on the golden altar let them smoke before the Most High. Then shall we see the Lord at work, and His will shall be done on earth as it is in Heaven.

God send His blessing with these words, for Christ's sake. Amen.

CURTIS HUTSON
1934-

ABOUT THE MAN:

In 1961 a mail carrier and pastor of a very small church attended a Sword of the Lord Conference, got on fire, gave up his route and set out to build a great soul-winning work for God. Forrest Hills Baptist Church of Decatur, Georgia, grew from 40 people into a membership of 7,900. The last four years of his pastorate there, the Sunday school was recognized as the largest one in Georgia.

After pastoring for 21 years, Dr. Hutson—the great soul winner that he is—became so burdened for the whole nation that he entered full-time evangelism, holding great citywide-areawide-cooperative revivals in some of America's greatest churches. As many as 625 precious souls have trusted Christ in a single service. In one eight-day meeting, 1,502 salvation decisions were recorded.

As an evangelist, he is in great demand.

At the request of Dr. John R. Rice, Dr. Hutson became Associate Editor of THE SWORD OF THE LORD in 1978, serving in that capacity until the death of Dr. Rice before becoming Editor, President of Sword of the Lord Foundation, and Director of Sword of the Lord Conferences.

All these ministries are literally changing the lives of thousands of preachers and laymen alike, as well as winning many more thousands to Christ.

Dr. Hutson is the author of many fine books and booklets.

VII.

Conditions to Answered Prayer

CURTIS HUTSON

(Message preached on VOICE OF REVIVAL radio broadcast)

"Ask, and it shall be given you; seek, and ye shall find; knock, and it shall be opened unto you: For every one that asketh receiveth; and he that seeketh findeth; and to him that knocketh it shall be opened." — Matt. 7:7,8.

Did you ever ask for something and not get it? Did you pray and not receive an answer? Someone suggested that God answers all prayer: to some He answers "yes," to others He answers "no." I disagree.

In his book, *Prayer—Asking and Receiving*, Dr. John R. Rice says prayer is asking and the answer to prayer is receiving. God does not answer *yes* to some prayers and *no* to others. When He says *no*, the prayer is simply not answered. *No* is not an answer to prayer. The answer to prayer is receiving.

In this promise of Matthew 7:8, Jesus said if we ask we shall receive; if we seek we shall find; and if we knock it shall be opened. Many have said to me, "I do not always receive an answer to prayer." Neither do I. But there are ways to get an answer, so I share with you today the conditions to answered prayer.

First, we must

CLEAR THE WAY

Psalm 66:18 says, "If I regard iniquity in my heart, the Lord WILL NOT HEAR ME." If I tolerate known sin in my life, I cannot expect to get my prayer answered. This verse states: "If I regard iniquity in my heart, the Lord WILL NOT HEAR ME." Isaiah 59:1, 2 says, "The Lord's hand is not shortened, that it cannot save; neither his ear heavy, that it cannot hear: But your iniquities have separated between you and your God, and your sins have hid his face from you, that he will not hear."

The Bible makes it very clear that God can hear prayer; but if we tolerate known sin in our life, He will not hear us. If one is to receive an answer to prayer, he must meet the requirement laid down in I John 1:9. Once you have cleared the way by receiving forgiveness and cleansing for every known sin, then you can sing, "Nothing between my soul and the Saviour"; and you are ready to move on to the next step.

The second condition to answered prayer is

A RIGHTEOUS LIFE

James 5:16 states, "Confess your faults one to another, and pray one for another, that ye may be healed. The effectual fervent prayer of a righteous man availeth much." Notice that prayer must be made by "a righteous man." First Peter 3:12 says, "For the eyes of the Lord are over the righteous, and his ears are open unto their prayers." Say, that's important! The Lord's ears are not open to any and everybody's prayers, only to the prayers of the righteous. Just be right, live the very best you know how, and His ears will be open unto your prayers.

Third, if you are to expect an answer when you pray, you must be

AN OBEDIENT CHRISTIAN

First John 3:22 states, "And whatsoever we ask, we receive of him, because we keep his commandments, and do those things that are pleasing in his sight." *Whatsoever* is a big word. The Bible says, "whatsoever we ask" we will receive. Why? Because we keep His commandments and do things pleasing in His sight. Obedience is a prerequisite to answered prayer. Learn to do everything He says. Learn to keep His commandments. Learn to be an obedient Christian. Not only that; we are to strive to please Him. We are not only to do those things which He commands, but the Bible says we are to do those things that are pleasing in His sight. Not only are we to obey Him, but we are to strive to please Him. There may not be a clear command concerning something we propose to do, but we should ask, "Will it please the Lord?"

If you expect an answer to prayer, you must clear the way by living a righteous life and by being obedient.

In the fourth place you must

ABIDE IN CHRIST

Jesus said in John 15:7, "If ye abide in me, and my words abide in you, ye shall ask what ye will, and it shall be done unto you." What a promise! But there is a condition: if we abide in Him and His words abide in us.

What does it mean to abide in Christ? The picture in John 15 is that of a branch abiding in the vine. To abide in the vine doesn't necessarily mean to stay connected to it. Connection to the branch has nothing to do with abiding. The result of not abiding is the withering of the branch so that it doesn't bear fruit.

Why does a branch not bear fruit? Why does it wither? Because the life of the vine does not flow into it. The branch is to receive from the vine. The branch does not reach down into the earth for moisture and fertilizer. The roots of the vine reach out and pull in the moisture, fertilizer, and food from the ground and take these up through the vine and out through the branches so the branches bear fruit. The branch that is abiding in the vine is simply yielding or opening and allowing the life of the vine to express itself through it. So to abide in Christ means that we yield, we surrender, we allow Christ to express Himself through us and to live out His life through us.

The Christian life is not so much an imitation of the Christ life as it is Christ living His life through us. In Galatians 2:20 Paul said, "I am crucified with Christ: nevertheless I live; yet not I, but Christ liveth in me: and the life which I now live in the flesh I live by the faith of the Son of God, who loved me, and gave himself for me." It is Christ living in me.

If we are to expect an answer to prayer, we must abide in Christ. To abide in Christ means yielding to Him, allowing Him to control every part of our being, allowing Him to live out His life through us, even as the branch abides in the vine, allowing the life of the vine to express itself through the branch.

If we are to expect an answer to prayer, we must not only clear the way, live a righteous life, be an obedient Christian and abide in Christ, but we must

HAVE FAITH

Notice Mark 9:23: "Jesus said unto him, If thou canst believe, all things are possible to him that believeth." We must expect an answer. James 1:5-7 declares, "If any of you lack wisdom, let him ask of God, that giveth to all men liberally, and upbraideth not; and it shall be given him. But [he qualifies it] let him ask in faith, nothing wavering. For he that wavereth is like a wave of the sea driven with the wind and tossed. For let not that man think that he shall receive any thing of the Lord."

If we are to receive an answer to prayer, we must believe, we must expect. Emerson said, "They can conquer who believe they can." Henry Ford said, "If you think you can, you are right; if you think you can't, you are right again," meaning you won't be able to do it. "For as he thinketh in his heart, so is he," says the Scripture.

One cannot expect an answer to prayer without believing. Hebrews 11:6 says, ". . . for he that cometh to God must believe that he is, and that he is a rewarder of them that diligently seek him." One must believe that God exists and that He rewards those who seek Him. Believe— and receive.

I am not saying that is the only condition to answered prayer. I have certainly prayed at times when my faith was very weak. But the very fact that I prayed indicated that I thought I would get an answer. I wouldn't waste my time praying if I didn't have some faith. My faith is not always as strong as I wish it were, but faith is a condition to answered prayer. Jesus said, "If thou canst believe, all things are possible to him that believeth."

When one of Napoleon's soldiers made a great request, the other soldiers laughed and said, "You have asked too much. You will never get it." But to their surprise the request was granted. Napoleon said to the soldier, "You have honored me by the magnitude of your request."

Friends, you honor God by the magnitude of your requests. You cannot ask too much from Him.

Did you know that God likes big-mouthed people? Psalm 81:10 says, "I am the Lord thy God, which brought thee out of the land of Egypt: open thy mouth WIDE, and I will fill it." God can fill a big mouth. We cannot get enough from God to leave Him with less than He had when He started giving.

If you are to receive an answer to prayer, then you need

THE RIGHT MOTIVES

James 4:3 says, "Ye ask, and receive not, because ye ask amiss [or wrong], that ye may consume it upon your lusts." You want it for a selfish purpose or for the wrong reason. I am sure God answers my prayers; but if I had a selfish, fleshly desire for something I did not need, then I would not get it because that would be "to consume it upon my own lust," my own selfish desires.

When we pray, we must have the right motives, want things for the right reason—to honor and glorify Christ. That is not to say God doesn't care about your needs. We are to ask for daily bread, for the Lord taught us to pray, "Give us this day our daily bread." According to that prayer, He expects us to pray every day. He didn't teach us to pray, "Give us our bread supply for this week," or, "Give us our month's supply of bread. Then we will pray again next month." Rather He said, "After this manner therefore pray ye . . . Give us this day our daily bread." He expects our prayers to be daily.

We can get and have a right to expect an answer to our prayer if our motives are right. We are not to ask for foolish things but for that which will glorify Christ.

If an answer doesn't come, just believe it wasn't God's will, that God knew best, because we must also pray

ACCORDING TO THE WILL OF GOD

First John 5:14, 15: "And this is the confidence that we have in him, that, if we ask any thing according to his will, he heareth us: And if we know that he hear us, whatsoever we ask, we know that we have the petitions that we desired of him." If we ask anything "according to his will," He heareth us. Prayer must be according to the will of God.

How can we be sure we are praying in the will of God? One way is to be led by the Holy Spirit. "The Spirit also helpeth our infirmities: for we know not what we should pray for as we ought," says Romans 8:26. We don't always know what to pray for, but He leads us in prayer.

Did you ever have an intense desire to pray for something? You felt strongly, *I should pray for this*? That was the Holy Spirit leading you. It was God's will for you to have the thing He was leading you to pray for. It is good to pray, "Lord, if it is not Your will, then withhold it. You know more what I need than I."

When I was a boy, my father would not let me play with his pocketknife. I thought then he was selfish, but now I know why. He was a barber, and he kept that knife sharp as a razor. I could have cut off a finger or maybe done worse. I now look back and thank him for withholding from me something I really thought I ought to have. It was his will for me not to have it, and his will was best. So God's will is always best for us.

How do you get an answer to prayer? By praying in the will of God. Another way to get an answer is by

NOT GIVING UP

In Matthew 7:7 Jesus said, "Ask, and it shall be given you." And verse 8 says, "For every one that asketh receiveth." "Ask" is in the continual sense: "He who keeps on asking receives, he who keeps on seeking finds, and he who keeps on knocking, to him the door shall be opened."

If you recall, Paul besought the Lord to remove a thorn from his flesh. Paul prayed, "Lord, I have this thorn; I could be a better preacher without it." But God didn't answer Paul's prayer. God didn't remove his thorn.

Paul prayed again, "Lord, I am still praying about this thorn which You haven't removed. If You will remove it, I could be a better preacher." Still no answer.

Paul prayed again: "Lord, this is the third time I have prayed about this thorn, but it is still here! I want it removed. I can be a better preacher and serve You better without it." God still didn't remove it. Rather, He told Paul, "My grace is sufficient for thee: for my strength is made perfect in weakness."

Then Paul changed that prayer: "Most gladly therefore will I rather glory in my infirmities, that the power of Christ may rest upon me."

To get an answer, you have to keep on praying. Persistent praying— not giving up. He who keeps on asking receives. He who keeps on seeking finds. If Paul had kept on asking, he would have received. But God changed Paul's prayer.

I promise you this: if you start praying for something and keep on praying for it and keep on praying for it and keep on praying for it, one of two things will happen: God will either give you what you are asking for, based on His promise in Matthew 7:7, 8, or He will change your prayer, as He did with Paul.

Have you prayed for something, then given up? You concluded that you were not going to get it, so you never prayed for it again. I suggest you now pray, "Lord, I'm going to keep on praying for this until You either give it to me or make it clear that I am not supposed to have it and change my prayer."

I heard the story of a man drilling for oil who ran out of money. Borrowing more money again and again, he drilled deeper but with no success. Finally he gave up, pulled the drill from the well and left. A few months later another man came by, dropped a drill in the same well, drilled a few feet deeper, and struck a gusher. The first man had quit too soon.

Have you, too, prayed for things but quit too soon? Jesus said, "Every one that asketh receiveth; and he that seeketh findeth; and to him that knocketh it shall be opened." Keep on asking, keep on seeking, keep on knocking. Don't give up. The song admonishes

> **Just keep on praying**
> **'Til light breaks through.**
> **The Lord will answer,**
> **He'll answer you.**
> **God keeps His promise,**
> **His Word is true.**
> **Just keep on praying**
> **'Til light breaks through.**

Then, if you are to expect an answer to prayer,

IDOLS CANNOT BE IN THE HEART

Ezekiel 14:3 says, "Son of man, these men have set up their idols in their heart, and put the stumbling block of their iniquity before their face: should I be inquired of at all by them?" These people set up idols in their heart, and God asks, "Should they even pray to Me at all?"

If you have idols in your heart—that is, something above God—then the question is raised as to whether you should even pray at all.

If you want an answer to prayer, there must be

A RIGHT RELATIONSHIP BETWEEN HUSBAND AND WIFE

First Peter 3:7 states, "Likewise, ye husbands, dwell with them according to knowledge, giving honour unto the wife, as unto the weaker vessel, as being heirs together of the grace of life; *that your prayers be not hindered.*"

Here the Bible teaches that a wrong relationship between husband and wife keeps prayers from being answered. Don't expect God to answer prayer when there are constant bickering and fussing in the home. Get your home relationship right; then you can get an answer. God does not mock us by saying, "Call unto me, and I will answer thee" (Jer. 33:3). God is not kidding when He says, "Open thy mouth wide, and I will fill it" (Ps. 81:10). He means it when He says, "Hitherto have ye asked nothing in my name: ask, and ye shall receive, that your joy may be full" (John 16:24).

God expects us to get an answer to prayer. He wants us to get an answer to prayer, but He gives certain conditions, and one of those conditions is a right relationship between the husband and wife.

God suggests, too, that when you pray,

BE SPECIFIC

Ask for what you want. The Bible says in John 14:13, "*Whatsoever ye shall ask in my name, that will I do.*" Underline the two words *whatsoever* and *that*. Be specific. Don't pray in general, such as, "Lord, we need Your blessings," but be specific in what blessings you need.

In Luke 11 the story is told of a man who went to a friend pleading for bread because he had some hungry friends who came to him wanting to be fed. Verse 5 says, "Friend, lend me three loaves." He didn't say, "Friend, I have some hungry folks at my house, and I need some bread." Rather, he told exactly how many loaves he wanted: "Lend me *three* loaves."

I have heard people pray, "Dear Lord, forgive us of all our sins." The promise in I John 1:9 is, "If we confess our sins, he is faithful and just to forgive us our sins." Confess your sins by name. You did not commit them in a bunch, so don't confess them as a bunch.

When the man lost the ax head in II Kings 6, and Elisha asked, "Where fell it?" the Bible says, ". . . he showed him the place." He didn't say, "Somewhere in this river," but pointed to the exact place where it fell.

Be specific. Tell the Lord exactly, explicitly what you want.

Cameron V. Thompson wrote a little book entitled *Master Secrets of Prayer*, published by Back to the Bible Publishers. Cam Thompson lived in Atlanta where I lived. He is now with the Lord. His wife and daughters visited Forrest Hills Baptist Church one night; and, after the service as we talked about Cam and his prayer life, his wife told me a story about one of their daughters.

The little girl, seeing a doll that she wanted in a window, asked, "Daddy, how much would that doll cost?"

He answered her, "$4.98."

"How many pennies is that?"

"Four hundred and ninety-eight."

Then she asked her daddy to pray with her that God would give her 498 pennies.

He prayed. A few days later a lady knocked on the front door of the Thompson residence. Mrs. Thompson answered the door, and the lady held up a jug filled with pennies. She said, "Mrs. Thompson, I have been dropping pennies in this jug for some time. This week when I dropped in some, they filled the jug. When I asked the Lord what I should do with this jug of pennies, your daughter came to mind. May I give them to her?"

She called in the little one, and the lady gave her the pennies. The little girl emptied the jug and began to count.

How many pennies do you think were in that jug? Was it 495? No, no! Was it 501? Not on your life. How many pennies? Yes, 498—exactly what the girl had asked for. She didn't pray, "Lord, give me $4.98." Her childlike prayer was, "Lord, give me 498 pennies," and God gave her exactly what she asked for—498 pennies! Isn't that exciting!

A man in our church with a Sunday school class prayed that God would double his attendance the next Sunday. Since he had twelve the Sunday before, he expected maybe twenty-four; but the children kept coming in the classroom—25, 30, 35, 40, 45, 50—exactly 50 children came into that class. They had to remove all of the chairs and let the children stand. The teacher was frustrated. He stuttered and said, "Boys, I don't know what happened! When we prayed last week for God to double our attendance, I expected maybe 24, but not 50!"

One little boy in the back of the room raised his hand. The teacher saw it and said, "Yes, Son, what is it?"

The little fellow responded, "Teacher, it is all my fault. Last week when you all prayed for 24, I prayed for 50."

When the Sunday school teacher told me that story, I literally shouted! I thought, *Get that boy! Let's hire him to conduct prayer meetings in this church! Let's have him pray for our needs. That child gets what he wants!*

The truth is, all of us ought to get what we want. God wants to answer our prayers. You should be specific when you pray. Tell God exactly what you want.

Jesus promised, "Ask, and it shall be given you; seek, and ye shall find; knock, and it shall be opened unto you: For every one that asketh receiveth; and he that seeketh findeth; and to him that knocketh it shall be opened."

Have you been praying for something that you didn't get? Then did you give up? Why not follow these simple suggestions: start over, pray again, and keep on praying until God either gives you what you ask for or changes your prayer?

THOMAS L. MALONE
1915-

ABOUT THE MAN:

Tom Malone was converted and called to preach at the same moment! At an old-fashioned bench, the preacher took his tear-stained Bible and showed Tom Malone how to be saved. He accepted Christ then and there. Arising from his knees in the Isbell Methodist Church near Russellville, Alabama, he shook the circuit pastor's hand; and this bashful nineteen-year-old farm boy announced: "I know the Lord wants me to be a preacher."

Backward, bashful and broke, yet Tom borrowed five dollars, took what he could in a cardboard suitcase and left for Cleveland, Tennessee. Immediately upon arrival at Bob Jones College, Malone heard a truth that totally dominated his life and labors for the Lord ever after—soul winning!

That day he won his first soul! The green-as-grass Tom, a new convert himself, knew nothing of soul-winning approaches or techniques. He simply asked the sinner, "Are you a Christian?" No. In a few minutes that young man became Malone's first convert.

Since that day, countless have been his experiences in personal evangelism.

Mark it down: Malone began soul winning his first week in Bible college. And he has never lost *the thirst* for it, *the thrill* in it, nor *the task* of it since. Pastoring churches, administrating schools, preaching across the nation have not deterred Tom Malone from this mainline ministry.

It is doubtful if young Malone *ever* dreamed of becoming the man he is today. He is now Doctor Tom Malone, is renowned in fundamental circles for his wise leadership and great preaching, is pastor of the large Emmanuel Baptist Church of Pontiac, Michigan, Founder and President of Midwestern Baptist Schools, and is eagerly sought as speaker in large Bible conferences from coast to coast.

Dr. John R. Rice often said that Dr. Tom Malone may be the greatest gospel preacher in all the world today!

VIII.

"Is Any Thing Too Hard for the Lord?"

There Is No Promise Too Hard for God to Fulfill; No Problem Too Hard for God to Solve; No Place Where God Can't Send a Revival; No Person Too Hard for God to Save.

TOM MALONE

(Preached at Sword of the Lord Conference in Danville, Illinois, in 1961)

Only three times does the Bible say, "The Lord appeared to Abraham."

He Appeared to Abraham to Reveal His Power. The first appearance is in Genesis, chapter 12. In verse 6 is this expression, "The Canaanite was then in the land." God's Word said that just before He made a great promise, verse 7: "And the Lord appeared unto Abram, and said, Unto thy seed will I give this land." God said, "It doesn't matter if the Canaanite is in the land, nor how strong he is, nor how long he has been there, nor how warlike he is. No matter how well-walled his villages are, how big the giants are, I am going to give you the land." God seems to have appeared to Abraham in this instance to reveal His power.

We, too, need that revelation. We, too, need to know that God is powerful. We dare not limit God.

We are living in a strange age. Many are talking themselves into a state of despondency and discouragement. We talk today about the strength of liberalism and modernism and how it is growing. We talk today about the downfall of schools, the modernism and liberalism in these institutions of learning. We talk about the coldness of the Christians, the compromise of churches. We talk about drugs and alcohol and sex and how these are affecting America.

All of it is true. But that doesn't affect God. His power is not limited.

I admire Elisha. Every time I read about a great character in the Bible, I say, *He is my favorite.* And he is for that day—until I get on to another one; then he becomes my favorite. I like Elisha because he was kind of a farmer boy. He was plowing with twelve yoke of oxen when one day Elijah came along. Elisha was called to be Elijah's successor. One day—oh, what a great day it was—God was going to take Elijah home. Elijah, I think, through the Lord, was putting Elisha to the test.

Elijah said, "You wait here; I am going to Gilgal."

Elisha answered, "No, you are not going anywhere without me! Something is going to happen today, and when it does, I am going to be there."

Elijah said, "You wait here."

"No, I am going to go with you."

There were fifty young preachers looking on, the young prophets and the young preachers. And Elijah said, "I am going over the Jordan; you stay on this side."

But Elisha said, "No, I will go with you. Something is going to happen."

And the young preachers spoke up. All fifty of them had to get their piece in. They kept saying to Elisha, "Your master is going to be lifted up today. He is going to go home today."

Elisha answered, "Hold your peace." That was a nice, polite Bible way of saying, "Shut your mouth! I know what is going to happen."

When Elijah said, "Stay on this side of Jordan," Elisha answered, "No, if you are going over Jordan, I am going with you."

So Elijah came to the Jordan, took off his coat, rolled it up and—*whop!*—hit the waters, and the Jordan rolled back and they walked over to the other side. After awhile the chariot of God came and Elijah was taken up.

Someone has counted eight miracles Elijah performed. When he asked Elisha, "What do you want? What is your request? What is the desire of your heart? What's your aspiration? What do you want?" Elisha answered, "I want a double portion of the Spirit of God."

If it had been we and God had asked, "What do you want?" most of us would have said, "Well, Elijah performed eight miracles. I know I can never do what he did. I would like to perform one, maybe two, maybe four." But not this preacher! "I want a double portion of your Spirit."

Elisha wrought exactly twice as many miracles as Elijah did. He got just what he asked for. He got what he had faith to believe. He got what he expected. He got what he wanted. Elisha wrought many miracles. He comes back to the River Jordan, rolls up his coat, and—whop!—hits the water and says, "Roll back, Jordan!" and Jordan rolled back.

Today we need to believe that God is not limited, that God is not confined to circumstances. God is not bound by the fact that there is modernism and compromise and coldness and deadness everywhere. He is still a God of infinite power.

So He appeared to Abraham to reveal His power.

God Appeared to Abraham to Reveal His Sufficiency. In chapter 17, verse 1, He appeared to Abraham again when he was ninety years old and nine, and said unto him, "I am the Almighty God; walk before me, and be thou perfect." The second appearance is to reveal His sufficiency: "El Shaddai—I am the God who is enough. I am all you need. I am the God who is sufficient."

We need that today, too. We need to believe today that if we have God, He is enough.

People say, "Brother Tom, what group do you belong to?" Or, "What association are you a member of?" None. They always want to know, "Where are your headquarters?" I don't have any. We have God, El Shaddai, a God who is enough. God revealed to Abraham His sufficiency.

God Appeared to Abraham to Reveal That He Was His Friend. In chapter 18, it seemed as if God wanted Abraham to know He was his friend. In this chapter He assured and encouraged him. Thus out of this chapter comes the question, "Is any thing too hard for God?"

I would like this morning to have every one of us leave this service believing that absolutely nothing is too hard for God. There are many discouraged preachers. Many Christians are discouraged. Many good women are discouraged. Many leaders are discouraged. Many are like old Elijah under the juniper tree.

If you will examine discouragement, you will find that it usually comes when there is no reason for it. It came to Elijah when there was no reason for it. Why on earth would a man fresh from a Mount Carmel experience get discouraged and get under a juniper tree? Elijah all day had watched modernist preachers pray; and no victory came, no answer came, no windows of Heaven opened, no fire fell, no revival—no answer. This same man then gets the God of glory to open the windows of Heaven, send down the fire, answer his prayer, and vindicate his call. How could he witness all this—then get under a juniper tree!

Why would he get despondent and filled with melancholy? Why would he get a persecution complex and talk about suicide, wanting to be alone, and all that kind of stuff that never should be in the language of a Christian?

This is the attitude of many Christians today. But is anything too hard for the Lord?

Four things come to us out of this text. First,

I. NO PROMISE TOO HARD FOR GOD TO FULFILL

Oh, the promises of God! I feel a little bit reluctant to even talk on the subject of prayer after Dr. Rice has spoken on it and after the great book he has written on prayer. But I have to pray, too. I, too, have to know what it means to claim the promises of God. So do you. Dr. Rice can't do your praying for you. He can't do mine for me. We ourselves need to know something about the promises of God.

Someone has said there may be at least thirty thousand promises in the Bible. Then I want God to give me one that I can claim for any phase of life.

For instance, so often we get in an airplane. A few years ago Mrs. Malone and I were going to cross the Atlantic Ocean. As we walked out of the hotel lobby to get in the limousine to go to the airport, in great big black letters was the headline, "PLANE DOWN IN THE ATLANTIC." I thought, *Why couldn't it have been in the Pacific!*

We had two children. We were going seven thousand miles from them. So I claimed the promise of Deuteronomy 33:27, "The eternal God is thy refuge, and underneath are the everlasting arms." I never get on an airplane but that I claim that promise. Then I rest in that promise.

God wants His people to launch out on His promises.

Numbers 23:19 is a wonderful verse: "God is not a man, that he should lie; neither the son of man, that he should repent: hath he said, and shall he not do it? or hath he spoken, and shall he not make it good?"

A young preacher went through our school, Charles Whitefield. Charles was saved in our church some years ago on an Easter Sunday. Then the Lord called him to preach. He got his training. He went to pastor the Grace Baptist Church in Birmingham, Michigan, between Pontiac and Detroit, where the elite live, where the well-to-do people live—folks who are hard to reach, people who think they don't need God. Many talked about what a hard field it was.

This young man went there to build a church. He started in the basement of a home. The crowd grew. After about sixty people came, he had to move out of the recreation room of the home. About that time a building was for sale for forty thousand dollars—a lot of money for a church just starting out. Charles began praying about it.

One day while reading the Bible he came across that promise, "Wherever you set the sole of your foot, I will give it thee." He didn't have sense enough to know that was in the Old Testament! You see, he was an ignorant preacher who hadn't gone to seminary. He hadn't learned all about dispensational truth. He hadn't learned that God said that to the Jew and that it could mean nothing to the Gentile. He hadn't graduated that far yet.

About one o'clock in the morning he pulled off his shoes, rolled up his trouser legs, got down on his knees, looked up into the heavens, and prayed: "Now, Lord, if it means what it says, that the sole of my foot must touch the ground, then I have my shoes off. I am going to step this off, Lord, and claim Your promise."

He stepped it off in the moonlight. Poor little old guy! You see, he didn't know it was for somebody else. He didn't know it was for some other dispensation. He hadn't as yet gotten that deep, that spiritual, that pious, like you and I have.

He launched out on the promises of God. He stuck out his neck. He launched out into the deep. He dived off the end of the diving board and said, "I am just going to claim this promise."

Well, to make a long story short, he built a good strong church. People are being saved and being baptized.

God sometimes says some things in the Bible not meant directly to me, but He never uttered one word that wasn't meant for me. "Whatsoever things were written aforetime were written for our learning" (Rom.

15:4). "And they are written for our admonition, upon whom the ends of the world are come" (I Cor. 10:11).

All people of God in this dark and troublesome hour need the promises of God. Oh, God's promises! How sweet! How beautiful! How wonderful! How true!

I think of the dear old lady who was dying. She had been talking about how sweet it was to trust the Lord; how dear were His promises! Someone said to her, "Suppose after you die, you find it is all a mistake, that the promises of God were not true, that you are not really saved after all and you will lose your soul."

The old saint's response was, "I may lose my soul, but God would lose more. God would lose His honor."

How true! I speak reverently, but God's honesty, God's honor is at stake.

A preacher I know built a great church. Somebody asked him, "How did you build it?"

He answered, "On John 14:13." "And whatsoever ye shall ask in my name, that will I do." That is a strange verse upon which to build a church, isn't it? Oh, may God help us to make great use of His promises!

Notice something else. There is no promise too hard for God to fulfill. There is no prayer too hard for God to answer. There is nothing that God can't do in answer to prayer.

God laid it on my heart a few years ago to start into a large building program. The school buildings cost $625,000; furnishings, thousands and thousands of dollars more—about $700,000 in all. I had no money. No rich people were in our church. We had no millionaires to draw from.

One day I got something in the mail which read—it is not near as good as the promises of the Bible, but it is all true—"When God is going to do something wonderful, He starts with the difficult. When God is going to do something very wonderful and miraculous, He starts with an impossibility." I took that little card and stuck it under the glass on my desk and looked at it every day. I said, *God will start with an impossibility.*

Needless to say, God has answered many of my prayers. The Lord has been wonderful. Oh, how good God is!

If I were to ask this group here this morning, "How many of you have had a prayer answered for you?" every Christian here would lift his hand.

But if I were to say to you, "Tell us about the prayer," some of you would go back ten years and tell when God saved your boy or girl. That is wonderful. Some of you would go back five years. Some of you would go back six months. But a good Christian ought not have to go back too far in order to tell about God's specifically answering his prayer.

We have this building program and a great indebtedness. We are trusting God for it. Good Christian people have invested their money in a bond program. And we tell them, "When you need your money, call for it."

A few days ago a registered letter came from one of our church members who had invested $3,600.00 in our building program. She said, "I have to have my money this week."

We had stated, "Whenever you need it, ask for it." I didn't go to the folks in the church and say, "We have got to have $3,600.00 by a certain day." But we went to God and prayed.

The other day I got a letter from the state fairgrounds in Minnesota from a lady who wrote, "I am having trouble with my nerves. I am ill and am really not as responsible as I ought to be. Invest the enclosed for me before I lose it or something happens to it."

There was an envelope with two or three money orders in it which amounted to $2,300.00. I opened another letter from Atlanta, Georgia, and a man said, "I am a Christian. I have heard of your building program. I want to invest $1,000.00 in the building program."

With some other gifts, God, in one mail, in one day, miraculously answered prayer. He has never failed.

God Almighty is not limited to circumstances. Oh, get out from under the juniper tree and believe that the God who parted the river when Elijah went over can part it for us when we want to go. God can do anything in answer to prayer. It is God's way out. It is our way in. It is the way over. It is the way of victory. No prayer is too hard for God to answer.

II. NO PROBLEM TOO HARD FOR GOD TO SOLVE

Now don't tell me you don't have any problems. No matter who you are—everybody gets in tight places. If you say, "I never get in a tight place," then you are different from the characters of the Bible. They really got in tight places—Gideon, Abraham, Moses, Paul. If he attempts something for God, any Christian comes to great times of crises. Many people face a problem, then come to believe that the problem is too great. God will solve it, provided you put first things first in your life.

A fellow came to our church some years ago. He is now teaching in our seminary. He has a bachelor's degree and a master's degree. He had done some teaching in a Christian college and university. When he came to us, he had been pastor of a little church in the Southern Baptist Convention. But over Convention matters, he lost his church. He had not been entirely happy in his teaching, so had given that up. He said, "Brother Tom, I want to get a job and make a living for my family while I think and pray and find out just exactly where God wants me. I need to get these problems cleared up in my life and get them solved." So he stayed in our church.

Our Sunday school superintendent at that time was a great soul winner. So for six months this man followed the Sunday school superintendent around like a little puppy, learning everything he could about the work of God—how to win people, how to build a church, how to reach large groups of people with the Word of God.

One day he came to me and said, "I believe the Lord has straightened out some things in my life. Pray with me that God will put me where He wants me."

One day the phone rang. This person calling said, "Brother Tom, we need a preacher for Sunday at a little church out in the country called Andersonville. Could you recommend somebody?" I told him I could. So I asked this fellow if he would like to go.

He preached that appointed Sunday. The church at that time was 107 years old. The largest crowd they ever had was on the celebration of their one hundredth anniversary when people came back home from many states around. About a hundred people were there on that hundredth anniversary. So this preacher went there to preach.

In a few days he came back with a troubled face and said, "Brother Tom, I don't want to go out there as pastor."

I said, "Who told you that you had to? I am not a bishop. I don't tell folks where to go. God takes care of that."

He said again, "Well, I don't want to go."

I said, "Then don't go."

He said, "But all last night I was troubled. I couldn't sleep. I had a burden on my heart. I think maybe God is calling me out there to that little country church. Brother Tom, you can't see twelve houses from that church. It is way out in the country."

I said, "Well, I didn't put the church out in the country, and I didn't call you, so don't blame me. If God has called you, then you do what God says."

He went. And he said, "If God has put me in this place, by His grace I will see what God can do."

So he set out doing the right thing. He preached the Gospel. And he preached about Jesus. You know, you can do fundamental preaching; you can preach the Bible and preach orthodoxy, yet stay from Jesus an awful long ways. He preached Jesus. He preached not to appeal to people's intellect but to their hearts, to get people saved. He preached the Gospel, first of all. He set out to do what God said— house-to-house visitation. The houses were half a mile apart. It was a rural area. You couldn't see a dozen houses from where the church was. He set out to have a visitation program. This is a hard place. It is not easy. It is a country place. It is a little place. It is a place where the people had never had any vision.

He got twelve people together. He organized them into six visitation couples. He took his wife, and that made seven couples. It was the highest number they ever had to go visiting, but they did it every week. He said, "We will have a visitation program if we never have anything else. We won't quit."

These couples drove up and down those country roads, knocking on the doors of those farmhouses.

That little church began to get full. People began to be saved. The spirit of revival prevailed all the time. It grew until the people had to stand around the walls. They far exceeded the greatest crowd they had ever had (and that was the crowd on their hundredth anniversary), with one and two, four, five and six getting saved every Sunday in a place nobody wanted to pastor, in a place that was hard.

It was not too hard for God. No place is too hard for God. No problem is too hard for Him.

I ask preachers sometimes how they are getting along, but then I wish I hadn't asked them. I can be on the mountain top, can almost feel the zephyr from angel's wings, then say to some preacher, "How are you getting along?" and when he gets through telling me, I have to go to the Bible and pray and get straightened out again myself! Oh, what discouraging conversation you get from the average Christian today!

It just thrills my soul when I ask some preacher, "How are you getting along?" and he smiles and says, "Praise God, things are going good! Folks are being saved. The church is growing. The Lord is answering prayer."

So surprised am I when a fellow says that to me anymore that I say, "Oh, He is?" I am not expecting that. I am expecting preachers to believe that God can't solve their problems, can't send revivals in hard places, can't give victory in difficult situations.

If we preach without enthusiasm, without victory, without encouragement in our own souls, our people will get in the same frame of mind. God help us to believe today that nothing is too hard for God.

III. NO PLACE WHERE GOD CAN'T SEND A REVIVAL

I am not going to be a hypocrite. I am not going to lie to you. I have been to places where I know I failed. I don't know whether you ever have or not. I believe that God can send a revival anywhere in the world. I have seen Him do it when not many people wanted a revival. I have seen God send a revival when they had never had one before. I have known God to give a revival when everything was against it.

You know, we try everything except God's way. We try advertising. We try to get people to realize what a great preacher is coming. We publicize, we organize, we do everything but agonize before God in prayer and claim His promises.

I shall never forget one place I went when still a student at Bob Jones College. It wasn't a town. It was a little crossroads. There was no church there, but there was an old school building. It was a little place called Village Farm, Alabama. The reason I wanted to go there was that a good many of my relatives, some of them very distant relatives, lived in that community. My grandfather who lived to be 91 and died in his 70th wedding year, left 109 living descendents. I have known more brilliant men, more educated men, but I have never known a greater man in some ways. He read the Bible through after he was 70 years of age. He read the New Testament through 28 times and the Old Book, as he called it, through a good many times. He read with a pencil in his hand, and he put that pencil under every word as he thought about it and meditated on it. He literally devoured it. He ate it. He literally saturated himself with it.

Grandfather had heavenly wisdom. He would take the big print Bible I gave him and out in the margin write questions he wanted to ask me or someone else. He would make comments. He thoroughly read it through.

Many of these 109 living descendents lived out in that rural farm area. So I wanted to go out to that area and have a revival.

The authorities gave permission to use that school building. I cleaned it out and fixed it up and started out to preach. The crowds came! Those country people took to that revival in that school. You could look out just before sundown in the afternoon and see the roads full. They came walking, riding mules and horses, in pickup trucks. They came in wagons with hay in the bed and the wagon filled with people. There would be five times more people on the outside in the yard than could get in the school building. And the Lord was blessing.

A few were being saved. The Devil was fighting. The old school building had a tin roof on it. The rough country boys would get out there in the woods at night and pick up big limestone rocks and throw them through the dark, and they would fall on the school building and in the middle of the people outside.

One night as I was preaching, a cat came sailing right through the air—anything to distract. A few were getting saved, but it was hard. There was deep conviction but not much freedom and liberty.

One morning during a testimony meeting an aunt of mine stood up to testify. The minute I looked at her, I knew there was something unusual about her. With lips trembling and big tears rolling down her face, she said, "Son [she helped rear me; she was still at home at my grandfather's farm when I was a boy], revival is going to come to this community. Our loved ones and friends are going to be saved."

Then she said why she knew. "Last night when I went home from the service, I had such a burden for my neighbor family who lives across the road, with not a one in the family saved. I thought of our loved ones, many of them still lost—cousins and aunts and uncles—and I went home burdened. Since I couldn't sleep, I arose and went to a room and got alone and closed the door. All night long I begged God for revival. This morning about daylight God assured me revival was going to come."

Then she dried her tears and sat down. She made me and everybody else believe it.

Oh, how the revival came! Folks began to be saved. Many of my loved ones were saved in that meeting who are serving the Lord this very day—neighbors and friends and country people. In one afternoon, even before the meeting was over, I baptized twenty-one.

A little church that had a meeting not long after that near there had not one person saved. A large group of folks joined the church who were saved in the little country school where I preached and where folks were saved by the scores.

Listen! There is no place on this earth where God can't send a revival. "If my people, which are called by my name, shall humble themselves, and pray, and seek my face, and turn from their wicked ways; *then* will I hear from heaven"—not before, not when you need ten thousand other things—but "*then* will I hear from heaven."

Oh, if after this conference we do not go back to our churches and have a revival, then we haven't had the right kind of a conference. O God, help us to believe that there is nothing too hard for You.

IV. NO PERSON TOO HARD FOR GOD TO SAVE

Now I have known some hard ones. Dr. Rice has. Some of you do. Some of you good women may be saying, "I am living with one." There is nobody God can't save. No person is too hard for the Lord to save.

There is one incident in the Bible that I think gives me as much thrill as anything I ever read, outside of what Jesus did for me personally. And that is these four men who got the paralytic to Jesus. I have often tried to decide where I would like to have been had I been there. Sometimes I think I would like to have been on the rooftop and listened to what they said to one another and what went on. And from the rooftop I would like to have looked down when Jesus looked up, and I would like to have seen the look on Jesus' face.

Then again I think I would like to have been down there where Jesus was and when the plaster began to fall and make all that noise and everybody wondering what was going on, except Jesus; then all of a sudden the hole appeared and there was a cot with a man on it and four men sticking their heads in that hole and looking down—I would like to have been down there and looked up and have seen it.

I don't know exactly how it happened, but I think maybe one day out there near Capernaum a man said to three of his neighbors, "Here is our neighbor. He is paralytic. We love him. He has a great need.

He needs Jesus." I suppose he went on to say, "One thing for sure. If we can get our neighbor in contact with Jesus, Jesus will take care of everything. Now our responsibility is to get him from here to there and under the attention of Jesus."

So they placed him on a bed and started out. You can imagine what people said to them along the way. They wanted to know all about it.

Here they are—these four men carrying a cripple. They go to where Jesus is preaching in the house. When they arrive, they confront a big crowd, keeping them from getting in the door.

The Bible doesn't say this, but being human, I know one fellow out of the four said, "Now men, it can't be done. We have gone as far as we can go. Nobody could ever say we haven't tried. Now let's don't be irrational about this thing. Let's don't make a big to-do about it. Let's take him back home."

When you get four people together in the work of God, when they hit a hard place, one of them is bound to say, "This is as far as you can go." So one of the four surely said, "Let's go back home."

But I know also that one in that crowd would not give up. "No, we are not going to give up. We started out to get this man to Jesus. So come hell or high water, we are going to accomplish our goal."

Carrying the bed and the paralytic, they start up the stairway that leads up on the rooftop. As they go slowly up the stairs, I can imagine one saying, "Now wait a minute! I never saw it done that way before." What difference does that make! I like for us to attempt some things never done that way before. Don't you?

Our congregation knows just about what we are going to do next. We start out with the Doxology, then we sing the sevenfold Amens, then we have responsive reading—all so cut-and-dried. I thank God when I can do something nobody has done before.

So in the crowd somebody must have said, "I never saw it done that way before." I don't know which one of the quartet did the talking, but one of them said to the crowd, "So what! You are going to see it now."

They start up to the roof, and another says, "Wait just a minute, boys! Has it been voted on by the board of deacons?"

One of the four said, "Board of deacons, my hind leg! We don't even have a board!"

On up they go. In a little bit another says, "Now wait just a minute! Did you get your orders from the denominational headquarters?" One of them answered, "We don't have any headquarters, sir. We don't even have any hind quarters. Come on, boys! Let's get this cot on up here on the roof."

They get up on the roof and start digging. Somebody else speaks up, "Wait just a minute! It is going to cost some money to get that hole patched." There is always somebody to ask, "Where are you going to get the money?" when you start out to do a soul-winning work.

Well, they opened up the hole. The plaster was flying, tile was breaking, people were standing out there criticizing, some maybe even attempting to stop them. But they got the hole broken, and one of these four said, "Now let's be careful not to drop him." And these eight tender hands let him down through the hole.

When they get him down at the feet of Jesus, Jesus looks up, and "when he saw their faith" —not his; *theirs*—He looked down at the man and said, "Son, thy sins be forgiven thee" (Mark 2:5).

Something else I would like to have seen. I would like to have seen that quintet go home, wouldn't you? I can just see them now, hugging one another and running over people. They are arm in arm, five of them, trying to get through the narrow streets and to home. There are five of them now, all hugging and crying. This man must be looking down at his feet and saying, "I was carried over here—but look at me! I can walk! Praise God!" I can just see him popping his heels together and shouting and praising God.

Why? Somebody believed. If we can get him to Jesus, his needs are going to be met, and his soul is going to be saved.

No person is too hard for God.

DWIGHT LYMAN MOODY
1837-1899

ABOUT THE MAN:

D. L. Moody may well have been the greatest evangelist of all time.

In a 40-year period, he won a million souls, founded three Christian schools, launched a great Christian publishing business, established a world-renowned Christian conference center, and inspired literally thousands of preachers to win souls and conduct revivals.

A shoe clerk at 17, his ambition was to make $100,000. Converted at 18, he uncovered hidden gospel gold in the hearts of millions for the next half century. He preached to 20,000 a day in Brooklyn and admitted only non-church members by ticket!

He met a young songleader in Indianapolis, said bluntly, "You're the man I've been looking for for eight years. Throw up your job and come with me." Ira D. Sankey did just that; thereafter it was "Moody will preach; Sankey will sing."

He traveled across the American continent and through Great Britain in some of the greatest and most successful evangelistic meetings communities have ever known. His tour of the world with Sankey was considered the greatest evangelistic enterprise of the century.

It was Henry Varley who said, "It remains to be seen what God will do with a man who gives himself up wholly to Him." And Moody endeavored to be, under God, that man; and the world did marvel to see how wonderfully God used him.

Two great monuments stand to the indefatigable work and ministry of this gospel warrior—Moody Bible Institute and the famous Moody Church in Chicago.

Moody went to be with the Lord in 1899.

IX.

Prevailing Prayer Requires Faith

D. L. MOODY

An element in prevailing prayer is FAITH. It is as important for us to know how to pray as it is to know how to work. We are not told that Jesus ever taught His disciples how to preach, but He taught them how to pray. He wanted them to have power with God. He knew that then they would have power with man.

In James we read: "If any of you lack wisdom, let him ask of God . . . and it shall be given him; but let him ask in faith, nothing wavering."

So faith is the golden key that unlocks the treasures of Heaven. It was the shield that David took when he met Goliath on the field. He believed that God was going to deliver the Philistine into his hands. Someone has said that faith could lead Christ about anywhere. Wherever He found it, He honored it. Unbelief sees something in God's hand and says, "I cannot get it." Faith sees it and says, "I will have it."

The new life begins with faith. Then we have only to go on building on that foundation. "I say unto you, What things soever ye desire, when ye pray, believe that ye receive them, and ye shall have them." But bear in mind, we must be in earnest when we go to God.

I do not know of a more vivid illustration of the cry of distress for help going up to God, in all the earnestness of deeply realized need, than the following story supplies:

Carl Steinman, who visited Mount Hecla, Iceland, just before the great eruption in 1845 after a repose of eighty years, narrowly escaped death by venturing into the smoking crater against the earnest entreaty of his guide. On the brink of the yawning gulf he was prostrated by a convulsion of the summit and held there by blocks of lava upon his feet. He graphically writes:

Oh, the horrors of that awful realization! There, over the mouth

of a black and heated abyss, I was held suspended, a helpless and
conscious prisoner, to be hurled downward by the next great throe
of trembling Nature!

"Help! help! help!—for the love of God, help!" I shrieked, in the
very agony of my despair.

I had nothing to rely upon but the mercy of Heaven; and I prayed
to God as I had never prayed before, for the forgiveness of my
sins, that they might not follow me to judgment.

All at once I heard a shout, and, looking around, I beheld, with
feelings that cannot be described, my faithful guide hastening down
the sides of the crater to my relief.

"I warned you!" said he.

"You did!" cried I, "but forgive me, and save me, for I am
perishing!"

"I will save you, or perish with you!"

The earth trembled, and the rocks parted—one of them rolling
down the chasm with a dull, booming sound. I sprang forward;
I seized a hand of the guide, and the next moment we had both
fallen, locked in each other's arms, upon the solid earth above.
I was free, but still upon the verge of the pit.

Bishop Hall, in a well-known extract, thus puts the point of earnestness
in its relation to the prayer of faith.

An arrow, if it be drawn up but a little way, goes not far; but,
if it be pulled up to the head, flies swiftly and pierces deep. Thus
prayer, if it be only dribbled forth from careless lips, falls at our feet.
It is the strength of ejaculation and strong desire which sends it to
Heaven and makes it pierce the clouds. It is not the arithmetic of
our prayers, how many they are; nor the rhetoric of our prayers,
how eloquent they be; nor the geometry of our prayers, how long
they be; nor the music of our prayers, how sweet our voice may
be; nor the logic of our prayers, how argumentative they may be;
nor the method of our prayers, how orderly they may be—which
God cares for. He looks not for the horny knees which James is
said to have had through the assiduity of prayer. We might be like
Bartholomew, who is said to have had a hundred prayers for the
morning, and as many for the evening, and all might be of no avail.
Fervency of spirit is that which availeth much.

Archbishop Leighton says:

It is not the gilded paper and good writing of a petition that
prevails with a king, but the moving sense of it. And to that King
who discerns the heart, heart-sense is the sense of all, and that
which He only regards. He listens to hear what that speaks, and

takes all as nothing where that is silent. All other excellence in prayer is but the outside and fashion of it. This is the life of it.

Brooks says:

> As a painted fire is no fire, a dead man no man, so a cold prayer is no prayer. In a painted fire there is no heat, in a dead man there is no life; so in a cold prayer there is no omnipotency, no devotion, no blessing. Cold prayers are as arrows without heads, as swords without edges, as birds without wings; they pierce not, they cut not, they fly not up to Heaven. Cold prayers do always freeze before they get to Heaven.
>
> Oh, that Christians would chide themselves out of their cold prayers, and chide themselves into a better and warmer frame of spirit, when they make their supplications to the Lord!

Take the case of the Syrophenician woman. When she called to the Master, it seemed for a time as if He were deaf to her request. The disciples wanted her to be sent away. Although they were with Christ for three years and sat at His feet, yet they did not know how full of grace His heart was.

Think of Christ sending away a poor sinner who had come to Him for mercy! Can you conceive such a thing? Never once did it occur. This poor woman put herself in the place of her child. "Lord, help me!" she said.

I think when we get so far as that in the earnest desire to have our friends blessed—when we put ourselves in their place—God will soon hear our prayer.

Having Faith for Others

I remember a number of years ago at a meeting I asked all those who wished to be prayed for to come forward and kneel or take seats in front. Among those who came was a woman. I thought by her looks that she must be a Christian, but she knelt down with the others.

I said, "You are a Christian, are you not?"

She said she had been one for so many years.

"Did you understand the invitation? I asked those only who wanted to become Christians."

I shall never forget the look on her face as she replied, "I have a son who has gone far away; I thought I would take his place today and see if God would not bless him."

Thank God for such a mother as that!

The Syrophenician woman did the same thing—"Lord, help *me!*" It was a short prayer, but it went right to the heart of the Son of God. He tried her faith, however, by saying, "It is not meet to take the children's bread and cast it to dogs." She replied, "Truth, Lord; yet the dogs eat of the crumbs which fall from their masters' table."

"O woman, great is thy faith!" What a eulogy He paid to her! Her story will never be forgotten as long as the church is on the earth. He honored her faith and gave her all she asked for.

Everyone can say, "Lord, help me!" We all need help. As Christians, we need more grace, more love, more purity of life, more righteousness. Then let us make this prayer today. I want God to help me to preach better and to live better, to be more like the Son of God. The golden chains of faith link us right to the throne of God, and the grace of Heaven flows down into our souls.

I do not know but what that woman was a great sinner; still, the Lord heard her cry. It may be that up to this hour you have been living in sin; but if you will cry, "Lord, help me!" He will answer your prayer, if it is an honest one.

Very often when we cry to God we do not really mean anything. You mothers understand that. Your children have two voices. When they ask you for anything, you can soon tell if the cry is a make-believe one or not. If it is, you do not give any heed to it; but if it is a real cry for help, how quickly you respond! The cry of distress always brings relief.

Your child is playing around, and he says, "Mama, I want some bread"—but he goes on playing. You know that he is not very hungry, so you let him alone. But by and by when the child drops the toys and comes tugging at your dress and saying, "Mama, I am so hungry!" then you know that the cry is a real one; you soon go to the pantry for some bread.

When we are in earnest for the bread of Heaven, we will get it. This woman was terribly in earnest; therefore her petition was answered.

I remember hearing of a boy brought up in an English almshouse. He had never learned to read or write, except that he could read the letters of the alphabet. One day a man of God came there and told the children that if they prayed to God in their trouble, He would send them help.

After a time this boy was apprenticed to a farmer. One day he was sent out into the fields to look after some sheep. He was having rather a hard time. Remembering what the preacher had said, he thought he would pray to God about it. Someone going by the field heard a voice behind the hedge. They looked to see whose it was and saw the little fellow on his knees, saying, "A, B, C, D," and so on.

The man asked, "My boy, what are you doing?" He looked up and said he was praying. "Why, that is not praying; it is only saying the alphabet." He told the man he did not know just how to pray, but a man once came to the poorhouse who told them that, if they called upon God, He would help them. So he thought that, if he named over the letters of the alphabet, God would take and put them together into a prayer and give him what he wanted. That little fellow was really praying.

Sometimes when your child talks, your friends cannot understand what he says, but Mother understands very well. So if our prayer comes right from the heart, God understands our language.

It is a delusion of the Devil to think we cannot pray. We can, if we really want anything. It is not the most beautiful or the most eloquent language that brings down the answer; it is the cry that goes up from a burdened heart. When this poor Gentile woman cried out, "Lord, help me!" the cry flashed over the divine wires, and the blessing came. So you can pray if you will; it is the desire, the wish of the heart, that God delights to hear and to answer.

Expect to Receive When You Pray

Then we must *expect* to receive a blessing. When the centurion wanted Christ to heal his servant, he thought himself not worthy to go and ask the Lord; so he sent his friends to make the petition to the Master and to say, "Do not trouble Yourself to come; all You have to do is to speak the word, and the disease will go." Jesus said to the Jews, "I have not found so great faith, no, not in Israel." He marveled at the faith of this centurion; it pleased Him so that He healed the servant then and there. Faith brought the answer.

In John we read of a nobleman whose child was sick. The father fell on his knees before the Master, saying, "Come down, ere my child die." Here you have both earnestness and faith. And the Lord answered the prayer at once. The nobleman's son began to amend that very hour. Christ honored the man's faith.

In his case there was nothing to rest upon but the bare word of Christ, but this was enough.

It is good to bear always in mind that the object of faith is not the creature but the Creator—not the instrument but the Hand that wields it. Richard Sibbes puts it for us thus:

> The object in believing is God, and Christ as Mediator. We must have both to found our faith upon. We cannot believe in God, except we believe in Christ. For God must be satisfied by God; and by Him, that is, God, must that satisfaction be applied—the Spirit of God—by working faith in the heart, and for raising it up when it is dejected. All is supernatural in faith. The things we believe are above nature; the promises are above nature; the worker of it, the Holy Ghost, is above nature; and everything in faith is above nature.
>
> There must be a God in whom we believe, and a God through whom we may know that Christ is God—not only by that which Christ hath done, the miracles, which none could do but God, but also by what is done to Him.
>
> And two things are done to Him, which show that He is God— that is, faith and prayer. We must believe only in God, and pray only to God; but Christ is the object of both. Here He is set forth as the object of faith and of prayer in that of Saint Stephen, "Lord Jesus, receive my spirit." And, therefore, He is God; for that is done unto Him which is proper and peculiar only to God.
>
> Oh, what a strong foundation, what bottom and basis our faith hath! There is God the Father, Son and Holy Ghost, and Christ the Mediator. That our faith may be supported, we have Him to believe on who supports Heaven and earth.
>
> There is nothing that can lie in the way of the accomplishment of any of God's promises, but it is conquerable by faith.

As Samuel Rutherford says, commenting on the case of the Syrophenician woman:

> See the sweet use of faith under a sad temptation; faith trafficketh with Christ and Heaven in the dark, upon plain trust and credit, without seeing any surety of dawn: Blessed are they that have not seen, and yet have believed. And the reason is because faith is sinewed and boned with spiritual courage; so as to keep a barred city against Hell, yea, and to stand under impossibilities; and here is a weak woman, though not as a woman, yet as a believer, standing out against Him who is "the Mighty God, the Father of Ages, the Prince of Peace." Faith only standeth out, and overcometh the sword, the world, and all afflictions. This is our victory, whereby one man overcometh the great and vast world.

Bishop Ryle has said of Christ's intercession as the ground and sureness of our faith:

The bank note without a signature at the bottom is nothing but a worthless piece of paper. The stroke of a pen confers on it all its value. The prayer of a poor child of Adam is a feeble thing in itself, but once endorsed by the hand of the Lord Jesus, it availeth much.

An officer in the city of Rome was appointed to have his doors always open, in order to receive any Roman citizen who applied to him for help. Just so, the ear of the Lord Jesus is ever open to the cry of all who want mercy and grace. It is His office to help them. Their prayer is His delight.

Reader, think of this. Is not this encouragement?

Let us close this chapter by referring to some of our Lord's own words concerning faith in its relation to prayer:

"And when he saw the fig tree in the way, he came to it, and found nothing thereon, but leaves only, and said unto it: Let no fruit grow on thee henceforward for ever. And presently the fig tree withered away. And when the disciples saw it, they marvelled, saying, How soon is the fig tree withered away! Jesus answered and said unto them, Verily I say unto you, If ye have faith, and doubt not, ye shall not only do this which is done to the fig tree, but also if ye shall say unto this mountain, Be thou removed, and be thou cast into the sea; it shall be done. And all things, whatsoever ye shall ask in prayer, believing, ye shall receive."—Matt. 21:19-22.

So again our Lord says:

"Verily, verily, I say unto you, He that believeth on me, the works that I do shall he do also; and greater works than these shall he do; because I go unto my Father. And whatsoever ye shall ask in my name, that will I do, that the Father may be glorified in the Son. If ye shall ask any thing in my name, I will do it."

And further:

"If ye abide in me, and my words abide in you, ye shall ask what ye will, and it shall be done unto you."

"Verily, verily, I say unto you, Whatsoever ye shall ask the Father in my name, he will give it you. Hitherto have ye asked nothing in my name: ask, and ye shall receive, that your joy may be full."—John 14:12-14; 15:7; 16:23, 24.

(From the book, *Prevailing Prayer—What Hinders It*, in Moody Colportage Series)

X.

Prayers of the Bible

D. L. MOODY

Those who have left the deepest impression on this sin-cursed earth have been men and women of prayer. You will find that prayer has been the mighty power that has moved not only God, but man.

Abraham was a man of prayer, and angels came down from Heaven to converse with him.

Jacob's prayer was answered in the wonderful interview at Peniel that resulted in his having such a mighty blessing and in softening the heart of his brother Esau.

The child Samuel was given in answer to Hannah's prayer.

Elijah's prayer closed up the heavens for three years and six months, and he prayed again and the heavens gave rain.

The Apostle James tells us that the Prophet Elijah was a man "subject to like passions as we are." I am thankful that those men and women who were so mighty in prayer were just like ourselves. We are apt to think that those prophets and mighty men and women of old time were different from what we are. To be sure, they lived in a much darker age, but they were of like passions with ourselves.

WONDERFUL BIBLE EXAMPLES OF PRAYERS ANSWERED

We read that on another occasion Elijah brought down fire on Mount Carmel. The prophets of Baal cried long and loud, but no answer came. The God of Elijah heard and answered his prayer.

Let us remember that the God of Elijah still lives. The prophet was translated and went up to Heaven, but his God still lives, and we have the same access to Him that Elijah had. We have the same warrant to go to God and ask the fire from Heaven to come down and consume our lusts and passions—to burn up our dross, and let Christ shine through us.

Elisha prayed, and life came back to a dead child. Many of our children are dead in trespasses and sins. Let us do as Elisha did. Let us entreat God to raise them up in answer to our prayers.

Manasseh the king was a wicked man who had done everything he could against the God of his father; yet in Babylon, when he cried to God, his cry was heard, and he was taken out of prison and put on the throne at Jerusalem. Surely if God gave heed to the prayer of wicked Manasseh, He will hear ours in the time of our distress.

Is not this a time of distress with a great number of our fellow men? Are there not many among us whose hearts are burdened? As we go to the throne of grace, let us remember that God answers prayer.

Look again at Samson. He prayed, and his strength came back so that he slew more at his death than during his life. He was a restored backslider, and he had power with God. If those who have been backsliders will but return to God, they will see how quickly God will answer prayer.

Job prayed, and his captivity was turned. Light came in the place of darkness, and God lifted him up above the height of his former prosperity—in answer to prayer.

Daniel prayed to God, and Gabriel came to tell him that he was a man greatly beloved of God. Three times that message came to him from Heaven in answer to prayer. The secrets of Heaven were imparted to him, and he was told that God's Son was going to be cut off for the sins of His people.

We find also that Cornelius prayed. And Peter was sent to tell him words whereby he and his should be saved. In answer to prayer, this great blessing came upon him and his household. Peter had gone up to the housetop to pray in the afternoon when he had that wonderful vision of the sheet let down from Heaven. It was when prayer was made without ceasing unto God for Peter that the angel was sent to deliver him.

So all through the Scriptures you will find that, when believing prayer went up to God, the answer came down. I think it would be a very interesting study to go right through the Bible and see what has happened while God's people have been on their knees calling upon Him. Certainly the study would greatly strengthen our faith—showing, as it would, how wonderfully God has heard and delivered when the cry has gone up to Him for help.

Look at Paul and Silas in the prison at Philippi. As they prayed and sang praises, the place was shaken, and the jailer was converted. Probably that one conversion has done more than any other recorded in the Bible to bring people into the Kingdom of God. How many have been blessed in seeking to answer the question—"What must I do to be saved?" It was the prayer of these two godly men that brought the jailer to his knees and that brought blessing to him and his family.

You remember how, as Stephen prayed and looked up, he saw the heavens opened and the Son of man at the right hand of God. The light of Heaven fell on his face so that it shone. Remember, too, how the face of Moses shone as he came down from the Mount; he had been in communion with God.

So when we get really into communion with God, He lifts up His countenance upon us. And instead of our having gloomy looks, our faces will shine because God has heard and answered our prayers.

JESUS, A MAN OF PRAYER

I want to call special attention to Christ as an example for us in all things; in nothing more than in prayer. We read that Christ prayed to His Father for everything. Every great crisis in His life was preceded by prayer. Let me quote a few passages.

I never noticed till a few years ago that Christ was praying at His baptism. As He prayed, the heavens were opened, and the Holy Ghost descended on Him. Another great event in His life was His Transfiguration. "As he prayed, the fashion of his countenance was altered, and his raiment was white and glistering."

We read again: "It came to pass in those days that he went out into a mountain to pray, and continued all night in prayer to God." This is the only place where it is recorded that the Saviour spent a whole night in prayer.

What was about to take place? When He came down from the mountain, He gathered His disciples around Him and preached that great discourse known as the Sermon on the Mount—the most wonderful sermon that has ever been preached to mortal men. Probably no sermon has done so much good, and it was preceded by a night of prayer. If our sermons are going to reach the hearts and consciences of the people, we must be much in prayer to God that there may be power with the Word.

In the Gospel of John we read that Jesus at the grave of Lazarus lifted up His eyes to Heaven and said: "Father, I thank thee that thou hast heard me; and I knew that thou hearest me always; but because of the people which stand by I said it, that they may believe that thou hast sent me."

Notice that before He spoke the dead to life, He spoke to His Father. If our spiritually dead ones are to be raised, we must first get power with God. The reason we so often fail in moving our fellow men is that we try to win them without first getting power with God. Jesus was in communion with His Father, and so He could be assured that His prayers were heard.

We read again, in the 12th of John, that He prayed to the Father. I think this is one of the saddest chapters in the whole Bible. He was about to leave the Jewish nation and to make atonement for the sin of the world. Hear what He says: "Now is my soul troubled, and what shall I say? Father, save me from this hour; but for this cause came I unto this hour."

He was almost under the shadow of the cross. The iniquities of mankind were about to be laid upon Him. One of His twelve disciples was going to deny Him and swear he never knew Him. Another was to sell Him for thirty pieces of silver. All were to forsake Him and flee. His soul was exceeding sorrowful, and He prays. When His soul was troubled, God spoke to Him. Then in the Garden of Gethsemane, while He prayed, an angel appeared to strengthen Him. In answer to His cry, "Father, glorify thy name," He hears a voice coming down from the glory—"I have both glorified it, and will glorify it again."

Another memorable prayer of our Lord was in the Garden of Gethsemane: "He was withdrawn from them about a stone's cast, and kneeled down and prayed."

I would draw your attention to the recorded fact that four times the answer came right down from Heaven while the Saviour prayed to God. The first time was at His baptism, when the heavens were opened, and the Spirit descended upon Him in answer to His prayer. Again, on the Mount of Transfiguration God appeared and spoke to Him. Then when the Greeks came desiring to see Him, the voice of God was heard responding to His call. And again, when He cried to the Father in the midst of His agony, a direct response was given. These things are recorded, I doubt not, that we may be encouraged to pray.

We read that His disciples came to Him and said, "Lord, teach us to pray." It is not recorded that He taught them how to preach. I have often said that I would rather know how to pray like Daniel than to preach like Gabriel. If you get love into your soul so that the grace of God may come down in answer to prayer, there will be no trouble about reaching the people. It is not by eloquent sermons that perishing souls are going to be reached. We need the power of God in order that the blessing may come down.

The prayer our Lord taught His disciples is commonly called the Lord's Prayer. I think that the Lord's Prayer, more properly, is that in the 17th of John. That is the longest prayer on record that Jesus made. You can read it slowly and carefully in about four or five minutes.

I think we may learn a lesson here. Our Master's prayers were short when offered in public. When He was alone with God, that was a different thing. And He could spend the whole night in communion with His Father.

My experience is that those who pray most in their closets generally make short prayers in public. Long prayers are too often not prayers at all, and they weary the people.

How short the publican's prayer was: "God be merciful to me a sinner!" The Syrophenician woman's was shorter still: "Lord, help me!" She went right to the mark, and she got what she wanted. The prayer of the thief on the cross was a short one: "Lord, remember me when thou comest into thy kingdom!" Peter's prayer was, "Lord, save me!"

So if you go through the Scriptures, you will find that the prayers that brought immediate answers were generally brief. Let our prayers be to the point, just telling God what we want.

In the prayer of our Lord, in John 17, we find that He made seven requests—one for Himself, four for His disciples around Him, and two for the disciples of succeeding ages. Six times in that one prayer He repeats that God had sent Him. The world looked upon Him as an imposter; and He wanted them to know that He was Heaven-sent. He speaks of the world nine times and makes mention of His disciples and those who believe on Him fifty times.

Christ's last prayer on the cross was a short one: "Father, forgive them, for they know not what they do." I believe that prayer was answered. We find that right there in front of the cross, a Roman centurion was converted. It was probably in answer to the Saviour's prayer. The con-

version of the thief, I believe, was in answer to that prayer of our blessed Lord. Saul of Tarsus may have heard it, and the words may have
followed him as he traveled to Damascus; so that when the Lord spoke
to him on the way, he may have recognized the voice. One thing we
do know—that on the day of Pentecost some of the enemies of the
Lord were converted. Surely that was in answer to the prayer, "Father,
forgive them!"

MEN OF GOD ARE MEN OF PRAYER

Hence we see that prayer holds a high place among the exercises
of a spiritual life. All God's people have been praying people.

Look, for instance, at Baxter! He stained his study walls with praying
breath. And after he was anointed with the unction of the Holy Ghost,
sent a river of living water over Kidderminster, and converted hundreds.

Luther and his companions were men of such mighty pleading with
God that they broke the spell of ages and laid nations subdued at the
foot of the cross.

John Knox grasped all Scotland in his strong arms of faith. His prayers
terrified tyrants.

Whitefield, after much holy, faithful closet-pleading, went to the Devil's
fair and took more than a thousand souls out of the paw of the lion
in one day.

See a praying Wesley turn more than ten thousand souls to the Lord!

Look at the praying Finney, whose prayers, faith, sermons and writings have shaken this whole country and sent a wave of blessing
through the churches on both sides of the sea.

Dr. Guthrie thus speaks of prayer and its necessity:

> The first true sign of spiritual life, prayer, is also the means of
> maintaining it. Man can as well live physically without breathing,
> as spiritually without praying. There is a class of animals—the
> cetaceous, neither fish nor sea-fowl—that inhabits the deep. It is
> their home. They never leave it for the shore. Yet, though swim-
> ming beneath its waves and sounding its darkest depths, they have
> ever and anon to rise to the surface that they may breathe the air.
> Without that, these monarchs of the deep could not exist in the
> dense element in which they live, and move, and have their being.
>
> And something like what is imposed on them by a physical
> necessity, the Christian has to do by a spiritual one. It is by ever
> and anon ascending up to God, by rising through prayer into a

loftier, purer region for supplies of Divine grace, that he maintains his spiritual life.

Prevent these animals from rising to the surface, and they die for want of breath. Prevent the Christian from rising to God, and he dies for want of prayer. "Give me children," cried Rachel, "or else I die." "Let me breathe," says a man gasping, "or else I die." "Let me pray," says the Christian, "or else I die."

"Since I began," said Dr. Payson, when a student, "to beg God's blessing on my studies, I have done more in one week than in the whole year before."

Luther, when most pressed with work, said, "I have so much to do that I cannot get on without three hours a day praying."

And not only do theologians think and speak highly of prayer; men of all ranks and positions in life have felt the same.

General Havelock rose at four o'clock, if the hour for marching was six, rather than lose the precious privilege of communion with God before setting out.

Sir Matthew Hale says, "If I omit praying and reading God's Word in the morning, nothing goes well all day."

"A great part of my time," said M'Cheyne, "is spent in getting my heart in tune for prayer. It is the link that connects earth with Heaven."

A comprehensive view of the subject will show that there are nine elements which are essential to true prayer.

The first is adoration. We cannot meet God on a level at the start. We must approach Him as One far beyond our reach or sight.

The next is confession. Sin must be put out of the way. We cannot have any communion with God while there is any transgression between us. If there stands some wrong you have done a man, you cannot expect that man's favor until you go to him and confess the fault.

Restitution is another. We have to make good the wrong, wherever possible.

Thanksgiving is the next. We must be thankful for what God has done for us already.

Then comes forgiveness, and then unity. And then for prayer, such as these things produce, there must be faith.

Thus influenced, we shall be ready to offer direct petition. We hear a good deal of praying that is just exhorting, and if you did not see the man's eyes closed, you would suppose he were preaching. Then, much that is called prayer is simply finding fault. There needs to be more *petition* in our prayers.

After all these, there must come submission. While praying, we must be ready to accept the will of God.

—From *Prevailing Prayer*

JOHN R. RICE
1895-1980

ABOUT THE MAN:

Preacher...evangelist...revivalist...editor...counselor to thousands...friend to millions—that was Dr. John R. Rice, whose accomplishments were nothing short of miraculous. Known as "America's Dean of Evangelists," Dr. Rice made a mighty impact upon the nation's religious life for some sixty years, in great citywide campaigns and in Sword of the Lord Conferences.

At age nine, after hearing a sermon on "The Prodigal Son," John went forward to claim Christ as Saviour. In 1916, with only $9.35 in his pocket, he rode off on his cowpony toward Decatur Baptist College. He was now on the road to becoming a world-renowned evangelist, although he was then totally unaware of God's will for his life.

There was many a twist and turn before Rice rode through the open door into full-time preaching—the army, marriage, graduate work, more seminary, assistant pastor, pastor—then FINALLY, where God planned to use him most—in full-time evangelism.

Dr. Rice and his ministry were always colorful (born in Cooke county, in Texas, December 11, 1895, and often called "Will Rogers of the Pulpit" because of their likeness and mannerisms)—and controversial. CONTROVERSIAL—and correctly so—because of his intense stand against modernism and infidelity and his fight for the Fundamentals.

Dr. Rice lived and died a man of convictions—intense convictions. But, like many other strong fighters for the Faith, Rice was also marked with a sincere spirit of compassion. Those who knew him best knew a man who loved them. In preaching, in prayer, and in personal life, Rice wept over sinners and with saints. But there is more....

Less than seventy-one hours before the dawning of 1981, one of the most prolific pens in all Christendom was stilled. Dr. John R. Rice left behind a legacy in writing of more than 200 titles, with a combined circulation of over 61 million copies. And through October of 1981, a total of 24,058 precious souls reported trusting Christ through his ministries, not counting those saved in his crusades nor in foreign countries where his literature has been translated.

And who but God knows the influence of THE SWORD OF THE LORD magazine which he started and edited for forty-six years!

And while "Twentieth Century's Mightiest Pen"—and man—has been stilled, thank God, the fruit remains! Though dead, he continues to speak.

XI.

"Open Thy Mouth Wide"

A Great God Pleads With Christians to Try Great Works, Make Tremendous Requests That Fit With His Power and Grace

JOHN R. RICE

"I am the Lord thy God, which brought thee out of the land of Egypt: open thy mouth wide, and I will fill it."—Ps. 81:10.

It is the fault of our "besetting sin" of unbelief that Christians now do not usually believe that God is as able and willing to do great and mighty things now as He did for saints in Bible times.

We hear that "the day of miracles is past," though the Bible says nothing of the kind. In fact, the new birth is itself a miracle. Direct leading of the Holy Spirit is a miracle. Every saved soul involves a future bodily, physical miracle in the resurrection. And many supernatural, miraculous events are prophesied in connection with the rapture of the saints, the tribulation time, Christ's return in glory, etc. But people excuse themselves for unbelief by supposing that God now is not willing to do the same kind of great things that He did for saints in the past.

Some, with an overemphasis on dispensationalism and with some encouragement from the beloved and useful Scofield Bible, have said that the Jews were an earthly people and could have physical blessings in answer to prayer, while Christians are a spiritual people and must pray only for spiritual things. Thus people are taught that the wonderful answers to prayer and dealings of God in physical matters are not to be expected now as they were in Bible times.

Others have set out to approximate the date for Christ's return to receive His saints. And they have taught of a "great falling away" with certain signs which they insist make sure that the end of the age is approaching. Therefore, they reason that we cannot now have as great revivals, that we need not expect God to show so mightily His power; so there is a wicked and disastrous effect of defeatism.

This tends to leave the impression that the God of the Bible is not now as willing, not now as able to do the wonderful things for His saints which He has done in other ages, particularly in Bible times.

But all this is a mistake. And here in Psalm 81:10 we are told that the mighty God who brought His children of Israel out of Egypt with signs and wonders is the same today and just as willing today. And this God, who proudly points back to His mercies and blessings of the past, now invites all of us in effect, saying, "That is the kind of God I still am! Open your mouth wide and let Me fill it. Try Me. Let Me show what mighty things I will do for My people out of My love and grace."

I. WHAT OUR WONDERFUL GOD IS LIKE

Here God reminds both His people Israel and us that He is the God that brought Israel out of the land of Egypt.

That wonderful series of events—the call of Moses, the plagues and miracles in Egypt, the crossing of the Red Sea, the wilderness journey and the conquest of the land of Canaan—is a marvelous story to which God loves to refer in the Bible.

In Nehemiah 9:20 God's power and deliverance and provision are repeated. And again in Psalm 135:8-12. In Psalm 136:10-22 that wonderful story is again repeated and praise encouraged for such a God and Saviour, "for his mercy endureth for ever." In Romans 9:7 the dealing of God with Pharaoh is held up as an example of His mercy and grace, along with judgment.

Yes, God takes great delight in calling attention to the fact that He is a mighty God, a miracle-working God, a God who yearns to help His people. Here the Lord invites us to consider the kind of God we have, and His great power and willingness to bless.

1. God Heard the Cry of Distressed and Troubled Israel

It is good to remember that God heard the groanings and prayers of His people Israel in Egypt. They were enslaved; they were abused and exploited by Pharaoh and all his taskmasters. But they cried to God and He heard. God was preparing Moses for their deliverance during his forty years in the wilderness. So God called Moses, ordained and empowered him for the task of freeing Israel.

Then the great deliverance began. Not only at that time but again and again when Israel called in time of trouble and need, God delivered them.

It is one of the sweetest themes in the Bible to find that God remembers His own.

"God remembered Noah" when he was in the ark on a desolate, landless sea.

God remembered Hannah, the barren woman who cried to Him again and again.

We read again and again how God remembered those in trouble and helped them. One of the wonderful things about God is that He hears the cry of the distressed. A helpless widow can get His attention and help quicker than can a wife with a strong husband. The orphan calls upon God with assurance that his cry will be heard before that of a child who has plenty of care, a prosperous home, and a father and mother. The man who is poor has more claim on God than the rich man. The one in trouble and grief has more encouragement to call on God than the man who is in prosperity and ease. It is still true today, "Blessed are the poor," and "Blessed are they that mourn" (Matt. 5:3,4). God hears the cry of His troubled people.

2. God Delivers With Mighty Power

I love to read again the story, that glad saga so often repeated in the Scriptures, of how God delivered Israel with a mighty hand. He turned the waters of the Nile into blood. He brought a plague of frogs. He brought lice and flies and hail. He brought a murrain upon cattle. He brought the midnight darkness over all the land of Egypt, darkness that could be felt. And then with proper warning, wherever there was no blood upon the door, He brought the death angel and the death of the first-born of every family, from Pharaoh's first-born to the son of the servant woman.

Oh, it is wonderful that God did deliver His people!

They gained favor among the Egyptians, who showered them with gold, silver and other gifts. They started to leave the land but Pharaoh repented of his decision and with an army rushed after them. God had opened the Red Sea for Israel; and Pharaoh and his army, lured to follow them, were there confounded and drowned in the sea which God let return to its natural bounds.

Their story of deliverance went before Israel into the land of Canaan. Heathen people wondered at such a God. Oh, how foolish we are to forget the God who delivers His people with an outstretched arm and with mighty power and with signs and wonders!

Do you think that God cares less for His people now than when He destroyed Sennacherib's army surrounding Jerusalem, speaking blasphemous threats (Isa. 37)? Do you think God would do less now for some humble, believing saint than He would in delivering Elisha from the Syrian army (II Kings 6:13-23)?

This is the kind of God we have—one who delivered Israel from Egypt and brought them safe to Canaan.

3. God Provided for Millions Through Forty Years of Wilderness Wandering

How would you feed three and a half million people out in a wilderness with no fields, no crop, no income? God settled that very easily. He sent the manna from Heaven. Every day it was carefully measured, an omer for every man, woman and child. On Friday there would come enough also for the Jewish Sabbath on Saturday. If any was kept over on other days, it bred worms and stank.

That must have been wonderfully balanced food, for it was called "angel's food." It could be eaten raw or baked or stewed. And for forty years Israel was well and healthy and happy on this divinely given food from Heaven. What a pantry, what a storehouse, what a source of supply for the people of God!

That is the kind of God we have today. He can provide for His own as freely now as He provided for the children of Israel. Do not many, many promises say so?

We are told that "their garments waxed not old" (Deut. 8:4; 29:5; Neh. 9:21). When a boy six years old came out of Egypt, he would find his shoes or sandals growing as he grew, and forty years later when he went into the land of Canaan he would be wearing the same shoes!

When they came to the wilderness where there was no water, the people murmured. But God told Moses to smite the rock with his blessed rod. When he did, there came out such a flood of water as to satisfy the needs of those three and a half million people with all their flocks.

Later when they came to this place, God told Moses to speak to the rock. Irritated, Moses struck the rock, yet water came again for the multitude.

God not only provided food, water and clothing for His people, but guidance and protection as well, as they crossed the Red Sea. The pillar of cloud was darkness to the Egyptians but light to the Israelites. Later there hovered over the camp, directly over the Tabernacle of the congregation, the pillar of cloud in the daytime and a pillar of fire at night. I wonder how many wanderers or travelers many miles away could see the flaming torch of that Shekinah glory, the literal presence of God Himself in the fiery column? When that pillar of cloud and fire went forward, Israel broke camp and followed. When that pillar of cloud and fire stopped, the people rested.

Oh, what leadership and perfect assurance of God's presence in the visible pillar of cloud and fire!

But does a Christian have less? No, but more because the Spirit of God dwells within our bodies. He guides into all truths. He is the Comforter, the Paraclete. He it is who helps us pray. The conscious presence of the Holy Spirit is the privilege of every Christian. That is the kind of God we have—the God who led the children of Israel out of Egypt.

4. The Text Implies That God Is the Same Today

The Lord says, "I am the Lord thy God, which brought thee out of the land of Egypt: open thy mouth wide, and I will fill it" (Ps. 81:10). Surely He means that now, many hundreds of years later, He is the same God and as willing to stretch out His mighty arm to defend His people, or to provide for their needs, or to guide them in the way everlasting!

Any honest interpretation of this Scripture means that God is now as willing and able to show Himself in mighty power for His people as He had been before when He brought Israel from the land of Egypt into Canaan.

There is an ageless, timeless, everlasting quality to the Scripture. "For ever, O Lord, thy word is settled in heaven" (Ps. 119:89). And the Lord Himself says, "Heaven and earth shall pass away, but my words shall not pass away" (Matt. 24:35). Every promise that God makes is an eternal promise. Every delineation and description of the goodness, power, grace and love of God are good for as long as any eye can read the Bible, as long as any broken heart can pray! The Bible does not pass out of date. The promises are forever.

This is because God Himself is unchangeable. In Malachi 3:6 He said, "For I am the Lord, I change not. . . ." In Hebrews 13:8 we are told, "Jesus Christ the same yesterday, and to day, and for ever." The God who delivers, the God of the mighty power, the God who is willing to show Himself, is now offering to do for us as much as He did for Israel when He brought them out of Egypt. Oh, what a wonderful God we have! He is a God who hears prayer, who works wonders, a God who is more willing to give than we are to receive.

II. THE CHRISTIAN SHOULD ATTEMPT
GREAT THINGS WITH GOD

Hudson Taylor had a motto, "Attempt great things for God; expect great things from God." In Psalm 81:10 the Lord says that in view of such a wonderful program as we have, we should open our mouth wide and let Him fill it. Surely He means we should launch out into the deep, that we should loosen cords and strengthen stakes, that we should attempt great things for God, expect God to make possible that which otherwise would not be possible.

And the Lord reminds us, "I am the Lord thy God, which brought thee out of the land of Egypt." And that reminds us that by obeying God a nation of slaves came out to make a great independent nation. That means that when they obeyed Him in attempting to go out, all the power of Pharaoh and the organized government in Egypt could not hold whom God called.

1. God Had Moses and Joshua Attempt
Tremendous Deeds

Particularly the Lord wants us to remember how He led Moses to attempt the impossible. Moses was met in the wilderness and out of a burning bush God told him that he should go back to Egypt, call the elders of Israel together and tell them that God had pressed him to deliver them and lead them out. These Israelites would not know Moses, so they would naturally doubt him. Only by supernatural signs could he manifest that God had given him leadership and would empower him to lead them out. If Moses could not believe God to furnish the signs and provide the power, it would have been useless for him to go.

And to face the mighty Pharaoh! Moses knew how Pharaoh had enslaved the whole Jewish race, how he had murdered countless thousands, and how his word was absolute law. Yet Moses was ordered to go before Pharaoh and demand, "Thus saith the Lord God of Israel, Let my people go!"

Oh, to lead a nation through the Red Sea, after God had freed them from Egypt, would take great faith, a miracle of God. To take the responsibility to lead three and a half million people and their cattle into a wilderness where there was no food and water would be a tremendous undertaking. Moses must open his mouth wide. To get manna from Heaven, to get water out of a rock, to deliver them from the Amalekites, to lead them across flooded Jordan into the land of Canaan, to attack walled cities and seize the whole land, was a mighty project which God led Moses to attempt until the end of the forty years. In this matter Moses was to open his mouth wide.

Moses was followed by Joshua who was given tremendous promises. God said to him:

*"Moses my servant is dead; now therefore arise, go over this Jordan, thou, and all this people, unto the land which I do give to them, even to the children of Israel. Every place that the sole of your foot shall tread upon, that have I given unto you, as I said unto Moses. From the wilderness and this Lebanon even unto the great river, the river Euphrates, all the land of the Hittites, and unto the great sea toward the going down of the sun, shall be your coast. There shall not any man be able to stand before thee all the days of thy life: as I was with Moses, so I will be with thee: I will not fail thee, nor forsake thee. Be strong and of a good courage: for unto this people shalt thou divide for an inheritance the land, which I sware unto their fathers to give them. Only be thou strong and very courageous, that thou mayest observe to do according to all the law, which Moses my servant commanded thee: turn not from it to the right hand or to the left, that thou mayest prosper whithersoever thou goest. This book of the law shall not depart out of thy mouth; but thou shalt meditate therein day and night, that thou mayest observe to do according to all that is written therein: for then thou shalt make thy way prosperous, and then thou shalt have good success."—*Josh. 1:2-8.

God would be with Joshua as He had been with Moses. He marked off tremendous boundaries for the prospective nation Israel, greater than they ever actually took, perhaps, until the days of David and Solomon. God promised, "Every place that the sole of your foot shall tread upon, that have I given unto you." He said that if Joshua would meditate in the book of the law day and night and observe it, "then thou shalt make thy way prosperous, and then thou shalt have good success." Joshua was called to tremendous leadership. He was to open his mouth wide and God would fill it. He was to attempt great things for God, which could not be done unless God in mercy sent His miraculous power.

2. The Same Challenge to Expect God's Power and to Undertake the Impossible Is Offered Us

Many times God invites us to attempt great things for Him. In John 14:12 the Lord Jesus said: "Verily, verily, I say unto you, He that believeth on me, the works that I do shall ye do also; and greater works than these shall ye do; because I go unto my Father." A Christian should attempt to do great things, even greater things than Christ in His earthly ministry accomplished, since many live much longer than Christ and have physically greater contacts and opportunities than He had in Palestine.

I feel sure that D. L. Moody preached to more people and won more souls than Christ did in His personal ministry. And in the days of radio, television, the printed page and the smallness of the world, surely God expects us to attempt greater things in reaching millions for Christ than others have done.

In II Kings we find the story that the aged and ailing Elisha sent for Joash, king of Israel, and told him to take bow and arrows and open the window toward the east. Then with the old prophet's hands upon the king's hands, he was commanded to shoot an arrow, "the arrow of the Lord's deliverance, and the arrow of deliverance from Syria." And Elisha said, "Thou shalt smite the Syrians in Aphek, till thou have consumed them" (II Kings 13:17).

As a symbol of his faith and acceptance of the task given him, Joash was commanded to take the arrows in his hands and then Elisha commanded, "Smite upon the ground." The king smote only three times. The man of God was wroth with him and said, "Thou shouldest have smitten five or six times; then hadst thou smitten Syria till thou hadst consumed it: whereas now thou shalt smite Syria but thrice" (II Kings 13:19).

God planned that the nation Syria would be destroyed and never again be a thorn in the flesh, a trial and temptation, never again bring oppression and war to Israel. But the doubting king timidly struck the earth only three times, not smiting again and again with a holy zeal and faith to accomplish what God has ordered. And so now he was to be victorious in only three battles and was not to utterly consume the Syrians, as God had planned.

The king should have opened his mouth wide. God was ready to fill it.

The unbelieving nine disciples left by Jesus at the foot of the Mount of Transfiguration could not cast out the demons from the boy brought to them. And Jesus said, "O faithless and perverse generation, how long shall I be with you? how long shall I suffer you? bring him hither to me" (Matt. 17:17). Jesus cast out the devils. He told the disciples they could not cast out the demons

". . . because of your unbelief: for verily I say unto you, If ye have faith as a grain of mustard seed, ye shall say unto this mountain, Remove hence to yonder place; and it shall remove; and nothing shall be impossible unto you. Howbeit this kind goeth not out but by prayer and fasting."—Matt. 17:20,21.

It is quite clear that the Lord was sad at the unbelief of His disciples. They did not believe they could cast out demons.

So many preachers have not faith that they can win drunkards or infidels or Catholics or Jews or heathens.

This passage is written in India. Night after night we have seen Catholics, Hindus, the fire-worshiping Parsis, the oh-so-difficult Moslems come to Christ. God has saved all kinds of sinners, old as well as young, and His presence has been wonderful. How He must be grieved when we do not attempt the hard cases, when we do not believe that the Gospel is adequate to reach the worst sinners.

3. Some Wonderful Examples of Attempting Great Things for God

In history, we have heart-warming examples of some men who undertook great things for God. One familiar with the life of D. L. Moody will remember how that Spirit-filled man with a less than grade school education led in building Farwell Hall for the Y.M.C.A. in Chicago, built a great Sunday school which became the great Moody Church; how he built Moody Bible Institute; how he united God's people for some of the greatest revival campaigns this world has ever seen; how he built one of the most important Christian literature programs in modern times; how he developed the Northfield conferences, the Northfield and Mount Hermon schools, the Tent Hall in Scotland, etc.

An illustration of the old days of D. L. Moody to attempt things others thought impossible was told by Dr. R. A. Torrey in his great message on "Why God Used D. L. Moody."

Moody decided that during the World's Fair in Chicago he would unite the people of God in great revival campaigns to cover the area in that time. For example, he decided to have a noonday meeting in the giant auditorium theater in downtown Chicago while the Fair was in progress out at the lake.

Dr. R. A. Torrey says:

> On "Chicago Day," in October 1893, none of the theatres of Chicago dared to open because it was expected that everybody in Chicago would go on that day to the World's Fair; and, in point of fact, something like four hundred thousand people did pass through the gates of the Fair that day. Everybody in Chicago was expected to be at that end of the city on that day. But Mr. Moody said to me, "Torrey, engage the Central Music Hall and announce meetings from nine o'clock in the morning till six o'clock at night."
>
> "Why," I replied, "Mr. Moody, nobody will be at this end of Chicago on that day; not even the theatres dare to open; everybody is going down to Jackson Park to the Fair; we cannot get anybody out on this day."
>
> Mr. Moody replied, "You do as you are told"; and I did as I was told and engaged the Central Music Hall for continuous meetings from nine o'clock in the morning till six o'clock at night. But I did it with a heavy heart. I thought there would be poor audiences.
>
> I was on the program at noon that day. Being very busy in my office about the details of the campaign, I did not reach the Central Music Hall till almost noon. I thought I would have no trouble getting in. But when I got almost to the Hall I found to my amazement that not only was it packed but the vestibule was packed and the steps were packed, and there was no getting anywhere near the door; and if I had not gone round and climbed in a back window they would have lost their speaker for that hour.
>
> But that would not have been of much importance, for the crowds had not gathered to hear me; it was the magic of Mr. Moody's name that had drawn them. And why did they long to hear Mr. Moody? Because they knew that while he was not versed in many of the philosophies and fads and fancies of the day, he

did know the one Book that this old world most longs to know—
the Bible.

One thinks also of Hudson Taylor who founded the China Inland
Mission because he made much of the motto, "Attempt great things
for God; expect great things from God."

Going to China without any regular and definite promise of support,
to grow a missionary force of nearly a thousand workers, all of them
going out by faith to the interior of China and trusting the Lord to supply
their need, never taking any collections for the mission work, was a
gigantic enterprise of faith. The faith missionary societies now have
workers to secure committal of support from some churches, instead
of having a guaranteed salary by a denominational mission board. So
the missionaries with faith missionary societies now deserve great credit.
But Hudson Taylor got hundreds of missionaries to go without any
definite committal of support, as I understand it, and he joined them
in praying down the money for passage, salaries, equipment and needs
and furlough.

Hudson Taylor opened his mouth wide, and God filled
it. He attempted great things for God and expected God to do great
things with him, through him and for him. And God did not fail him,
as He never fails any who trust Him.

A classic example of faith that attempts the large things, faith that
opens the mouth wide to receive great things from God, is that of George
Mueller of Bristol, England, who launched out into the deep on God's
promises! He set out to build an orphans' home, to staff and house it
and supply its needs by asking God alone, without ever taking a public
collection and without letting anyone know of his needs. He set out
to prove that there is a God who answers the prayer of faith.

Mueller did not believe and, of course, we do not believe that it is
wrong to take collection, wrong to let God's people know about God's
work and what it needs. But he felt led not only to build an orphans'
home, but to be a particular, specific case of daily answered prayer that
would build the faith of millions.

And in literally thousands of detailed answers to prayer, God gave
the land, the buildings, brought the teachers, supplied the daily needs
for as many as 2,300 orphans, year after year, decade after decade,
until long after Mueller died. The food was supplied, the clothes, the
teachers, the buildings. The money came on the same basis for print-

ing Christian literature and for sending missionaries far and near.

We are told that George Mueller got from God in answer to prayer, without ever taking a collection or telling anyone about his needs or the needs of God's work, some seven and a half million dollars. That amount would be more nearly thirty million today.

Mueller learned the secret of God's provision. By faith he opened wide his mouth, and God filled it.

My own small faith and small labors are not worthy to be compared with those of the blessed men of God I have mentioned. But as one who has found God faithful, let me praise His name. There was a day when everywhere the best Christian leaders had decided there were to be no more great revivals, when the term "evangelist" was one of reproach, when the leaders of my own Southern Baptist denomination despised and slandered me, when Moody Bible Institute, which ought to have been a center of evangelism like that of Moody and Torrey, published the infamous book, *True Evangelism*, by Lewis Sperry Chafer, slandering evangelists, deriding evangelistic preaching and the evangelistic invitation and the calling of evangelists. It was a day when the greatest summer Christian assembly—Winona Lake, founded and built by Evangelist J. Wilbur Chapman, W. E. Biederwolf and Billy Sunday—shut its doors against me and old-fashioned revival preaching.

But I set out to bring back citywide revival campaigns in America, and God, in mercy, gave great citywide campaigns in Buffalo, Cleveland, Chicago, Seattle, Miami for this poor preacher and raised up a crop of evangelists with open doors everywhere.

This poor evangelist felt a great need to get the Gospel in print for common people, following the example of Spurgeon, Talmage, Moody and Torrey. God graciously expanded our ministry in print to over 60 million copies of books and pamphlets, published in more than thirty-eight languages around the world, and to an extensive and blessed ministry of THE SWORD OF THE LORD for forty-five years. I never opened my mouth as wide as I should, but I have proved God.

III. GOD IS DELIGHTED WHEN HIS PEOPLE ASK GREAT THINGS OF HIM

This is the most obvious meaning of the text. After reminding people of all the great things God has done in the past, the inspired psalmist says, "Open thy mouth wide, and I will fill it." Christians should ask big things of a big God.

Let us consider this matter of large and believing prayers.

1. Proper Praying Connected With Faith in God

The promise in Psalm 81:10 presumes faith. God reminds us of the great things He has done in the past. The more one dwells on the Scriptures and what God has done and promises to do, the more faith arises in the heart. "So then faith cometh by hearing, and hearing by the word of God" (Rom. 10:17).

This is no slight-of-the-hand way of praying. This is no bit of mysterious magic. Faith grows as it is fed and exercised, as it leans upon God and waits for Him. One who opens his mouth wide and expects God to fill it must turn in faith to God, not away from God.

It necessarily implies that one who comes to open his mouth wide for God to fill loves God and wants to please Him, and is trying to ask in the will of God. The wonderful Bible promises about prayer are not intended as a way for the worldly-minded and unspiritual to twist God's arm in order to get things without any reference to the will and plan of God.

Psalm 81:10 is not to be taken as nullifying other Scriptures or making void plans and principles God has expressed elsewhere in the Bible. All the promises of God fit together and belong together, and this promise is to one who waits on God, who wants what God wants, who earnestly wants to please God. One who willfully, without any reference to God's plan as set forth in the Scriptures and without any concern for and without trying to find the leadership of God as to what he should ask, brazenly asks for carnal or spiritual things to suit a carnal order, may be sadly disappointed.

A young minister's wife read my book, *Prayer—Asking and Receiving*, and was thrilled to be reminded how often God had answered prayer, even that of this poor preacher. So she wrote something like this:

> Brother Rice, I have read your book on *Prayer* and see that you can get things from God. I want you to join me in prayer that God will give my husband $10,000 so he can buy a good car, pay his expenses for four years in college, and can be free from any trouble and concern about finances during these college days. Thus he will do better schoolwork and have greater peace of mind. Will you agree with me to ask for $10,000 now for my husband?

I wrote that I could not join in any such request. I did not believe it the will of God. I do not think God takes care of His preachers that way. I told her that if I had the $10,000 to give, I would not give it for that purpose. I said that, if her husband had a rich father with millions who gave away thousands of dollars each year, I still thought it would be folly for that indulgent father to put $10,000 cash in his son's hands at one time to prepare for four years in the future.

It might be that if that young preacher learned the lessons God teaches preachers by poverty and daily waiting on God, living with some hardship but with constant evidence of God's care, he might later have some enterprise for God that would justify asking for $10,000 and that God might give it. But this promise of Psalm 81:10 is not the pleasing of a spoiled child but the promise of a good and loving God made to His own children.

We should open our mouths wide and let God fill them. But we should determine ahead of time that we want what God wants. We should try to find His will, then be willing to go a step at a time. We should ask for today's daily bread, not necessarily for bread for next year. So this promise is inevitably connected with faith and with the principles of answered prayer laid down in the Scriptures.

2. How Often the Scripture Teaches Us to Ask Great Things of God!

God insisted that Abraham ask for a son even when he was one hundred years old and when Sarah was ninety. And when Abraham seemed to waver, God asked him, "Is any thing too hard for the Lord?" (Gen. 18:14).

God encouraged Jeremiah to expect the return of Israel from captivity, that captivity he had been warning the nation of for months. And Jeremiah was to buy property, seal the deed, after weighing out the seventeen shekels of silver and having the witnesses sign the evidence. When Jeremiah prayed unto the Lord saying, "Ah, Lord God! behold, thou hast made the heaven and the earth by thy great power and stretched out arm, and there is nothing too hard for thee" (Jer. 32:17), we are told, "Then came the word of the Lord unto Jeremiah, saying, Behold, I am the Lord, the God of all flesh: is there any thing too hard for me?" (vss. 26,27). And there is that much loved promise in Jeremiah 33:3, "Call unto me, and I will answer thee, and shew thee great and mighty things, which thou knowest not."

You remember the incident of Jesus' cursing the fig tree and its withering away. In Matthew 21:22, we have Jesus' promise, "And all things, whatsoever ye shall ask in prayer, believing, ye shall receive." And His promise as given in Mark 11:22-24,

"And Jesus answering saith unto them, Have faith in God. For verily I say unto you, That whosoever shall say unto this mountain, Be thou removed, and be thou cast into the sea; and shall not doubt in his heart, but shall believe that those things which he saith shall come to pass; he shall have whatsoever he saith. Therefore I say unto you, What things soever ye desire, when ye pray, believe that ye receive them, and ye shall have them."

Does not Jesus offer us the greatest things we ever need in answer to prayer?

When the distraught prophet brought his demon-possessed boy to Jesus saying, "If thou canst do anything, have compassion on us and help us," Jesus said unto him, "If thou canst believe, all things are possible to him that believeth." All things? Yes, all things!

How big is your mouth? Open it wide. Then if that opened mouth represents faith, the mouth that opens the widest will be filled with the answer from God!

The promise in John 14:13,14 means the same thing: "And whatsoever ye shall ask in my name, that will I do, that the Father may be glorified in the Son. If ye shall ask any thing in my name, I will do it."

"If ye shall ask ANY THING in my name, I will do it." Jesus said ask anything in the world! God is pleased for us to ask big things.

God wants glory in the church which He loves and for which Jesus died. And how can He be glorified? Ephesians 3:20,21 says:

"Now unto him that is able to do exceeding abundantly above all that we ask or think, according to the power that worketh in us, Unto him be glory in the church by Christ Jesus throughout all ages, world without end."

"That is able." Oh, that the church of the living God to which the saints bought by the blood belong, would only believe that He is exceeding abundantly able to do more than we can even ask or think! God delights in big prayers from His people.

3. Our Little Faith Can Hardly Believe How God Answered the Big Prayers in the Bible

We have here a theme too great for a limited space. Even in the Bible the inspired writer did not have room to tell it all, but says in Hebrews 11:32-35:

"And what shall I more say? for the time would fail me to tell of Gideon, and of Barak, and of Samson, and of Jephthah; of David also, and Samuel, and of the prophets: Who through faith subdued kingdoms, wrought righteousness, obtained promises, stopped the mouths of lions, Quenched the violence of fire, escaped the edge of the sword, out of weakness were made strong, waxed valiant in fight, turned to flight the armies of the aliens. Women received their dead raised to life again: and others were tortured, not accepting deliverance; that they might obtain a better resurrection."

At the word of Moses, the Nile River turned to blood, a plague of frogs covered the land, then billions of flies, then the other plagues in Egypt. His rod could become a snake or could bring water out of a rock or could open the Red Sea for His people or close it on Pharaoh's horsemen. Moses opened his mouth wide. As long as his hands were upheld, the armies of Israel could defeat the Amorites.

So with a boldness that must have shocked the angels (but strangely did not displease God!), Joshua commanded the sun to stand still, and it did. I have often thought that the sun itself must have been shocked at such a command.

Elijah risked his life in believing that God would send the fire from Heaven to burn up the sacrifices and that He would send the rain when he prayed.

When the Hebrew children faced the fiery furnace and Daniel the lions' den, they expected deliverance and got it.

Then we have the faith of Paul saying the word and Elymas the sorcerer being struck blind; Peter saying the word and Ananias and Sapphira falling dead!

Think of Peter asking God to raise Dorcas from the dead or Paul bringing to life the young man who fell out of the third-story loft at Troas, or Paul in the shipwreck explaining that God had given him all their lives and not a hair of their heads would be harmed, then how he shook off the terrible snake in the fire and was not harmed.

Think of the audacity of the New Testament Christians setting out to conquer the Roman world with the Gospel and how far they carried it in the first century!

We can only hint at the amazing way God was pleased to hear the prayers of people who asked and got miraculous things from God.

Look through the Bible: did ever God rebuke one who came with a great request?

Was He not pleased with the centurion who could simply say, "Speak the word only, and my servant shall be healed" (Matt. 8:8)?

Was He not pleased at the insistence of the Syrophenician woman who would not take no for an answer?

Did He not encourage us to be like the widow before the unjust judge who could not be shut up but would have her justice?

Was not God pleased at the persistence of Jacob who wrestled with the angel and, with his thigh out of joint, could not be persuaded to let go until he got the blessing?

Preachers tend to tell us to go slow, not to ask for too big a thing, not to ask anything selfish, nor for more than bare necessities. But God never says anything like that, never puts on the brakes.

A dear layman in Dallas, Texas, came for a time of prayer with me. We prayed for daily radio broadcasts costing hundreds of dollars, for a heavy printing bill, for a blessed tent revival that was about to start, for the money for a large brick tabernacle 90 by 146 feet we were building. After we had agreed on all these things for which we would ask God's help, he prayed and then rather apologetically said, "Lord, if You will please give us these things this time, we will try never to ask for so much anymore"!

But if men feel that God is embarrassed by much asking, they are wrong. Preachers would have us limit our requests to bare necessities, but God says, "I am the Lord thy God, which brought thee out of Egypt: open thy mouth wide, and I will fill it."

4. God Has Graciously Answered Prayer for This Poor Servant

In the words of the psalmist, "This poor man cried, and the Lord heard him, and saved him out of all his trouble" (34:6). If it was proper for David to tell it, it is proper for me to tell it to the glory of God. Some who read this doubtless have had just as great answers to prayer; if so, then tell it. But let me mention some ways that God has graciously showed His power in times of need.

When I was about fifteen my father, after a very serious and extended illness, was expected to die soon. Two doctors consulted said he would not live until morning. My stepmother, my elder sister and I, without prearrangement and separately, prayed for God to raise him up.

The next morning when he awoke he asked, "Where are my pants?" He put on his clothes and walked up to the little store to attend to some business. His sickness was over. He would take a little rest each day until he recovered his strength, but God seemed to have instantly healed my dad who should have died!

When she was five, our daughter Grace had diphtheria. The doctor sent a culture from her throat to the medical laboratory, and it was confirmed. Our home was quarantined by the county health officer. My wife and I knelt down by her bed and prayed.

That afternoon the fever disappeared. The next morning at our earnest request the county health officer sent the nurse, tests were renewed, and the nurse said, "This girl doesn't have diphtheria." I said, "I know she doesn't now, but she did have yesterday."

Another time Mrs. Rice and I agreed to pray for a car. On Monday evening we prayed together. Again Tuesday evening we prayed together. We had never mentioned the need to anyone. No one had mentioned to us a prospect. Wednesday night we drove home in a new sedan.

In the time of terrible drought in Peacock, Texas, some of us joined in prayer for a great rain within twenty-four hours. "If it does not come by 11:00 tomorrow night, it is not in answer to our prayers," I said. People agreed.

That next afternoon there came boiling clouds and a cloudburst of rain that soaked an area within a radius of about five miles in a county where already farms had been abandoned, houses boarded up and where drinking water was shipped in by train!

God answers prayer. He commands, "Open thy mouth wide, and I will fill it."

God Says to Open YOUR Mouth Wide

After reading my large book, *Prayer—Asking and Receiving,* hundreds have written to ask me to join them in prayer about certain projects. I appreciate their sharing with me their burden and letting me share with them the prayer. But I fear that all such people largely miss the point of the teaching here.

God has wonderfully answered my prayers. He has wonderfully answered prayers of other men who have witnessed to God's faithfulness, such as George Mueller, Hudson Taylor, D. L. Moody and R. A. Torrey. But it would be a sad mistake to believe that God had chosen certain men He would rather hear pray than others or that God meant the blessed promises in the Bible to only a chosen few. The death of Christ made atonement for the sins of the whole world. Everybody who ever gets saved, gets saved by grace alone. Every preacher who was ever called to preach was "counted worthy" when he was not, and by God's grace was allowed to preach the Gospel. There is no respect of persons with God.

So when He makes a blessed promise that He will answer prayer, He is anxious for the humblest Christian to call upon Him, to make his requests known, to implore God, to wait on God, to persistently supplicate before God. When the Lord said, "I am the Lord thy God, which brought thee out of the land of Egypt: open thy mouth wide, and I will fill it," the promise of blessing was as universal as the deliverance of the whole nation Israel, of which we are thus reminded.

I am glad to tell how God has wonderfully answered my prayer. But I do not mean to leave the impression that I have learned some particular secret, that I have some special favor with God, or that God would rather answer my prayer than yours. God, who will save one sinner as well as another when he comes in penitent faith, will answer the prayer of one humble Christian the same as another, if he comes in faith to ask for the glory of God and according to real needs and in dependence on the promise of God.

God wants you, dear reader, to open your mouth wide. He wants you to attempt great things, ask great things. The intent of this message will be lost if you simply ask someone else to do your praying for you.

I beg you to take your burden to the Lord and persistently wait on God for His great blessings. He has more for you than you have ever taken. More is provided than you have ever asked. His promises are greater than you have ever claimed. So "open thy mouth wide" for the filling you need.

HARRY J. HAGER
1899-1983

ABOUT THE MAN:

Dr. Hager attended Hope College and later became professor of Bible and Biblical Literature there. He graduated from Western Theological Seminary as class valedictorian and graduated from Chicago University with a Ph.D. He did extensive research and traveled in Egypt, Palestine and other Bible lands from 1926-29.

Dr. Hager was pastor of Bethany Reformed Church, Chicago, from 1929-1975. In addition to his parish of some 3,000—the largest congregation of his denomination—he conducted several evangelistic campaigns and Bible conferences a year, directed America's largest summer DVBS and had a radio ministry of five hours weekly on two major Chicago stations.

Prior to his ministry at Bethany, he pastored a Presbyterian church in Volga, South Dakota, and a Reformed church at Forest Grove, Michigan.

Some of the other positions he enjoyed were: Bible conference speaker at Winona Lake and American Keswick, a speaker at the historic Congress on Prophecy at Calvary Baptist Church, New York City; a frequent speaker at the noonday meetings of the Chicago Christian Businessmen's Committee which broadcast over WJJD; was a frequent speaker on WMBI; a member of the Advisory Council of the World Christian Fundamentals Association, National Association of Evangelicals, and the International Child Evangelism Fellowship.

Dr. Hager crossed the Atlantic eleven times in the interests of worldwide evangelism. In 1949 he made a worldwide tour of foreign mission fields. In 1950 he made his third visit to the Holy Land. In 1952 he conducted a two-week evangelistic crusade in the Dutch language in Amsterdam under the auspices of Youth for Christ.

He is the author of *The Dutch School of Radical N.T. Criticism.*

He was a good friend of Dr. John R. Rice and the Sword of the Lord ministries. Many Sword of the Lord conferences on evangelism were held in his large church on the south side of Chicago.

Dr. Hager resigned his church in 1976 and died in 1983 in Holland, Michigan.

XII.

The Power to Prevail

HARRY J. HAGER

"And he said, Let me go, for the day breaketh. And he said, I will not let thee go, except thou bless me." —Gen. 32:26.

Alone! alone! all, all alone!
Alone on the wide, wide sea,
And never a saint took pity on
My soul in agony.

These weird lines from the *Rime of the Ancient Mariner* suggest something of the desolation in those words: Jacob was left alone.

Across the rocky and roaring Jabbok, Jacob's family and flocks are nestling in two camps in quiet and peaceful slumber under the stars. But the head of the clan remains behind. No rest for this weary man, no sweet dreams and visions of angel-visitants ascending and descending from Heaven on the ladder of God; but a fierce conflict raging back and forth from midnight till break of day.

As the evening darkness deepens into the blackness of the night, the wary Jacob comes upon a stranger unawares and, sensing it may be one of Esau's henchmen, he leaps like a panther to the combat, just as he had previously engaged many a cattle thief in the darkness in the plains of Padan-Aram.

But for once the wily, aggressive supplanter discovers that his spirited offensive fails to turn the tide of combat in his favor. The stranger is every whit his equal, pits strength against strength, matches hold for hold, till the struggle drags out into an all-night endurance contest with neither gaining the advantage.

Then suddenly the agile stranger touches the hollow of Jacob's thigh, the thigh-bone springs from socket, and the sinew is strained. From that moment the contest is over. Jacob is limp and helpless now, and his only hope is to clinch and hang on.

There you have the scene. I am sure it has provoked three questions in your minds. First, what was this contest all about; second, how went the course of the battle; and finally, what was its outcome?

I. THE ISSUE

It is apparent that this incident at Peniel was the great crisis in Jacob's life, a crisis with which very significant issues were linked. This young sheikh, so successful in the land of Padan-Aram, suddenly discovered himself face to face with a new situation which he was utterly unable to meet. He had employed every device of ingenuity in an attempt to allay his brother Esau's passion for revenge.

"And Jacob sent messengers before him to Esau his brother unto the land of Seir, the country of Edom. And he commanded them, saying, Thus shall ye speak unto my lord Esau; Thy servant Jacob saith thus, I have sojourned with Laban, and stayed there until now: And I have oxen, and asses, flocks, and menservants, and womenservants: and I have sent to tell my lord, that I may find grace in thy sight. And the messengers returned to Jacob, saying, We came to thy brother Esau, and also he cometh to meet thee, and four hundred men with him." — Gen. 32:3-6.

It was the specter of this armed force that haunted Jacob that night. He saw plainly that since these overtures for peace had failed, he was now threatened with the loss of everything in a single hour of ruthless revenge. The fruits of all his ambition, industry, and ingenuity would be swept away, his loved ones either killed or enslaved, and himself possibly tortured to death. It was most certainly an hour of crisis.

There are similar crises in the life of every believer. It may be an inner conflict precipitated by an outward circumstance—the sudden loss of employment, the prospect of a long illness, the base ingratitude of a prodigal son, or the death of a beloved child or lifelong companion. There are times when we have done all to fortify ourselves against an impending crisis, only to find that our human resources have utterly failed. All that human wisdom can devise and human ingenuity can provide have been mustered to the battle in an effort to stem the tide that is turning against us. Yet the divine destiny seems to move us irrepressibly to the hour of defeat. Do whatsoever we will in such times, we are helpless and can but wait to see what will happen next.

It was thus with Jacob. He had paid every price that the world demands for its rewards of success. He said, "In the day the drought consumed me, and the frost by night; and my sleep departed from mine eyes" (Gen. 31:40).

But that night on hither side of the Jabbok Jacob was slowly awaking to the realization that hard work alone was not enough. Nor was his wealth sufficient to meet this new situation. It became dimly apparent to the resourceful ranchman that while he had acquired much, he had missed the best that life could give him. He had oxen and asses and flocks and menservants and maidservants, but he had not the spirituality and the devout character to prevail with God as a pleader of the covenant—and at this moment he needed his covenant God very badly. God had withheld this larger blessing for the reason that Jacob had never seriously sought it.

In spite of the early vision at Bethel, Jacob, after twenty years of spiritual privilege, was of the earth earthy. He was a strange mixture—this carnal son of the covenant. How beautiful his love for Rachel! With what devotion did he love and provide for his clan! Yes, he was a good enough sheikh measured by any standards of the hills and plains.

But that night Jacob began to ask: *How do I look to God? How do I stand in His sight?* Since Bethel he had not met with the ground of reality, and as he ventured into the Promised Land, he needed God more than all else. God had a great purpose to fulfill through him as His covenant heir, but Jacob could not be used till the "Jacob" nature was subdued. Jacob's problem was not Esau. His greatest problem was himself.

Such times of testing come to every Christian who heeds the call to leave the shallows of a carnal Christian life and launch forth into the deep of a consecrated spirituality. There are times when we Christian parents discover that our children are not really converted and our homes are not really Christian, and at such times we may well pause to examine ourselves. Is it that we have no power with God because of our own unsurrendered lives? Again, how often we ministers run upon stretches of extreme barrenness in our ministry. The flame of love flickers in our congregation, the prayer life weakens, the passion for souls begins to languish, and the unsaved are utterly unmoved.

Have you ever awakened in such a time to the discovery that it is your own carnality, worldliness, selfishness, pettiness, and prayerlessness which have held back the flow of blessings? How long since you have been alone with yourself and have sought to discover the issues involved in your Christian growth and usefulness?

II. THE STRUGGLE

Let us return to Jacob. In the fierceness of this introspection, Jacob begins to pray alone.

"And Jacob said, O God of my father Abraham, and God of my father Isaac, the Lord which saidst unto me, Return unto thy country, and to thy kindred, and I will deal well with thee: I am not worthy of the least of all the mercies, and of all the truth, which thou hast shewed unto thy servant; for with my staff I passed over this Jordan; and now I am become two bands. Deliver me, I pray thee, from the hand of my brother, from the hand of Esau: for I fear him, lest he will come and smite me, and the mother with the children. And thou saidst, I will surely do thee good, and make thy seed as the sand of the sea, which cannot be numbered for multitude."—Gen. 32:9-12.

There is a confession of unworthiness in this prayer, there is an acknowledgment of gratitude, there is an admission of helplessness, and a pleading of the promise, but Jacob has not yet touched the vital issue in the great spiritual conflict which now begins.

With a sense of caution that was active even in the moment of apparent annihilation, he draws up his caravan in a line of separate camps. The company is lodged for the night.

"And he rose up that night, and took his two wives, and his two womenservants, and his eleven sons, and passed over the ford Jabbok. And he took them, and sent them over the brook, and sent over that he had."—Gen. 32:22, 23.

Then it is that Jacob meets the stranger and wrestles with Him until the breaking of the day. There can be but little debate as to the identity of this stranger. He was none other than the Angel of the Covenant, the Second Person of the Godhead, the discarnate Son of God, clothed with the vesture of an angel.

But why did the Angel of the Covenant appear at this juncture in Jacob's life? The answer is this: humanly speaking, this covenant patriarch would have lived another half a century without any spiritual improvement had not the real weakness of his life been divinely exposed. Jacob's doublemindedness had to be conquered once for all. He could no longer be half for the world and half for God. Jacob must henceforth live on a new and higher plane of righteousness, spirituality, and faith. And so the Angel strikes his body to touch his soul.

God must take from every one of His servants whom He uses the very staff which has hitherto been his mainstay.

Do you notice what the all-night conflict does for Jacob's soul? He no longer seeks mere deliverance. He no longer wishes merely to "get by." He is no longer concerned merely with the problem of Esau. With his thigh-bone sprung and the muscle strained, Jacob awakes to the fact that his adversary is none other than the Divine Messenger Himself. And as he clings to Him, Jacob begins to weep for his contradictions. Then, but not until then, does Jacob really see himself in all his energetic futility. Then, but only then, does Jacob discover the unlimited power of God.

And this is what the Angel of the Covenant is seeking to accomplish with this Son of the Promise. Jacob must not merely be converted; he must be surrendered. God will give him the blessing as soon as he is shaped that he can be trusted with the blessing. No longer does Jacob know his God afar off. Henceforth He is his All in all.

But there are Peniels in the life of the Christian today. Have you ever had your hour of extremity? Have you in sheer desperation turned to the God you thought you had always known and found Him withholding the coveted blessing until He could come to terms with you regarding some unsurrendered area of your life? Have you met with God Himself in the wrestlings of prayer? Have your doubts been settled once for all in that secret place of supplication? Have you forsworn all divided loyalties and halfhearted devotions, and surrendered yourself utterly to Him whate'er betide?

Can you honestly say that your life, in purpose, at least, is all for God? Have you accepted His plan for your life, taken His will for your motive, trusted in His resources for your dynamic? Such a Peniel is for the true follower of Christ life's crowning victory through life's most humbling defeat.

Let us try next to understand a little more fully the exact nature of that victory.

III. THE VICTORY

The triumph of Jacob was a victory over self through surrender, a victory with God through faith, and a victory over his fellowmen through prayer. The conquest of self involved a complete disavowal of all confidence in self or any other human resources. It implied a confession of the sinfulness of all unconsecrated means of self-advancement. It called forth a whole new attitude toward his life in the plan and purpose of God.

"What is thy name?" asked the Angel. And he said, "Jacob." It was a confession. "I am a supplanter, a deceiver, a double-dealer."

This same humiliating confession is wrung from the heart of every soul with whom the Holy Spirit deals in sanctification. What is your name? My name is "Look-Out-for-Yourself." What is your name? O God, I am "Facing-Both-Ways." And your name? My name is "Half-hearted." What weaknesses these names reveal! Here is "Little-Faith," there is "Temporary," over there is "Mrs. Timorous," and yonder is "Mr. Ready-to-Halt."

But to every surrendered life God gives a new name. And the Angel said, "Thy name shall be called no more Jacob, but Israel: for as a prince hast thou power with God and with men, and hast prevailed" (Gen. 32:28).

Do you know that name? Is it yours? Have you learned how to prevail with God upon your knees? Do you know how to cling to Him in wrestling prayer till the Holy Spirit has burned out the dross in confession and surrender, revealed the power of the Divine Presence, and sent you away to life's battle with the weapons of victory in your hands?

When the Divine grace has achieved this victory over self, victory over the world is inevitable. Jacob had power to prevail with Esau because he had prevailed with God. Israel limping is stronger than Jacob wrestling.

The church is today in desperate need of such spiritual champions. The power of prevailing prayer is an open secret. Why is it that more of God's children do not learn it? Is it not a true philosophy of conversion to say that no soul is ever won except as some believer has painfully travailed in the intercession for that soul?

Nor will the citadels of vice and wickedness ever be shaken without the wrestling of earnest prayer. The enemies within our gates will never be subdued by the weapons of a mere scientific apologetic. Our churches will not be revived until those who know God and have the promises learn to pray with dependent faith, surrendered life, and passionate love. We need today a church that has been to Peniel and has learned the secret of a limping dependence, and can prevail with men because she prevails with God.

But Jacob's greatest victory came in the moment of the divine revelation.

"And Jacob asked him, and said, Tell me, I pray thee, thy name. And he said, Wherefore is it that thou dost ask after my name? And he blessed him there. And Jacob called the name of the place Peniel: for I have seen God face to face, and my life is preserved."—Gen. 32:29, 30.

Jacob had learned that God could be mightily moved by the plea of human weakness. Little wonder after such a profound experience that Jacob felt the need of knowing better the God of his fathers. He had heard of Him at his father's knee when a boy, he had called upon Him as a youth on the threshold of life, he had raised altars to Him upon his return to the borders of his inheritance; but at Peniel he had come to grips with Him in the arena of a deep spiritual crisis. He had seen God face to face. He had gained a new vision of the covenant life. He must now know God as one who, like Abraham, walks with Him and enters into the counsels of His covenant. Was this knowledge vouchsafed to Him? Let Charles Wesley give us the answer:

> Come, O Thou Traveler unknown,
> Whom still I hold, but cannot see,
> My company before is gone,
> And I am left alone with Thee;
> With Thee all night I mean to stay,
> And wrestle till the break of day.
>
> I need not tell Thee who I am,
> My misery or sin declare;
> Thyself hast call'd me by my name;
> Look on Thy hands, and read it there!
> But who, I ask Thee, who art Thou?
> Tell me Thy name, and tell me now.
>
> In vain Thou strugglest to get free,
> I never will unloose my hold;
> Art Thou the Man who died for me?
> The secret of Thy name unfold.
> Wrestling, I will not let Thee go,
> Till I Thy name, Thy nature know.

'Tis all in vain to hold Thy tongue,
Or touch the hollow of my thigh;
Though every sinew be unstrung,
Out of my arms Thou shalt not fly;
Wrestling, I will not let Thee go,
Till I Thy name, Thy nature know.

What though my shrinking flesh complain,
And murmur to contend so long?
I rise superior to my pain;
When I am weak, then I am strong:
And when my all of strength shall fail,
I shall with the God-Man prevail.

Yield to me now, for I am weak,
But confident in self-despair;
Speak to my ear, in blessing speak,
Be conquer'd by my instant prayer!
Speak, or Thou never hence shalt move,
And tell me if Thy name is Love.

'Tis Love! 'tis Love! Thou diedst for me!
I hear Thy whisper in my heart!
The morning breaks, the shadows flee;
Pure universal Love Thou art!
Thy nature, and Thy name, is Love!
To me, to all, Thy heart doth move:

My prayer hath power with God; the grace
Unspeakable I now receive;
Through faith I see Thee face to face,
I see Thee face to face, and live;
In vain I have not wept and strove;
Thy nature, and Thy name, is Love.

I know Thee, Saviour, who Thou art;
Jesus, the feeble sinner's Friend!
Nor wilt Thou with the night depart,
But stay and love me to the end!
Thy mercies never shall remove,
Thy nature, and Thy name, is Love!

Contented now upon my thigh
I halt, till life's short journey end;
All helplessness, all weakness, I
On Thee alone for strength depend;
Nor have I power from Thee to move;
Thy nature, and Thy name, is Love!

Lame as I am, I take the prey,
Hell, earth, and sin, with ease o'ercome;

I leap for joy, pursue my way,
And as a bounding hart fly home!
Through all eternity to prove
Thy nature, and Thy name, is Love!

JOHN LINTON
1888-1965

ABOUT THE MAN:

The story of John Linton is another of those sagas that shine with the wonder-working grace of God.

One of twelve children, this immigrant boy from Scotland gravitated to the life of a wastrel, a wanderer. This wicked youth seemed to be destined to a life of cheating, lying and stealing.

But God moved in when John was thirteen. He had left home, had lied to suspecting police, had hid in barns; then finally he was taken in by a Christian woman and mothered. Here John learned the sweet lesson of the Heavenly Father's patience, tenderness and forgiveness to an erring child. So he confessed Christ and claimed His forgiveness. This was the turning point in his life.

Shortly he emigrated to Canada. And at James Street Baptist Church, Hamilton, Ontario, John Linton heard God's call to preach the Gospel.

He attended Gordon Bible College in Boston. Under the consecrated teaching there, Linton "grew like a hothouse plant." His pastor persuaded him to go to a Baptist college in Woodstock, where he could finish high school work as well.

College life became a geographical game of musical chairs—Boston, Woodstock, Toronto, Manitoba. All the while he was preparing to be a "good preacher," he was busy "practicing preaching."

He graduated with a master's degree, married a childhood sweetheart and became a pastor. It was during his pastorate at High Park Baptist Church, Toronto, that he became vitally interested in revival and evangelism. Linton entered evangelism—and God blessed—across Canada, across America, until his decease in 1965.

John Linton is not normally listed among the elite of the evangelists in this century: Moody, Sunday, Bob Jones, Sr., Appelman, John Rice. But he was not some lesser light—God mightily moved through his ministry. He left a trail of converts to Christ as well as revived, restored, rejoicing churches.

His gospel soundness, his compelling delivery, his Scotch brogue and his devotion to our Lord made him widely acceptable. You cannot hear the inimitable Scotch brogue in his sermon, but you can enjoy its sweet and powerful message.

He died at age 77 in the pulpit while conducting evangelistic services.

XIII.

Unanswered Prayer

JOHN LINTON

"Ye ask, and receive not." —James 4:3.

Here James raises the question of the prayers God does not answer. We would have known this fact even if James had not mentioned it, because unanswered prayer is recorded in our experience as well as in the Bible. We have asked, and we have not received.

Is then God unfaithful? Are His promises undependable? How are we to reconcile these Scriptures—"Ask, and ye shall receive," and "Ye ask, and receive not"?

I am going to make several observations concerning unanswered prayer, and I trust each one will be a window letting in some light upon our problem.

I remark first:

I. SOME PRAYERS ARE BETTER UNANSWERED

I fervently thank God for some prayers of mine which He has answered. It has proven God's faithfulness. It has encouraged others to ask and receive. It has resulted in the salvation of souls. But I thank God just as fervently today for the prayers of mine He has not answered.

When I was a lad I worked as an apprentice molder in a small foundry. It employed about eight or ten men and was owned and managed by an elderly man. I was ambitious to succeed, and it became the desire and prayer of my heart that I might one day become the owner and manager of that little foundry.

I thank God He did not answer that prayer. God had better things in store for me. Instead of spending my life molding castings to ornament buildings that would perish in time, God wanted me to stand in a pulpit and be used in molding character that would last for eternity.

I think of another preacher who thanks God for unanswered prayer. He is in Heaven today and has been a long time there. His name is Elijah. One day in a fit of despondency this good man fled into the wilderness, lay down under a scrub tree, and prayed that he might die.

God in mercy did not answer that prayer. He had far better things for Elijah than a grave under a juniper tree. Even while Elijah was praying for death, God was preparing a chariot of glory to take him to the skies. God planned to give to the world, through Elijah's translation, a pre-intimation of the glorious ascension to Heaven of Jesus Christ.

Elijah was to be taken up alive into Heaven, but he would have missed all that, had God answered his prayer. Instead of going home in glory and victory to God, his dead body would have found a grave in the wilderness with a scrub tree as his only monument. What a poor end that would have been for the hero of Carmel! That would have spoiled the whole story of Elijah's life. The victory on Mount Carmel would have been overshadowed by his defeat in the wilderness. The ghost of his ultimate failure would have stalked through every sermon preached about Elijah. What preacher could become eloquent preaching about a man who died in the Slough of Despond?

No, God did not answer Elijah's prayer. And Elijah is walking the streets of Heaven today thanking God that some prayers are better not answered.

You may remember, too, that in Numbers 14, Israel cried, "Would God we had died in this wilderness," and God in judgment answered that prayer. He said in wrath, "As ye have spoken in mine ears, so will I do to you." That generation died in the wilderness just as they had prayed, but it was a judgment upon them that God answered their prayer. Some prayers are better not answered, and that was one of them.

Sometimes God speaks through the convicting Holy Spirit to souls unsaved. But instead of yielding, they resist the Spirit, they harden their hearts, they say,

> **Go, Spirit, go thy way,**
> **Some more convenient day**
> **On Thee I'll call.**

Yet God in mercy has not answered their prayer. He has not left them. In love and infinite patience He is still speaking to their hearts, still drawing them to Himself, and they ought to thank Him that some prayers are not answered.

II. SOMETIMES THE ANSWER COMES UNRECOGNIZED

We ask and God gives. Yet sometimes the answer is right before our eyes, and we do not recognize it. We are sure God will answer our request, so we glue our eyes to the front door looking for the answer. And because God sometimes chooses to send the answer in by the back door, it is unrecognized.

This is illustrated for us in chapter 12 of Acts. Peter was in prison sentenced to death. He was to be beheaded by Herod on the morrow in the public square of the city. But the church decided to hold an all-night prayer meeting, and they gave themselves to real, earnest, definite intercession for Peter's deliverance.

And that night deliverance came, even while they prayed. Yet when liberated Peter knocked at the door, only little Rhoda believed he was there! Here was the answer to their prayer standing right at the door, but they would not receive the answer. The answer came unrecognized.

Have you ever asked yourself why this was? Some tell me they evidently did not believe God would liberate Peter. They say it is quite clear they did not believe God would answer their prayers.

Now that is a lazy way of thinking. It is certainly not a reasonable explanation. You ask me to believe that this group of Christians, who have seen much of the supernatural, and with whom signs and wonders were almost a daily occurrence, so doubted that God would answer their prayer, that even when they held an all-night prayer meeting they were agreed in their unbelief that God would not or could not do what they asked. Well, I don't believe your explanation. Such doubting Thomases do not pray all night. They do not pray without ceasing, as this group did.

Why, then, was the answer unrecognized? I believe for my part that someone that night received the assurance of faith that Peter would be delivered. This assurance would spread from heart to heart. And then as nearly always happens with those who pray the prayer of faith, they began to speculate in their minds as to how God would work this deliverance.

And, of course, there was only one way for God to do it. On the morrow in the public square, with Herod and the enemies of the church gathered, with Peter's head on the block and the headsman's ax just about to fall—suddenly there would appear a mighty angel with voice of thunder, the ax would fall with a clatter to the pavement, Peter's chains would fall from his hands and, rising up a free man, he would walk through the midst of terrified Herod and Company with all the rejoicing Christians following him in a triumphal procession! Yes, they can see the deliverance, and I rather think someone was praying about that noonday triumphal procession when little Rhoda interrupted their prayer with—"Peter's at the door."

Of course, it could not be Peter! What? in the middle of the night? with nobody to see the miracle? Of course, God would not do it that way. Rhoda must be overexcited. And so liberated Peter, the answer to their prayer, stands unrecognized at the door.

My dear friends, I have seen the counterpart of this happen again and again. Some woman has claimed by faith her husband for God. Almost immediately that husband has become specially trying. He speaks against Christians and the church. He criticizes the Bible. He is more outspoken in his opposition than before she believed for his salvation. And this sudden antagonism has sent praying women to me in distress because it seemed the very opposite of what they expected would happen.

I tell such praying saints to rejoice and be exceeding glad for God is answering their prayers. I remind them that the Devil usually tears a man before he leaves him; that their loved ones will likely be worse before they are better; that God's Spirit is working, they are kicking— like Saul of Tarsus—against the pricks, and the very antagonism that dismays is the precursor of that soul's salvation.

Observe also:

III. THE ANSWER MAY ONLY BE DELAYED

You may recall that the angel of God came to an old man named Zacharias and said, "Zacharias, thy prayer is heard." Zacharias nearly fell over! He must have felt like saying, "What prayer?" The angel referred to his prayer for a child, which had been offered so long ago that Zacharias had almost forgotten it. The answer came, but it was delayed almost a lifetime.

George Mueller prayed sixty-two years for the salvation of two men. On his first visit to America, he said, "I have prayed daily for thirty-five years for the salvation of two men, and I will continue to do so until they are saved. On land or sea, sick or well, I will remember them before God."

Mueller lived twenty-seven years after that and died without seeing them saved. One of these men was saved at Mueller's funeral service; and the other, two years later. God honored Mueller's faith; and, although the prayer seemed to be unanswered, the answer was only delayed.

> **Unanswered yet, the prayer your lips have pleaded,**
> **In agony of heart those many years?**
> **Does faith begin to fail? Is hope departing?**
> **And think you all in vain those falling tears?**
> **Say not the Father hath not heard your prayer;**
> **You shall have your desire sometime, somewhere.**
>
> **Unanswered yet? tho' when you first presented**
> **This one petition at the Father's throne,**
> **It seemed you could not wait the time of asking,**
> **So urgent was your heart to make it known.**
>
> **Tho' years have passed since then, do not despair;**
> **The Lord will answer you sometime, somewhere.**
>
> —Ophelia G. Browning

The Bible tells of a man who waited fifteen hundred years for the answer to his prayer. Moses asked God to let him set foot in the Holy Land, but God—at that time—did not grant his desire. Centuries later the door of Heaven opened; and Moses, with Elijah, stepped down upon the Mount of Transfiguration in Palestine. When he set foot on that mountain, his prayer was answered—after fifteen hundred years.

When God delays the answer, there is a wise purpose in that delay. It tests the strength of our desire. It tests our faith. God is always honored when we believe despite delay. He says to angels and archangels, "Do you hear that mother praying down on the earth? She is thanking Me through her tears for her boy's salvation. She has prayed thirty years for that prodigal, and he is not saved yet. But her faith in Me is as strong now as when she first believed." Thus God is glorified, His Word is honored, and the wisdom of the delay is always justified. God's delays are always for our greater good and His highest glory.

Billy Bray, the Cornish miner, had built a little church in the town where he lived. He claimed that "Father" had promised him a pulpit for the church. Passing along the street one day, he stopped at a store where an auction sale was proceeding. The auctioneer pointed to a large handsome oak cabinet and asked for a bid. Billy said "Father" told him that was the pulpit, so he bid six shillings. A man behind Billy bid seven shillings; and since Billy had no more money, it was knocked down for seven shillings—to Billy Bray's dismay.

Billy took the matter to "Father" in prayer and asked if he had displeased "Father" in something so that his prayer was not answered. He was told that everything would be all right, that "Father" was not displeased. Billy went about his business.

That afternoon on his way home he saw a lorry outside a saloon and on the sidewalk were several men struggling to get a cabinet inside the door which was too small. While the men were grumbling over the size of the cabinet, Billy said, "I'll give you six shillings for it."

"It's yours," said the owner.

Billy said, "There's one condition—that you lend me the horse and lorry and these men."

"They are yours," said the saloonkeeper, and off Billy went.

He said later, "Father knew I had the six shillings to pay for the pulpit, but He also knew I had no money to hire a horse and lorry to deliver it!"

I remark further:

IV. THE CONDITIONS MAY NOT HAVE BEEN FULFILLED

The choicest blessings of God are conditional. There are certain conditions governing asking and receiving, and often prayer is not answered because these conditions have not been fulfilled.

Let me mention three of the major conditions of answered prayer.

1. We must ask with a clean heart.

"If I regard iniquity in my heart, the Lord will not hear me." No one can hope to prevail in prayer who is willfully disobeying God. It is quite true that God answers prayer for Jesus' sake and on the basis of His merit, not ours; nevertheless to knowingly harbor sin in our lives is to hinder the answer to prayer.

2. We must ask with a compelling plea.

What is the argument that moves God to answer prayer? Is it our desperate need? Is it our much asking? Is it the joy or comfort the answer will give us? These are doubtless all good arguments to present to God, but there is one compelling plea surpassing all others, one that never fails to move God, and that plea is that the Lord Jesus Christ may be glorified through the answer. He is the One whom the King delighteth to honor. God will answer prayer for Jesus' sake. His glory is our one prevailing plea.

When a woman asks God to save her husband so that she will have an easier time in the home, that is not a compelling plea. Jesus Christ died for her husband and deserves her husband's love and worship and service. It is an injustice and dishonor to Christ that her husband does not live for Him. If that woman will ask God to save her husband so that Jesus Christ will receive the glory and honor from her husband that is His due, then she is using a compelling argument, and in all likelihood God will honor that plea.

3. We must ask with a conquering faith.

James says, "But let him ask in faith, nothing wavering. For he that wavereth is like a wave of the sea driven with the wind and tossed. For let not that man think he shall receive any thing of the Lord."

To waver in faith is to hinder the answer. The waves of the sea are at the mercy of the wind. Whichever way the wind blows, the wave goes. The Christian who believes one day that the answer will come, and next day, because of some unfavorable circumstance, he begins to doubt, is unstable in his faith and will not receive the answer.

The man who really believes is not affected by circumstances. His faith remains unshaken whichever way the wind blows. Such faith is a conquering faith. It is independent of circumstances, and such faith brings the answer.

Note also that:

V. UNOFFERED PRAYER IS THE GREATEST CAUSE OF UNANSWERED PRAYER

James tells us, "Ye have not because ye ask not." My friends, we do not receive more because we do not ask. Prayer is essentially asking and receiving; and, of course, we have not if we ask not. Only God knows the blessings we have missed, the power we have forfeited, the fruitfulness we have lost, all because we did not pray.

I bless God for the day when I read of Dr. A. C. Dixon's one hundred people converted and baptized because he prayed the prayer of faith. God used that story to stir me to pray and to learn a little at least of the prayer of faith. In turn, I taught this truth to my converts and church members; and hundreds, literally hundreds, have been saved through the prayer of faith.

For twenty years in the pastorate I held a Saturday night prayer meeting, urging my people to concentrate their prayer on one petition only—that a soul or souls would be saved on the morrow. The result was that during those twenty years many hundreds were saved because we thus prayed.

I tremble to think of what my ministry in those churches would have been without this particular kind of prayer. Ordinary prayer brings ordinary results. Prevailing prayer made so by an all-conquering faith brought unusual results.

Now will someone tell me these people would have been saved anyway? Will anyone deny that we could have seen more saved if we had prayed more? What a sublime privilege therefore is prayer; and what an awful responsibility when we ask not!

VI. THERE IS ONE PRAYER THAT IS ALWAYS ANSWERED

This particular prayer is not only always answered, but it is answered immediately, it is answered the very moment it is offered. It is the believing prayer of a penitent who asks God to save him and to save him now. That prayer God answers always and at once.

There has been no exception to that. There can be no exception since He is faithful that promised. If a man asks God to save his soul and believes that very moment that God does so, that man is saved the very moment he believes.

Have you, my friend reading this message, offered such a prayer to God? If not, why not? The Holy Spirit will impart faith to you to believe savingly on Christ if you will take the humble place of a lost sinner. And the moment you believe, you will be saved and know it. "For by grace are ye saved through faith." And bear in mind that this faith "is not of yourself, it is the gift of God." God always honors the faith He inspires. This is one prayer that is always answered.

JESSE HENDLEY
1907-

ABOUT THE MAN:

Jesse Hendley was for fourteen years pastor of a great Southern Baptist church with a membership of over 2300, in East Point, Georgia, a suburb of Atlanta. For more than fifty years he has been director of the Radio Evangelistic Hour gospel broadcast. In addition, he was one of the most successful evangelists in the country in the 1940's and '50's. His preaching was unique and very effective. This devoted, humble Christian was easy to admire, easy to love, and easy to work with.

In a write-up by a Georgia journalist who "covered" one of his meetings in the earlier years, Hendley is described as one who "reads his Scripture from the Greek New Testament but preaches like Billy Sunday."

He was educated at Georgia Tech, Columbia Seminary and Southern Baptist Theological Seminary, Louisville. He is also a remarkable Greek scholar.

But Dr. Hendley is pre-eminently a soul winner with a passion that knows no bounds. This passion characterizes his preaching, making it at once fiery, fervent and penetrating. Who can ever forget his tremendous and famous message on "Sin—Hell—Salvation"!

Yes, evangelism was and is his very life.

Once in Atlanta he began a meeting in a large tent. When it turned out to be too small, he moved to the Atlanta baseball stadium. Hendley rigged up a mike over home plate and delivered his sermons from there, speaking to as many as 7,500. Hundreds were saved during that revival in 1945. He held other large campaigns in his heyday, and had God's blessings on each, leading thousands to Christ. Dr. Hendley was one of the main speakers at Sword of the Lord Conferences at Winona Lake, Indiana, in those early years.

The sermon in this volume is taken from an old edition of THE SWORD OF THE LORD. It is so good, we felt we must include it.

XIV.

The Greatest Sin in America Today

JESSE M. HENDLEY

(Sermon preached at Sword of the Lord Conference on Revival and Soul Winning, Lake Louise, Toccoa, Georgia, 1952)

We are living in dark days *physically*. War clouds continually hang over our heads.

We are living in dark days *mentally*. Never have I seen as much trash, filth, dirt and sin being poured out in booklets, magazines, pamphlets, novels, TV and every way else under the sun that people are goggling up. Then we wonder why we are out of touch with God! People are reading and thinking all sorts of evil instead of the things of God's holy Word.

Then we are living in dark days *spiritually*. As I travel around I find there are very few who seem to know definitely that they are right with God. They are muddled in their thinking and in their spiritual experience. And to multitudes, God seems to be very, very distant. We are living in dark days spiritually.

We are living in dark days of terrible sin, with sin abounding as never before. The greatest and most alarming fact is that we Christians seem not to be concerned about it.

I read a magazine telling how many millions of homosexuals there are in the United States of America, the same sin that brought down the power of God on the wicked cities of Sodom and Gomorrah. Some years ago a reporter from Russia came and traveled all over America. He went back and wrote an editorial in a Russian newspaper. They may lie about a lot of things, but this man didn't lie when he said that the symbol of America is the picture of a nude woman. Everywhere you turn it is sin, sin, sin.

In the last few years a professor of Southern California made research on the decay in morals. He made the statement that more than three-fourths of the brides who go to the altars today are not virgins. He said that more than fifty percent of illegitimate children are born of high school girls [this was preached in 1952; these figures are much higher in this day]. Now that is tragic.

God's Word says that "as the days of Noe were, so shall also the coming of the Son of man be" (Matt. 24:37). We are living in days of terrible sin. And God's judgments are upon us.

If God Almighty doesn't punish America for her sins, He is going to have to raise from the dead the inhabitants of Sodom and Gomorrah and apologize to them for burning them to death back about four or five thousand years ago, because the same sins that brought down the wrath of God on Sodom and Gomorrah and burned them down to the bare earth are going on in America today. And they are increasing.

We read in the book of Jude those terrible words:

"Even as Sodom and Gomorrha, and the cities about them in like manner, giving themselves over to fornication, and going after strange flesh, are set forth for an example, suffering the vengeance of eternal fire." —vs. 7.

God's almighty justice DEMANDS, God's almighty holiness DEMANDS that He punish America because of her sins. Beloved, do not look for things to get better. Look for a blood bath such as we have never dreamed about, *unless we have a revival.*

Prayerlessness of Christians Is the Sin that Damns America

Now to my subject. The greatest sin in America is not homosexuality. The greatest sin in America is not the dirty, filthy magazines which people are reading. The greatest sin in America is not the adultery and the fornication and the other awful, terrible sins that are going on. *The greatest sin in America is the sin of prayerlessness committed by Christians.*

The world is going to Hell because of sin, and the only thing that can drive back the tidal wave of sin and save America is revival. A revival can only come through God's people. But a revival can't come through God's people until they get right with Him and back to holy prayer. Our whole condition is dependent upon holy prayer.

Now our Lord Jesus Christ says in Matthew 6:6,

"When thou prayest, enter into thy closet, and when thou hast shut thy door, pray to thy Father which is in secret; and thy Father which seeth in secret shall reward thee. . . ."

Our Lord says, "When thou prayest. . . ." He does not say you ought to pray. He takes it for granted that every child of God—for He is speaking to the disciples here—will pray. So the Lord says, "When thou prayest, enter into thy closet."

A man says, "I pray while riding down the highway." Man, you had better be looking at that road! A woman says, "I pray when I wash dishes and sweep floors." If that is all the praying we do, we will never see a revival. Jesus said, "Enter into thy closet, and when thou hast shut thy door, pray to thy Father which is in secret." Why? Because prayer demands great concentration. It is impossible for us to concentrate on God and those things that are so high and holy that wrap up the interest of our souls and of our loved ones and of our nation and of the world, unless we are alone, in solitude. We must take time to pray.

One time there was a man who in one little sentence did more for me than all the books I ever read and all the sermons I have ever heard on prayer. He put in one of his sermons on prayer this little line, "How much do YOU pray?" He was pointing his finger at me—How much do YOU pray?

I decided to check me out. I got a clock, went down on my knees and went through my usual prayer. Believe me, I got the shock of my life when I rose up after the little praying that I was doing, the little time I was staying on my knees. You say, "Preacher, that's kind of a mechanical thing." Maybe it is, but it certainly shocked me. It awakened my mind and heart and life to find out actually how little time I was spending before God.

And we wonder why souls are lost! We wonder why we don't have power to win souls! We wonder why sin conquers us! We wonder why the Devil defeats us! We wonder why the inrush of sin and iniquity everywhere! My friends, we are not paying the price of prayer. How much do **YOU** pray?

The secret of power is coming from that prayer room, and from nowhere else. You and I can go down to the altar, get down on our knees and make dedications all we please, but if we do not go back yonder to that prayer room and day after day take time with God, it is not going to abide; we are going to lose our power and blessing.

At Winona Lake, Indiana, in one of Dr. Rice's great conferences, a group of us preachers and evangelists were together talking on the platform. The subject was prayer. Dr. Oswald Smith was there. One of the men said, "Dr. Smith, tell us something of the secret of your power and of your blessing." I will never forget how he answered:

> Gentlemen, I didn't get it all when I went to the altar for the first time. I didn't get it all by continually coming to the altar and making rededication. I found that I had to daily spend time alone with God.

Then he made this amazing statement:

> Every day except one time in forty years, right after breakfast I have gone alone and spent at least one hour on my knees before my God in prayer. If there is any secret of power in my life, it is that I have taken time with God in prayer.

Friends, we will never change ourselves, and God knows we need to be changed; we will never change our homes, and God knows our homes need to be changed; we will never change our churches, and God knows our churches need revival; we will never change our communities, and God knows our communities need to be turned upside down; we will never change this world until we Christians pay the price of holy prayer before God.

The greatest sin today is committed by believing Christians who have been born of the Spirit of God, but are not giving themselves to prayer. And if you are among those rare Christians who are paying the price, thank your God and tighten up; because the only hope of all of us is a revival. It is going to come no other way.

Abraham's Prayers Saved Lot From Destruction in Sodom

Now the Lord reveals in His Word some examples of prayer that bring to us great conviction. The greatest challenge I have ever had on prayer was the challenge of these men of the Bible. We are tempted to say, "Well, these men are demigods. They were half-gods. They weren't normal. They are not even as you and I with our temptations and our trials."

But God's Word reminds us that they were men subject to like passions even as we, but the difference is, they rose above the things of time and communed with God and brought to pass miracles.

I like to think of Abraham as a man of intercession, one so right with God that he could pray for somebody else. Some people have to spend so much time praying for themselves that there is no time to pray for others. We have to stay prayed up if we are going to pray for other people. Here's a man walking with God.

You remember how, in his great prayer, Abraham prayed unto the Lord for Sodom and Gomorrah, and how God saved Lot out of the midst of the judgment because of his prayers. We read these words:

"And Abraham drew near, and said, Wilt thou also destroy the righteous with the wicked? Peradventure there be fifty righteous within the city: wilt thou also destroy and not spare the place for the fifty righteous that are therein? That be far from thee to do after this manner, to slay the righteous with the wicked: and that the righteous should be as the wicked, that be far from thee: Shall not the Judge of all the earth do right? And the Lord said, If I find in Sodom fifty righteous within the city, then I will spare all the place for their sakes.

"And Abraham answered and said, Behold now, I have taken upon me to speak unto the Lord, which am but dust and ashes: Peradventure there shall lack five of the fifty righteous: wilt thou destroy all the city for lack of five? And he said, If I find there forty and five, I will not destroy it.

"And he spake unto him yet again, and said, Peradventure there shall be forty found there. And he said, I will not do it for forty's sake.

"And he said unto him, Oh let not the Lord be angry, and I will speak: Peradventure there shall thirty be found there. And he said, I will not do it, if I find thirty there.

"And he said, Behold now, I have taken upon me to speak unto the Lord; Peradventure there shall be twenty found there. And he said, I will not destroy it for twenty's sake.

"And he said, Oh let not the Lord be angry, and I will speak yet but this once: Peradventure ten shall be found there. And he said, I will not destroy it for ten's sake."—Gen. 18:23-32.

Then comes one of the greatest statements I have read in the holy Word of God:

"And the Lord went his way, as soon as he had left communing with Abraham: and Abraham returned unto his place."—Vs. 33.

There was a PLACE God came down to; Abraham came also to that PLACE; and God and Abraham talked over things of vital interest to themselves and to the loved ones of Abraham, and for which he was pleading.

I tell you, friends, the hope of America is not in jet planes, not in bombs, not in a fighting army or in any political things—but our only hope is a few Abrahams who are close enough to God to intercede.

Then you remember that God came down with the angels, and they finally had to drag Lot—yes, literally drag him—out of the city, saying to him about his loved ones, "Bring them out of this place. for the Lord hath sent us to destroy it" (Gen. 19:13). Then God said to him, "Haste thee, escape thither; for I cannot do any thing till thou be come thither" (vs. 22).

When I was first converted, I read that passage on a streetcar one morning, and it was all I could do to keep from shouting! I wrote in the margin of my Bible: "The prayers of godly Abraham tied the judgment hands of God." Even God Himself could not bring down fire upon the wicked cities of Sodom and Gomorrah until Abraham's prayer was answered and Lot was safe outside.

There may be some of us sitting here tonight who cannot talk any more to husbands, wives, children, loved ones, friends. We have talked until we can talk no more. They get mad with us, and it creates a hell. But, praise God, they cannot get beyond our prayers! They did not get beyond the prayers of Abraham. In other words, God said to Lot, "Get out of here! Because of the prayers of my friend Abraham, we can't bring down the fire from Heaven until you get out."

Then we read these great words,

"Abraham got up early in the morning to the place where he stood before the Lord: And he looked toward Sodom and Gomorrah, and toward all the land of the plain, and beheld, and, lo, the smoke of the country went up as the smoke of a furnace."—Vss. 27, 28.

And again, listen to these words:

"And it came to pass, when God destroyed the cities of the plain, that God remembered Abraham, and sent Lot out of the midst of the overthrow...."—Vs. 29.

It was not Lot who was saving himself; it was not Lot's prayers or Lot's holiness—he was in a backslidden, miserable condition. But it was the prayers of old, godly Abraham, old, separated Abraham that turned the tide and saved Lot in that tremendous hour.

Do not tell me that the God of Abraham is dead. And if God did it for Abraham, He has to do it for us. He is no respecter of persons. He has promised, and He will keep His word.

Now Abraham was a man of prayer. He was even as we. But he paid the price. He lived a holy life. And that is an expression that has gone out of our vocabulary. Our praying does not amount to anything if we are not living holy lives. God says, "Don't talk to Me with sin in your life. Get up off your knees and go on away."

But beloved, when our hearts are clean and right with God, and we come and claim these blessed promises, God has to do something or He is not God. The God of Heaven cannot lie.

The Prayers of Moses Saved Israel
From Destruction

There has never been a man like Moses. Perhaps he was the greatest man of all time. Seven hundred or more times his name is mentioned in the Bible. I do not know of anyone whose prayer life has matched his. On two different occasions he prayed and fasted forty days and nights!

What a man of God! What a man of prayer! No wonder he brought miracles to pass. Living close to God, He did marvelous things for and through him. We see so very little in our lives that is divine, that is miraculous, that is the Word of God.

Brother, when we have a revival, we will see miracles. When the Holy Ghost comes, we will see miracles take place. We will know that God is here when a great spiritual revival comes. We are getting some souls saved. Thank God for that! But the churches are not revived like they ought to be. God's people are jealous one of another. We are fighting one another, talking about one another. All kinds of sins are in the way. All that mess will go when we have a real spiritual awakening.

Moses is up yonder receiving the Ten Commandments on the tables of stone. Down below Israel begins making that golden calf and bowing down and worshiping it. Suddenly God's demeanor changes, and something happened. The Lord said unto Moses,

"Go, get thee down; for thy people, which thou broughtest out of the land of Egypt, have corrupted themselves: They have turned aside quickly out of the way which I commanded them: they have made them a molten calf, and have worshipped it, and have sacrificed thereunto, and said, These be thy gods, O Israel, which have brought thee up out of the land of Egypt.

"And the Lord said unto Moses:

"I have seen this people, and, behold, it is a stiffnecked people: Now therefore let me alone, that my wrath may wax hot against them, and that I may consume them: and I will make of thee a great nation."— Exod. 32:7-10.

What a man who can make the eternal God say, "Let me alone"! What a man! "Let me alone, Moses." He is talking to a human being, not to an archangel. This is just a little man, subject to like passions as we are; a man who came out of Egypt with all of its money and glory and splendor; a man who made such a surrender as I have never known in history. Here is one who had the whole of the greatest empire of his day at his feet but turned his back on it and went out and threw in his lot with a bunch of slaves. It would be comparable to the President of the United States of America leaving the White House and going down on a little South Georgia farm to take care of a few chickens. What a sacrifice! What a surrender according to the flesh! But Moses turned his back on it all because he looked at the payday, the day when God is going to pay off holy living. He knew it is the spiritual life that is going to pay off. He knew that it is what is done for God that is going to pay off. It is the time we pray and the holy living we do and the honest-to-goodness service we turn in. It is not jealousy one of another, not desire for position, not desire for the First Baptist or the First Methodist or First Presbyterian Church, and all that sort of tommyrot, but a desire to do a job for Jesus. That is the thing that will pay off. Knowing this, Moses went all out for God.

I have a little volume in my study which I keep in front of me because of the words of the title: "All Out for God." It is a challenge to my own heart. "All Out for God." Nothing reserved. Everything—from the top of my head to the bottom of my feet—all out for God. Nothing reserved—putting God first. If God does not bless the man who puts Him first, He is not God. He will, He must bless the fully surrendered life.

Here is one so surrendered that God admires him. Hear me, friends.

God respects the one who will turn his back on the world and go all out for Him, and spend time in prayer and give himself for others, as this meek, holy, godly Moses did.

Now Moses was not always that way. He had a battle to get like that. But he paid the price, and he fought his way through—and won! I know how he won. No man ever whips himself except by prayer. There is no other way you can put your foot on self, crush self, like the writhing serpent it is, down to the earth so that you can rise with God, except through holy prayer. Moses was a man of prayer.

Then Moses began to plead with God:

"Wherefore should the Egyptians speak, and say, For mischief did he bring them out, to slay them in the mountains, and to consume them from the face of the earth? Turn from thy fierce wrath, and repent of this evil against thy people."—Exod. 32:12.

I read repeatedly in this Book where God calls on men to repent, but here a man calls on God to repent. And the wonderful thing about it is, God repented of the destruction which He thought to do!

"And the Lord repented of the evil which he thought to do unto his people."—Vs. 14.

And He did it not! He was going to blot out the nation, but one man stood in the gap.

This Book does not say that it is going to take much people who are all out for God to bring revival and to bring down the blessings of God and save our nation and multitudes of souls and bring real revival; but God does say it is going to take a few who mean business. And in this particular case, it is one man, Moses.

Daniel Prayed Through for Israel in Captivity

Daniel was a man of prayer. We read of Daniel that he said, "I was mourning three full weeks"—twenty-one days. I like to put the title "praying through" over chapter 10 of the book of Daniel. Daniel prayed through.

Many, many times when we ask God for something, we may be in earnest at the moment, but we do not stay with it. God knows we don't mean business. If we did, we would pray through; we would come back time and again. Daniel determined to stay on his knees until the answer came.

Finally God sent an angel from Heaven to tell Daniel, "O man greatly beloved. . . the first day you got on your knees and started praying,
your prayer was heard in Heaven. But there was some trouble on the
line, and I had to do battle with the principalities and the powers in
the heavenlies."

We forget there is a Devil and demons to fight. We forget that every
time we win a soul to Christ, we have to tear a soul out of the hands
of Hell and the Devil. That is why soul winning is the hardest business
in this world. It has never been and never will be easy. But when we
pay the price, we will see souls snatched out of the hands of the Devil.
This is going to take holy living, holy witnessing, holy prayer—Christians
meaning business for God. And if we do not mean business, we might
as well quit, because God is not playing; He is in dead earnest. And
He will meet any man or woman, anywhere, any time, who will pay
the price.

The trouble with us is, we have not paid the price. God is saying,
"Prove Me now, right this minute. If you obey My voice and do what
I tell you to do—live a holy life, and pray—I will open the windows
of Heaven and pour out the blessings that you want."

Ezra and Nehemiah Saved the Remnant of Israel
and by Prayer Restored the Nation

Ezra was a priest, and in chapter 9 of the book that bears his name
we read that when he learns of Israel's great sin of intermarriage with
the heathen, he went to his knees and cried and prayed to God in one
of the holiest prayers that has ever been uttered. Read this prayer and
see that as this godly man poured out his heart for poor, suffering,
backslidden Israel, the people gathered about weeping very sore, and
a great revival broke out, until wives separated from heathen husbands
and husbands separated from heathen wives. When they got cleaned
up, God again visited His people!

I like to put over that chapter, "A man who saved his nation from
destruction." This is the second time the nation Israel has been saved
from extinction by the godly, holy life and praying of a man who walks
with God, just a human being even as you and I, but one who paid
the price in holy living and in holy praying. He won the victory for
the Lord.

You say, "These men you're talking about are preachers." But consider: Nehemiah was a layman, a cupbearer to Artaxerxes, the great king of Persia, a king who held Nehemiah's life in his hands. Remember how there came to him word that Israel was in a desperate condition. The walls were broken down, the gates burned with fire, and the heathen and the enemy were ravaging the people of God. Nehemiah began to pray and fast. It meant nothing to him personally, but he loved them.

Beloved, God cannot use us unless we love people. We see the unselfishness of Nehemiah. He prayed from December to April. You pray from December to April without proper food and drink and see if something doesn't happen to your body. When he goes into the presence of the king and the king sees his terrible condition, he says, "You're a sick man. And it isn't physical; it's heartsickness. Now tell me what is wrong with you." This scared Nehemiah, so he asked the God of Heaven what he should tell him. God said, "Tell that king just why you are fasting and praying. I'm going to take care of him and help you out." So when he told the king, the king said, "You can go back and rebuild those walls and gates. I'll give you supplies, protection and everything else needed."

Nehemiah went back and rebuilt the walls and the gates and did a tremendous job for God—a layman, who knew what it was to pray, a godly layman who, through prayer, moved a king to help the people of God. He fasted and prayed from December to April—and got an answer from God.

The Prayer Life of Jesus, Our Example

Do you want a revival in your church, preacher? Are you willing to pay a price? Then consider the life of Jesus. All of these are examples, but the great Example is the Saviour.

While studying the chronological life of Christ, I found we had only about sixty-two days in His life. And it is amazing how much prayer is in it. We read of His praying all night. We read that many times He arose a great while before day and went out into a desert place and there prayed.

If the Saviour had to pray and stay in communion with God, think you that you and I can get by without prayer and the walk with God?

Is this the reason God is distant? Is this the reason we have little power? The Devil is not afraid of prayerless sermons, or prayerless Bible teaching, or prayerless church services. But when a church gets down on its knees and means business for God, look out! The Devil is going to stir up troubles sure as we are here, because he knows something is going to happen. Mean business for God.

Jesus was praying at His baptism by John when the heavens were opened and the Holy Ghost came upon Him, and the Father's voice proclaimed, "This is my beloved Son, in whom I am well pleased."

That is the pattern of spiritual blessing. Do we have opened heavens? Do we know the Spirit's power? Do we hear Him say, "You are my beloved son"? No? Is it because we are not living with Him in prayer? The heavens do not open until men and women pray.

When Christ wanted to choose twelve apostles, He spent a whole night in prayer. And when the day came, the record says He called the disciples and picked out twelve men whom He named apostles to be with Him.

In the Garden of Gethsemane, when He was taking the weight of the world upon Himself, the Word of God said so crushing was the load that His sweatdrops became as it were great drops of blood, dropping to the earth.

Everywhere you turn, people are slipping into Hell without God and without hope. I very much question tonight that in my home city of Atlanta one-fourth the population is saved. Fifty-two percent never darken anybody's church door. Think of its twelve million in Greater New York and only a tiny fraction making any profession at all. We are living in a world that is going to Hell; and the real Christians are very, very few. BUT BROTHER, THOSE FEW ARE THE ONLY HOPE OF THIS WORLD.

On the cross Christ prayed, "Father, forgive them; for they know not what they do." And what has He been doing these two thousand years in Glory? Praying. "He ever liveth to make intercession for us."

Now if prayer was so vital to Jesus Christ, our great Example, can you and I get by with anything less than much prayer?

Souls Saved in Answer to Continued Prayer

Now you say, "Preacher, suppose I do pay the price. What will be the reward?"

The first reward of real holy praying is accomplishment of the greatest business in the world—the winning of souls to Jesus Christ. I never knew one soul winner who was not a man or a woman of prayer.

I was called up into the Tennessee mountains some years ago for a tent revival. Those mountaineers were all round about, and we were having a great victory. God was pouring out His Spirit.

One night at the close of the service, I noticed a little mountain woman sitting with her husband. A little babe was cradled in her left arm. I could tell by their dress that they were people of very humble circumstances. I took one look, and I thought, *I believe she is just holding him here, hoping I will come over and talk to him. He must be lost.*

So I slipped over and asked, "Fellow, are you saved?"

Lifting up his head he said, "No, sir."

"Well, let's go back to the prayer tent. Now is the time to settle it. You want to be saved, don't you?"

She looked up at him; he looked down at her. You could tell they really loved each other. She said with tears rolling down her cheeks, "Honey, won't you go?"

He beat it with me right back to the prayer tent. When one is convicted of sin, it is like ripe apples dropping off in a bucket. Down on our knees we went. That fellow wept as he came to the Lord. I took my Bible and showed him the promises of God and when I saw him safely on the old Rock, then I said, "Are you willing to go out there and tell your wife you're saved?"

"I sure am, Preacher," he replied.

I saw one of those tender sights that angels love to see. She was still sitting with that little babe cradled in her left arm. As he walked up to her and said, "Honey, I'm saved," she reached up that one good arm, put it on his head, pulled it down to her breast, and began to pat the back of his head, crying, "Honey, I've prayed such a long time for this!"

I walked out of that place wiping the tears out of my eyes, and I said, "Lord, I believe You sent me up here into these Tennessee mountains just to answer the prayers of a little mountain woman who prayed, 'God, I want my husband saved!' "

Oh, the greatest business in the world will take place in our lives when we pray.

As I came into this building tonight a young man walked up to me and said, "Preacher, I'm from Fort Lauderdale. I was saved in your meeting there." He said, "Five of us have driven up here." Oh, this wonderful business of soul winning!

Listen to me, beloved! Is there anything on earth like soul winning?

Tell me, is there? Is there anything that this world down here has ever tasted that can compare with the joy that comes to us when we are winning souls to Jesus Christ?

The second thing: when we pray we will have the consciousness of His divine presence. Now at the beginning I said that there is a thing that alarms me. A lot of people up and down the land have accepted Christ; they have made profession, and I believe that they were born again. But somehow God is away off! Now why? Invariably you will find these people have no consistent prayer life, though they know down in their souls that they are God's children and God is their Father.

I love that song:

Shut in with God in the secret place,
There in the Spirit beholding His face,
Gaining new power to run in the race.
I love to be shut in with God.

What a song! I have been in the presence of people in whose presence I felt the presence of God. And invariably they were men and women who lived in great communion with God. There is no other way to have the sense of His presence.

Then the final thing. If we pray, we will have the guarantee of our salvation. Now if you would ask me tonight of the dearest thing I have, I could not say it was my precious wife, or my girl or my boy, whom I love better than life itself. I could not say it is this, that or the other. I would have to say tonight that my dearest, most priceless treasure is the salvation of my soul. Let the godless crowd go on if they want to—but here is a man who is glad he is saved.

Every time I read in this Book about Hell, every time I read in this Book about judgment, every time I read in this Book about sin and its condemnation, every time I read about the awful, terrible threatenings of the doom of a lost sinner, I say, *Thank You, Lord, for saving my soul.* I am glad I am saved.

In Rome, Georgia, a medical doctor helped me while I was there in a campaign. We were pouring out the truth about the responsibility of Christians for prayer and soul winning, being filled with the Spirit, bringing the lost in, etc.

One day I said to him when I went in, "Doc, how are you feeling?"

He said, "I don't feel so well!"

"What's the matter?"

"Well, you have been talking to us every night from the Book about our responsibility to bring others to Jesus, haven't you?"

"Yes."

"There's an old man, a wealthy man, dying out here on his estate. I have treated that man's body for fifteen years, but I'm ashamed to say that I never asked him about his soul. The pressure was on me so terribly that I got in my car yesterday and drove out to his home. Sitting by his bedside, I said, 'Brother, I treated your body fifteen years, but I've never asked you, Is it well with your soul?' The man started crying and, shaking his head, said, 'No, Doctor, it isn't well with my soul.'" The doctor said, "I don't want to unduly disturb you, but let me ask you a second question: Will you right now accept Jesus as your Saviour and Lord? The man became excited and he said, 'Doctor, I've waited too late! Doctor, I've waited too late! I've waited too late!' Terror began to grip him. He became excited, and his loved ones came rushing in. They had to give him sedatives to calm him. With a heavy heart, I got into my car and drove back to the city."

That man lay there and died, admittedly, on his own testimony, without God and without hope, and went to Hell a lost soul. He admitted that in his seventy-two years he had never reached out and touched God in holy prayer, and now he is lost and lost forever!

Friend, if you have never reached out and touched God in holy prayer, or if you have somehow gotten out of touch with Him, won't you go alone, right now, and call upon Him, in holy prayer?

God bless you!

R. A. TORREY
1856-1928

ABOUT THE MAN:

Torrey grew up in a wealthy home, attended Yale University and Divinity School, and studied abroad. During his early student days at Yale, young Torrey became an agnostic and a heavy drinker. But even during the days of his "wild life," he was strangely aware of a conviction that someday he was to preach the Gospel. At the end of his senior year in college, he was saved.

While at Yale Divinity School, he came under the influence of D. L. Moody. Little did Moody know the mighty forces he was setting in motion in stirring young R. A. Torrey to service!

After Moody died, Torrey took on the world-girdling revival campaigns in Australia, New Zealand, England and America.

Like many another giant for God, Torrey shone best, furthest and brightest as a personal soul winner. This one man led 100,000 to Christ in a revival that circled the globe!

Dr. Torrey's education was obtained in the best schools and universities of higher learning. Fearless, quick, imaginative and scholarly, he was a tough opponent to meet in debate. He was recognized as a great scholar, yet his ministry was marked by simplicity.

It was because of his outstanding scholastic ability and evangelistic fervor that Moody handpicked Torrey to become superintendent of his infant Moody Bible Institute. In 1912, Torrey became dean of BIOLA, where he served until 1924, pastoring the Church of the Open Door in Los Angeles from 1915-1924.

Torrey's books have probably reached more people indirectly and helped more people to understand the Bible and to have power to win souls, than the writings of any other man since the Apostle Paul, with the possible exceptions of Spurgeon and Rice. Torrey was a great Bible teacher, but most of all he was filled with the Holy Spirit.

He greatly influenced the life of Dr. John R. Rice.

XV.

The Importance of Prayer

R. A. TORREY

(The American Standard Version of 1901 is referred to as the Revised Version [R.V.] which Dr. Torrey uses throughout this message.)

In Ephesians 6:18 we read words which put the tremendous importance of prayer with startling and overwhelming force:

"Praying always with all prayer and supplication in the Spirit, and watching thereunto with all perseverance and supplication for all saints."

When we stop to weigh the meaning of these words, then note the connection in which they are found, the intelligent child of God is driven to say, "I must pray, pray, pray. I must put all my energy, all my heart into prayer. Whatever else I do, I must pray."

The Revised Version is, if possible, stronger than the Authorized:

"With all prayer and supplication praying at all seasons in the spirit, and watching thereunto in all perseverance and supplication for all the saints."

Note the *all*s: "with *all* prayer," "at *all* seasons," "in *all* perseverance," "for *all* the saints." Note the piling up of strong words, "prayer," "supplication," "perseverance." Note once more the strong expression, "watching thereunto," more literally, "being sleepless thereunto." Paul realized the natural slothfulness of man, especially his natural slothfulness in prayer.

How seldom we pray things through! How often the church and the individual get right up to the verge of a great blessing in prayer and just then let go, get drowsy, and quit. I wish that these words, "being sleepless unto prayer," might burn into our hearts. I wish the whole verse might burn into our hearts.

But why is this constant, persistent, sleepless, overcoming prayer so needful?

1. Because there is a Devil.

He is cunning, he is mighty, he never rests, he is ever plotting the downfall of the child of God; and if we relax in prayer, the Devil will succeed in ensnaring us.

This is the thought of the context. Verse 12 reads:

"For our wrestling is not against flesh and blood, but against the principalities, against the powers, against the world rulers of this darkness, against the spiritual hosts of wickedness in the heavenly places."

Then comes verse 13:

"Wherefore take up the whole armor of God, that ye may be able to withstand in the evil day, and, having done all, to stand."

Next follows a description of the different parts of the Christian's armor which we are to put on if we are to stand against the Devil and his mighty wiles. Then Paul brings all to a climax in verse 18, telling us that to all else we must add prayer—constant, persistent, untiring, sleepless prayer in the Holy Spirit, or all else will go for nothing.

2. Prayer is God's appointed way for obtaining things, and the great secret of all lack in our experience, in our life, and in our work is neglect of prayer.

James brings this out very forcibly in chapter 4 and verse 2 of his epistle: "Ye have not because ye ask not." These words contain the secret of the poverty and powerlessness of the average Christian—neglect of prayer.

Many a Christian is asking, "Why is it I make so little progress in my Christian life?" "Neglect of prayer," God answers. "You have not because you ask not."

Many a minister is asking, "Why is it I see so little fruit from my labors?" Again God answers, "Neglect of prayer. You have not because you ask not."

Many a Sunday school teacher is asking, "Why is it that I see so few converted in my Sunday school class?" Still God answers, "Neglect of prayer. You have not because you ask not."

Both ministers and churches are asking, "Why is it that the church of Christ makes so little headway against unbelief and error and sin and worldliness?" Once more we hear God answering, "Neglect of prayer. You have not because you ask not."

3. Those whom God set forth as a pattern of what He expected Christians to be — the apostles — regarded prayer as their most important business.

When the multiplying responsibilities of the early church crowded in upon them, they

". . . called the multitude of the disciples unto them, and said, It is not reason that we should leave the word of God, and serve tables. Wherefore, brethren, look ye out among you seven men of honest report, full of the Holy Ghost and wisdom, whom we may appoint over this business. But we will give ourselves continually to prayer and to the ministry of the word."

It is evident from what Paul wrote to the churches and to individuals about praying for them that much of his time, strength and thought was given to prayer (Rom. 1:9; Eph. 1:15,16; Col. 1:9; I Thess. 3:10; II Tim. 1:3).

All the mighty men of God outside the Bible have been men of prayer. They have differed from one another in many things, but in this they have been alike.

4. Prayer occupied a very prominent place and played a very important part in the earthly life of our Lord.

Turn, for example, to Mark 1:35.

"And in the morning, rising up a great while before day, he went out, and departed into a solitary place, and there prayed."

The preceding day had been a very busy and exciting one, but Jesus shortened the hours of needed sleep that He might arise early and give Himself to more sorely needed prayer.

Turn again to Luke 6:12, where we read,

"And it came to pass in those days that he went out into a mountain to pray, and continued all night in prayer to God."

Our Saviour found it necessary on occasion to take a whole night for prayer.

The words "pray" and "prayer" are used at least twenty-five times in connection with our Lord in the brief record of His life in the four

Gospels, and His praying is mentioned in places where the words are not used. Evidently prayer took much of the time and strength of Jesus. A man or woman who does not spend much time in prayer cannot properly be called a follower of Jesus Christ.

5. Praying is the most important part of the present ministry of our risen Lord. This reason for constant, persistent, sleepless, overcoming prayer seems, if possible, even more forcible.

Christ's ministry did not close with His death. His atoning work was finished then, but when He rose and ascended to the right hand of the Father, He entered upon other work for us just as important in its place as His atoning work. It cannot be divorced from His atoning work; it rests upon that as its basis, but it is necessary to our complete salvation.

What that great present work is, by which He carries our salvation on to completeness, we read in Hebrews 7:25:

"Wherefore he is able also to save them to the uttermost that come unto God by him, seeing he ever liveth to make intercession for them."

This verse tells us that Jesus is able to save us unto the uttermost, not merely *from* the uttermost, but *unto* the uttermost, unto entire completeness, absolute perfection, because He not merely died, but because He also "ever liveth."

The verse also tells us for what purpose He now lives, *"to make intercession* for us," to pray. Praying is the principal thing He is doing in these days. It is by His prayers that He is saving us.

The same thought is found in Paul's remarkable triumphant challenge in Romans 8:34:

"Who is he that shall condemn? It is Christ Jesus that died, yea rather, that was raised from the dead, who is at the right hand of God, who also maketh intercession for us."

If we then are to have fellowship with Jesus Christ in His present work, we must spend much time in prayer; we must give ourselves to earnest, constant, persistent, sleepless, overcoming prayer.

I know of nothing that has so impressed me with a sense of the importance of praying at all seasons, being much and constantly in prayer, as the thought that that is the principal occupation at present of my risen Lord. I want to have fellowship with Him, and to that end I have asked the Father whatever else He may make me, to make me an intercessor, to make me one who knows how to pray and who spends much time in prayer.

This ministry of intercession is a glorious and a mighty ministry, and we can all have part in it. The man or woman shut away from the public meeting by sickness can have part in it. The busy mother; the woman who has to take in washing for a living can have part—she can mingle prayers, for the saints and for her pastor and for the unsaved and for foreign missionaries, with the soap and water as she bends over the washtub and not do the washing any more poorly on that account. The hard-driven man of business can have part in it, praying as he hurries from duty to duty.

But of course we must, if we would maintain this spirit of constant prayer, take time—and take plenty of it—when we shall shut ourselves up in the secret place alone with God for nothing but prayer.

6. Prayer is the means that God has appointed for our receiving mercy and obtaining grace to help in time of need.

Hebrews 4:16 is one of the simplest and sweetest verses in the Bible,

"Let us therefore come boldly unto the throne of grace, that we may obtain mercy, and find grace to help in time of need."

These words make it very plain that God has appointed a way by which we shall seek and obtain mercy and grace. That way is prayer, bold, confident, outspoken approach to the throne of grace, the most holy place of God's presence, where our sympathizing High Priest has entered in our behalf (vss. 14,15).

Mercy is what we need, grace is what we must have, or all our life and effort will end in complete failure. Prayer is the way to get them. There is infinite grace at our disposal, and we make it ours experimentally by prayer.

Oh, if we only realized the fullness of God's grace that is ours for the asking, its height and depth and length and breadth, I am sure that we would spend more time in prayer. The measure of our appropriation of grace is determined by the measure of our prayers.

Who does not feel a need for more grace? Then ask for it. Be constant and persistent in your asking. Be importunate and untiring in your asking. God delights to have us "shameless" beggars in this direction, for it shows our faith in Him. He is mightily pleased with faith. Because of our "shamelessness," He will rise and give us as much as we need

(Luke 11:8). What little streams of mercy and grace most of us know, when we might know rivers overflowing their banks!

7. Prayer in the name of Jesus Christ is the way Jesus Christ Himself has appointed for His disciples to obtain fullness of joy.

He states this simply and beautifully in John 16:24:

"Hitherto have ye asked nothing in my name; ask, and ye shall receive, that your joy may be fulfilled."

"Made full" is the way the American Revised Version reads. Who is there that does not wish his joy filled full? Well, the way to have it filled full is by praying in the name of Jesus.

We all know people whose joy is filled full; indeed, it is just running over, shining from their eyes, bubbling out of their very lips, and running off their fingertips when they shake hands with you. Coming in contact with them is like coming in contact with an electrical machine charged with gladness. Now people of that sort spend much time in prayer.

Why is it that prayer in the name of Christ brings such fullness of joy? In part, because we get what we ask. But that is not the only reason, nor the greatest. It makes God real. When we ask something definite of God and He gives it, how real He becomes! He is right there! It is blessed to have a God who is real, and not merely an idea.

I remember how once I was taken suddenly and seriously sick all alone in my study. I dropped upon my knees and cried to God for help. Instantly all pain left me—I was perfectly well. It seemed as if God stood right there and had put out His hand and touched me. The joy of the healing was not so great as the joy of meeting God.

There is no greater joy on earth or in Heaven than communion with God, and prayer in the name of Jesus brings us into communion with Him. The psalmist was surely not speaking only of future blessedness but also of present blessedness when he said, "In thy presence is fullness of joy" (Ps. 16:11). Oh, the unutterable joy of those moments when in our prayers we really press into the presence of God!

Does someone say, "I have never known any such joy as that in prayer"? Do you take enough leisure for prayer to actually get into God's presence? Do you really give yourself up to prayer in the time which you do take?

8. Prayer, in every care and anxiety and need of life, with thanksgiving, is the means that God has appointed for our

obtaining freedom from all anxiety, and the peace of God which passeth all understanding.

Paul says:

"Be careful for nothing, but in every thing by prayer and supplication with thanksgiving let your requests be made known unto God, and the peace of God which passeth all understanding, shall keep your hearts and minds through Christ Jesus."—Phil. 4:6,7.

To many this seems, at first glance, the picture of a beautiful life but beyond the reach of ordinary mortals. Not so at all. The verse tells us how the life is attainable by every child of God.

"Be careful for nothing," or as the Revised Version reads, "In nothing be anxious." The remainder of the verse tells us how, and it is very simple: "But in every thing by prayer and supplication with thanksgiving let your requests be made known unto God."

What could be plainer or more simple than that? Just keep in constant touch with God, and when any trouble or vexation, great or small, comes up, speak to Him about it, never forgetting to return thanks for what He has already done. What will the result be? The peace of God which passeth all understanding shall guard your hearts and your thoughts in Christ Jesus.

That is glorious, and as simple as it is glorious! Thank God, many are trying it. Don't you know anyone who is always serene? Perhaps he is a very stormy man by his natural makeup; but troubles, conflicts, reverses and bereavements may sweep around him; yet the peace of God which passes all understanding guards his heart and thoughts in Christ Jesus.

We all know such persons. How do they manage it? Just by prayer, that is all. Those who know the deep peace of God, the unfathomable peace that passes all understanding, are always men and women of much prayer.

Some of us let the hurry of our lives crowd prayer out, and what a waste of time and energy and nerve force there is by the constant worry! One night of prayer will save us from many nights of insomnia. Time spent in prayer is not wasted, but time invested at big interest.

9. Prayer is the method that God Himself has appointed for our obtaining the Holy Spirit.

Upon this point the Bible is very plain. Jesus says:

*"If ye then, being evil, know how to give good gifts unto your children,
how much more shall your heavenly Father give the Holy Spirit to them
that ask him?"*—Luke 11:13.

Men are telling us in these days, very good men too, "You must not
pray for the Holy Spirit." But what are they going to do with the plain
statement of Jesus Christ, "How much more will your heavenly Father
give the Holy Spirit *to them that ask him?"*

Some years ago when an address on the baptism with the Holy Spirit
was announced, a brother came to me before the address and said with
much feeling, "Be sure and tell them not to pray for the Holy Spirit."

"I will surely not tell them that, for Jesus says, 'How much more shall
your heavenly Father give the Holy Spirit to them that ask him?' "

"Oh, yes," he replied, "but that was before Pentecost."

"How about Acts 4:31? Was that before Pentecost, or after?" I asked.

"After, of course."

I said, "Read it. 'And when *they had prayed*, the place was shaken
where they were assembled together; and they were all *filled with the
Holy Ghost*, and they spake the word of God with boldness.' "

Then I asked, "How about Acts 8:15? Was that before Pentecost or
after?"

"After," he replied.

"Please read. 'Who, when they were come down, *prayed* for them,
that they might receive the Holy Ghost.' "

He made no answer. What could he answer? It is plain as day in
the Word of God that before Pentecost and after, the first baptism and
the subsequent fillings with the Holy Spirit were received in answer to
definite prayer. Experience also teaches this.

Doubtless many have received the Holy Spirit the moment of their
surrender to God before there was time to pray; but how many there
are who know that their first definite baptism with the Holy Spirit came
while they were on their knees or faces before God, alone or in company with others, and who again and again since that have been filled
with the Holy Spirit in the place of prayer!

I know this as definitely as I know that my thirst has been quenched
while I was drinking water.

Early one morning in the Chicago Avenue Church prayer room where
several hundred people had been assembled a number of hours in
prayer, the Holy Spirit fell so manifestly, and the whole place was so

filled with His presence that no one could speak or pray: only sobs of joy filled the place. Men went out of that room to different parts of the country, taking trains that very morning. Reports soon came back of the outpouring of God's Holy Spirit in answer to prayer. Others went out into the city with the blessing of God upon them. This is only one instance among many that might be cited from personal experience.

If we would only spend more time in prayer, there would be more fullness of the Spirit's power in our work. Many and many a man who once worked unmistakably in the power of the Holy Spirit is now filling the air with empty shoutings, and beating it with his meaningless gesticulations, because he has let prayer be crowded out. We must spend much time on our knees before God, if we are to continue in the power of the Holy Spirit.

10. Prayer is the means that Christ has appointed whereby our hearts shall not become overcharged with surfeiting and drunkenness and cares of this life, and so the day of Christ's return come upon us suddenly as a snare.

One of the most interesting and solemn passages upon prayer in the Bible is along this line.

"Take heed to yourselves, lest at any time your hearts be overcharged with surfeiting and drunkenness and cares of this life, and so that day come upon you unawares. For as a snare shall it come on all them that dwell on the face of the whole earth. Watch ye therefore, and pray always, that ye may be accounted worthy to escape all these things that shall come to pass, and to stand before the Son of man."— Luke 21:34-36.

According to this passage there is only one way in which we can be prepared for the coming of the Lord when He appears, that is, through much prayer.

The coming again of Jesus Christ is a subject that is awakening much interest and much discussion in our day; but it is one thing to be interested in the Lord's return and to talk about it, and quite another thing to be prepared for it. We live in an atmosphere that has a constant tendency to unfit us for Christ's coming. The world tends to draw us down by its gratifications and by its cares. There is only one way by which we can rise triumphant above these things—by constant watching unto prayer, that is, by sleeplessness unto prayer.

Watch in this passage is the same strong word used in Ephesians 6:18, and *always* the same strong phrase *in every season*. The man who spends little time in prayer, who is not steadfast and constant in prayer, will not be ready for the Lord when He comes. But we may be ready. How? Pray! Pray! Pray!

11. Because of what prayer accomplishes.

Much has really been said upon that already, but there is much also that should be added.

(a) Prayer promotes our spiritual growth as almost nothing else, indeed as nothing else but Bible study; and true prayer and true Bible study go hand in hand.

It is through prayer that my most hidden sin is brought to light. As I kneel before God and pray, "Search me, O God, and know my heart: try me, and know my thoughts: and see if there be any wicked way in me," God shoots the penetrating rays of His light into the innermost recesses of my heart, causing the sins I never suspected to be brought to view.

In answer to prayer, God washes me from mine iniquity and cleanses me from my sin (Ps. 51:2).

In answer to prayer, my eyes are opened to behold wondrous things out of God's Word (Ps. 119:18).

In answer to prayer, I get wisdom to know God's way (James 1:5) and strength to walk in it.

As I meet God in prayer and gaze into His face, I am changed into His own image from glory to glory (II Cor. 3:18). Each day of true prayer life finds me more like unto my glorious Lord.

John Welch, son-in-law to John Knox, was one of the most faithful men of prayer this world ever saw. He counted that day ill spent in which seven or eight hours were not used alone with God in prayer and study of His Word. An old man speaking of him after his death said, "He was a type of Christ."

How came he to be so like his Master? His prayer life explains the mystery.

(b) Prayer brings power into our work. If we wish power for any work to which God calls us, be it preaching, teaching, personal work, or the rearing of our children, we can get it by earnest prayer.

A woman with a little boy who was perfectly incorrigible once came to me in desperation and said: "What shall I do with him?"

I asked, "Have you ever tried prayer?"

She said she thought she had prayed for him. I asked if she had made his conversion and his character a matter of definite, expectant prayer. She replied that she had not been definite in the matter. She began that day, and at once there was a marked change in the child. He grew up into Christian manhood.

How many a Sunday school teacher has taught for months and years and seen no real fruit from his labors, then has learned the secret of intercession! By earnest pleading with God, he has seen his scholars brought one by one to Christ! How many a poor preacher has become a mighty man of God by casting away his confidence in his own ability and gifts and giving himself up to God to wait upon Him for the power that comes from on High!

John Livingstone spent a night, with some others likeminded, in prayer to God and religious conversation. Then when he preached the next day in the Kirk of Shotts, five hundred people were converted, or dated some definite uplift in their life to that occasion. Prayer and power are inseparable.

(c) Prayer avails for the conversion of others.

There are few converted in this world unless in connection with someone's prayers. I formerly thought that no human being had anything to do with my own conversion, for I was not converted in church or Sunday school or in personal conversation with anyone. I was awakened in the middle of the night and converted.

As far as I can remember, I had not the slightest thought of being converted or of anything of that character when I went to bed and fell asleep; but I was awakened in the middle of the night and converted probably inside of five minutes. A few minutes before I was about as near eternal perdition as one gets. I had one foot over the brink and was trying to get the other one over.

I say, I thought no human being had anything to do with it, but I had forgotten my mother's prayers. And I afterwards learned that one of my college classmates had chosen me as one to pray for until I was saved.

Prayer often avails where everything else fails. By prayer the bitterest enemies of the Gospel have become its most valiant defenders; the greatest scoundrels, the truest sons of God; the vilest women, the purest saints. Oh, the power of prayer to reach down, down, down where hope itself seems vain, and lift men and women up, up, up into fellowship with and likeness to God! It is simply wonderful! How little we appreciate this marvelous weapon!

(d) Prayer brings blessings to the church.

The history of the church has always been a history of grave difficulties to overcome. The Devil hates the church and seeks in every way to block its progress; now by false doctrine, again by division, again by inward corruption of life. But by prayer, a clear way can be made through everything.

Prayer will root out heresy, allay misunderstanding, sweep away jealousies and animosities, obliterate immoralities, and bring in the full tide of God's reviving grace. History abundantly proves this. In the hour of darkest portent, when the case of the church, local or universal, has seemed beyond hope, believing men and believing women have met together and cried to God and the answer has come.

It was so in the days of Knox; it was so in the days of Wesley and Whitefield; it was so in the days of Edwards and Brainerd; it was so in the days of Finney; it was so in the days of the great revival of 1857 in this country and of 1859 in Ireland. And it will be so again in your day and mine!

Satan has marshaled his forces. Christian Science with its false Christ—a woman—lifts high its head. Others making great pretensions of apostolic methods, but covering the rankest dishonesty and hypocrisy with these pretensions, speak with loud assurance.

Christians equally loyal to the great fundamental truths of the Gospel are glowering at one another with a Devil-sent suspicion. The world, the flesh and the Devil are holding high carnival. It is now a dark day. *But*—now "it is time for thee, Lord, to work; for they have made void thy law" (Ps. 119:126). And He is getting ready to work, and now He is listening for the voice of prayer. Will He hear it? Will He hear it from you? Will He hear it from the church as a body? I believe He will.

ROSALIND GOFORTH
1864- (unknown)

ABOUT THE PERSON:

Born in London, England, in 1864, Rosalind came to Montreal, Canada with her parents three years later. Her seven brothers and three sisters dubbed her "Rosie." In the ensuing years, these older ones teased, scolded, coddled and protected her, making for a stormy childhood. With a volcanic temper, one day she cried out to her mother with intense longing, "O Mother, if only I could be good! I do SO want to be good!"

At age twelve the discontented child found the peace and forgiveness that her passionate nature craved.

Her education, apart from art, was received chiefly in private schools or from her mother.

At age nineteen Rosalind began praying that if the Lord wanted her to marry, He would lead to her one wholly given up to God's service.

In 1885 she graduated from the Toronto School of Art and began preparations to leave for London to complete her art studies. But while on a scenic boat trip to Niagara Falls, she was introduced to "a very shabby fellow," Jonathan Goforth, called "Our City Missionary." He made no impression whatsoever upon her. But after hearing him once, she forgot the shabby clothes for the wonderful challenge in his eyes!

In a few days, at the Toronto Mission Union, she said to herself, *This is the man I would like to marry!* When Rosalind and the "shabby young man" were thrown together more and more, she soon realized that underneath the cheap, country clothes there beat a heart of sterling character.

When a few months later he asked, "Will you join your life with mine for China?" her answer was "yes" without a moment's hesitation.

It was a marriage of rare beauty, fellowship and unity in faith and work. They labored in Honan, China, training hundreds of Chinese pastors and evangelists. During the Boxer Rebellion of 1900, both barely escaped with their lives, though suffering severe wounds.

They returned to the Orient and helped start a revival in Korea in 1907. This revival seemed to follow them as they returned to China.

In 1925 they went to Manchuria and served there eight years before ill health forced them to return to Canada.

Although Goforth was blind the last years of his life, and Rosalind's hearing was impaired, both promoted missions until they went home to be with the Lord.

XVI.

How I Know God Answers Prayer

ROSALIND GOFORTH

After 48 years as missionary to China, Mrs. Goforth writes this classic testimony of amazing answers to prayer....

"Are not five sparrows sold for two farthings, and not one of them is forgotten before God?.... Fear not therefore: ye are of more value than many sparrows."—Luke 12:6,7.

This testimony deals almost wholly with just one phase of prayer—petition. The record is almost entirely a personal testimony of what petition to my heavenly Father has meant in meeting the everyday crises of my life.

A prominent Christian worker who read some of these testimonies in *The Sunday School Times* said to the writer, "To emphasize getting things from God, as you do, is to make prayer too material."

To me this seems far from true. God is my Father and I am His child. As truly as I delight to be sought for by my child when he is cold, hungry, ill or in need of protection, so is it with my heavenly Father.

Prayer has been hedged about with too many manmade rules. I am convinced that God has intended prayer to be as simple, as natural and as constant a part of our spiritual life as the communication between a child and his parent in the home. And as a large part of that communication between child and parent is simply asking and receiving, just so it is with us and our heavenly Parent.

Perhaps, however, the most blessed element in this asking and getting from God lies in the strengthening of faith which comes when a definite request has been granted. What more helpful and inspiring than a ringing testimony of **what *God* has done?**

As I have recalled the past in writing these incidents, one of the most precious memories is that of an evening when a number of friends had gathered in our home. The conversation turned to answered prayer. For more than two hours we vied with one another in recounting personal incidents of God's wonderful work; and the inspiration of that evening still abides.

A Christian minister once said to me, "Is it possible that the great God of the universe, the Maker and Ruler of mankind, could or would, as you would make out, take interest in such a trifle as the trimming of a hat! To me it is preposterous!"

Yet did not our Lord Jesus Christ say, "The very hairs of your head are all numbered"; and "not one sparrow is forgotten before God"; and again, "Your heavenly Father knoweth what ye have need of **before** ye ask him"?

It is true that "there is nothing too great for God's power"; and it is just as true that "there is nothing too small for His love!"

If we believe God's Word, we must believe, as Dan Crawford has tersely and beautifully expressed it, that "the God of the infinite is the God of the infinitesimal." Yes, He

**Who clears the grounding berg
And guides the grinding floe,
He hears the cry of the little kit fox
And the lemming of the snow!**

No more wonderful testimony, perhaps, has ever been given of God's willingness to help in every emergency of life than that which Mary Slessor gave when asked to tell what prayer had meant to her.

My life is one long daily, hourly record of answered prayer. For physical health, for mental overstrain, for guidance given marvelously, for errors and dangers averted, for enmity to the Gospel subdued, for food provided at the exact hour needed, for everything that goes to make up life and my poor service. I can testify, with a full and often wonder-stricken awe, that I believe God answers prayer. **I know God answers prayer!**

I have been asked the question, "Has God **always** given you just what you have asked for?"

Oh, no! For Him to have done so would have been great unkindness. For instance: when I was a young woman I prayed for three years that God would grant me a certain petition. Sometimes I pleaded for this as for life itself, so intensely did I want it.

Then God showed me very clearly that I was praying against His will.

I resigned my will to His in the matter, and a few months later God gave what was infinitely better. I have often praised Him for denying my prayer; for had He granted it, I could never have come to China.

Then, too, we must remember that many of our prayers, though always heard, are not granted because of some sin harbored in the life or because of unbelief or of failure to meet some other Bible-recorded condition governing prevailing prayer.

The following incidents of answered prayer are by no means a complete record. How could they be, when no record of prayer has been kept all these fifty years? Had there been, I doubt not that volumes could have been written to the glory of God's grace and power in answering prayer. But even from what is recorded here I, too, can say from a full heart, **I know God answers prayer.**

> **He answered prayer: so sweetly that I stand**
> **Amid the blessing of His wondrous hand**
> **And marvel at the miracle I see,**
> **The favors that His love hath wrought for me.**
> **Pray on for the impossible, and dare**
> **Upon thy banner this brave motto bear,**
> **"My Father answers prayer."**

EARLY LESSONS IN THE LIFE OF FAITH

"I love the Lord, because he hath heard my voice and my supplications."—Ps. 116:1.

When a very little child, so young I can remember nothing earlier, a severe thunderstorm passed over our home. Terrified, I ran to my mother, who placed my hands together and, pointing upward, repeated over and over again the one word "Jesus."

More than fifty years have passed since that day, but the impression left upon my child-mind of a Being invisible but able to hear and help, has never been effaced.

The most precious recollections of early childhood are associated with stories told us by our mother, many of which illustrated the power of prayer.

One that made a specially deep impression upon me was about our grandfather who, as a little boy, went to visit cousins in the south of England, their home being situated close to a dense forest. One day the children, lured by the beautiful wild flowers, became hopelessly lost in the woods. After trying in vain to find a way out, the eldest, a young girl, called the frightened, crying little ones around her and said, "When Mother died she told us to always tell Jesus if we were in any trouble. Let us kneel down and ask Him to take us home."

They knelt. And as she prayed one of the little ones opened his eyes to find a bird so close to his hand that he reached out for it. The bird hopped away, but kept so close to the child as to lead him on. Soon all were joining in the chase after the bird, which flew or hopped in front or just above and sometimes on the ground almost within reach. Then suddenly it flew into the air and away. The children looked up to find themselves on the edge of the woods and in sight of home!

With such influences bearing upon one at an impressionable age, it is not surprising that I came even as a very little child to just "tell Jesus" when in trouble.

Through the mists of memory one incident stands out clearly, which occurred when I was six or seven years of age. While playing one day in the garden, I was seized with what we then called "jumping" toothache. I ran to my mother for comfort, but nothing she could do seemed to ease the pain.

The nerve must have become exposed, for the pain was acute. Suddenly I thought, *Jesus can help me,* and just as I was, with my face pressed against my mother's breast, I said in my heart, *Lord Jesus, if You will take away this toothache right now, now, I will be Your little girl for three years.*

Before the prayer was fully uttered the pain was entirely gone. I believe that Jesus had taken it away; and the result was that for years, when tempted to be naughty, I was afraid to do what I knew was wrong lest, if I broke my part of what I felt to be a compact, the toothache would return.

This little incident had a real influence over my early life, gave me a constant sense of the reality of a divine Presence, and so helped to prepare me for the public confession of Christ as my Saviour a few years later, at the age of eleven.

About a year after my confession of Christ, an incident occurred which greatly strengthened my faith and led me to look to God as a Father in a new way.

When Easter Sunday morning came it was so warm only spring clothes could be worn. My sister and I decided at breakfast that we would not go to church, as we had only our old winter dresses. Going to my room,

I turned to my Bible to study it, when it opened at Matthew 6, and my eyes rested on these words: "Why take ye thought for raiment?. . . Seek ye first the kingdom of God. . . and all these things shall be added unto you."

It was as if God spoke the words directly to me. I determined to go to church, even if I had to humiliate myself by going in my old winter dress.

The Lord was true to His promise; I can still feel the power the resurrection messages had upon my heart that day so long ago. And further, on the following day, a box came from a distant aunt containing not only new dresses but much else that might well be included in the "all these things."

An unforgettable proof of God's loving care came to us as a family about this time, when my parents were face to face with a serious financial crisis. Isaiah 65:24 was literally fulfilled: "Before they call, I will answer; and while they are yet speaking, I will hear."

At that time it is necessary to state that we depended on a quarterly income, which came through my mother's lawyer in England. Unusual circumstances had so drained our resources that we found ourselves in the middle of the quarter with barely sufficient to meet a week's needs. My dear mother assured us that the Lord would provide, that He would not forsake those who put their trust in Him.

That very day a letter came from the lawyer in England enclosing a draft for a sum ample to meet our needs till the regular remittance should arrive. This unexpected and timely draft proved to be a bonus, which did not occur again.

Some years later, having moved to a strange city, a great longing came to do some definite service for my Master. One day there came to the Bible class I attended a call for teachers to aid in a Sunday school nearby. When I presented myself before the superintendent and offered my services, it is not much wonder I received a rebuff, for I was young and quite unknown. I was told that if I wished a class, it would be well for me to find my own scholars. I can remember how a lump seemed choking me all the way home that day.

At last, determining not to be baffled, I prayed the Lord to help me get some scholars. I went forth, praying every step of the way, the following Saturday afternoon; and canvassing just one short street near our home, I received the promise of nineteen children for Sunday school.

The next day a rather victorious young woman walked up to the Sunday school superintendent with seventeen children following. Needless to say, I was given a class.

In the autumn of 1885 the Toronto Mission Union, a faith mission, decided to establish a branch mission in the East End slums of that city. Three others and I were deputed to open this work. Everything connected with it was entirely new to me; but I found it most helpful and inspiring. For in face of tremendous difficulties, that seemed to my inexperienced eyes insurmountable, I learned that prayer was the secret which overcame every obstacle, the key that unlocked every closed door.

I felt like a child learning a new and wonderful lesson—as I saw benches, tables, chairs, stove, fuel, lamps, oil, even an organ coming in answer to definite prayer for these things. But best sight of all was when men and women, deep in sin, were converted and changed into workers for God, in answer to prayer. Praise God for the lessons then learned, which were invaluable later when facing the heathen.

The time came when two diverse paths lay before me—one to England, as an artist; one to China, as a missionary. Circumstances made a definite decision most difficult. I thought I had tried every means to find out God's will for me, and no light had come.

But in a day of great trouble, when my precious mother's very life seemed to hang in the balance, I shut myself up with God's Word, praying definitely for Him to guide me to some passage by which I might know His will for my life. My Bible, opening at John 15:16, seemed to bring a message to me: "Ye have not chosen me, but I have chosen you, and ordained you, that ye should go and bring forth fruit." Going to my dear mother and telling her of the message God had given me, she said, "I dare not fight against God."

From that time the last hindrance from going to China was removed. Surely the wonderful way God has kept His child for more than thirty years in China is proof that this call was not a mistaken one. "In all thy ways acknowledge him, and he shall direct thy paths" (Prov. 3:6).

During the summer of 1887 a book written by Dr. Hudson Taylor came into my hands. In *China's Spiritual Needs and Claims* the writer told many instances of God's gracious provision in answer to prayer. The incidents related impressed me deeply. A little later, a few weeks before my marriage, when I found I was short fifty dollars of what I would need to be married free of debt, I resolved not to let others know of my need but to just trust God to send it to me. The thought came, *If you cannot trust God for this, when Hudson Taylor could trust for so much more, are you worthy of being a missionary?*

It was my first experience of trusting quite alone for money. I was sorely tempted to give others just a hint of my need. But I was kept from doing so; and though I had a week or more of severe testing, peace of mind and the assurance that God would supply my need came at length. The answer, however, did not come till the very last night before the wedding.

That evening a number of my fellow workers from the East End Mission called and presented me with a beautifully illuminated gift, also a purse. After these friends had left I returned to my home circle, assembled in the back parlor, and showed them the gift and the purse unopened! Not for a moment did I think there was anything in the purse till my brother said, "You foolish girl! Why don't you open it?" I opened the purse and found it contained a check for fifty dollars!

This incident has ever remained peculiarly precious; for it seemed to us a seal of God upon the new life opening before us.

CHARLES ALBERT BLANCHARD
1848-1925

ABOUT THE MAN:

These two messages by Dr. Charles Blanchard were lifted from his famous Christian classic, *Getting Things From God,* which was the overflow of God's blessing upon this saintly associate of D. L. Moody and second president of Wheaton College, Wheaton, Illinois. This man knew that God answered prayer and was desirous to help others know that, and to get their prayers answered.

Dr. Blanchard had power with God because of prayerfulness. On Wheaton campus he was an abiding testimony of the faithfulness of God in response to the faith of man.

Your faith will be strengthened, your heart warmed and moved to trust God for all things, as you read these two tremendous messages or testimonies.

Other works by Dr. Blanchard, published by Moody Press were: *Light on the Last Days; An Old Testament Gospel; Who Wrote the Bible? Method in Biblical Criticism.* In addition, he had in print several tracts on: Christian Science, the Theatre, the Home, teaching concerning sickness; what we are to do with our troubles, confession of sin, and how to live a victorious life.

Some of his other accomplishments: President of Wheaton College, Chicago Hebrew Mission, National Christian Association, Federation of Illinois Colleges, and Director Chicago Tract Society.

XVII.

"Confess Your Faults One to Another, and Pray..."

CHARLES A. BLANCHARD

I take this title from the directions which the Holy Spirit gives through James for the care of the sick. He says in the fifth chapter of that letter, verses 14 and 15:

"Is any sick among you? let him call for the elders of the church; and let them pray over him, anointing him with oil in the name of the Lord: And the prayer of faith shall save the sick, and the Lord shall raise him up; and if he have committed sins, they shall be forgiven him."

I have heard this Scripture repeated all my life, but I have almost never heard it in public quotation:

"Confess your faults one to another, and pray one for another, that ye may be healed. The effectual fervent prayer of a righteous man availeth much."—vs. 16.

Francis Murphy used to say, "The three hardest words to pronounce in the English language are, 'I was wrong,' and the next three hardest to pronounce are, 'You were right.'"

Undoubtedly, Mr. Murphy was correct. Honest confession of faults is, if not the most difficult thing that Christians ever have to do, one of the most difficult. Of course, it is more difficult than thanksgiving, though this is sorely neglected by good people even, but the confession of faults is harder to do.

Satan knows that if we honestly confess our sins, they are forgiven; and he knows that if we honestly confess them, we cease from them; therefore, he fights every inch of the road that a Christian walks toward confession.

A Personal Incident

I remember some years ago when Mrs. Blanchard was quite sick. She is a physician and has been, by the grace of God, a very successful physician. I have myself seen her, under God, raise a young man from the very edge of the grave, when the physician in charge was letting him die as fast as he could.

I have never been particularly disturbed when she has reported illness, thinking that she knew what to do, would do it, and that shortly it would pass away. I felt and acted in this manner at the time of which I am speaking. She took the remedies which she had given to many others, but for some reason they produced no satisfactory results.

Days grew into weeks, and weeks into months, and there was no improvement. She began to look really haggard and sick.

She said to me one day, "I do not believe I shall be any better unless I go to the hospital and have an operation. If you will call up the Presbyterian Hospital and arrange for a room, I will see Dr. Sarah Hackett Stevenson and ask her if she will operate on me."

I called the hospital and arranged for the room. She saw Dr. Stevenson, who agreed to operate.

We were waiting a day or two, when she said to me, "I think perhaps I would like to go down to Detroit and see Belle before I go to the hospital. One cannot tell just how soon one can get out after an operation."

I said, "Yes, that is well. Go to Detroit."

So she went to Detroit and had her visit with our oldest daughter, her husband and baby, and returned no better, but rather worse.

At this time it dawned on me that I had not in a definite way committed her to God. I had not received because I had not definitely asked. So when I went to prayer, immediately the Holy Spirit said to me, "Have you confessed your faults?" Reflecting, I said, "No." He said, "You must confess your faults."

We were not living in an unkindly fashion, but there are many things in home lives which are not just as they ought to be. There were some of these things to my account, and I acknowledged them. Then I went to pray. I said, "Lord, You see that Your child is sick. We have been arranging for the hospital. You know that that takes time. It takes money. It involves danger; even the minor operations do not always result happily. You have the power; You can speak the word, if You will. Please help."

The next morning when I looked across to see her face, it showed evident improvement. She was better in appearance than she had been for weeks. When she spoke she said, "I feel differently; I have not felt so well for a long time." I thanked God but did not at that time tell her of my special prayer. Again, however, I asked God to perfect the work—to drive away the disease and make her well.

The second morning she looked like a young woman, though she was about fifty years of age at that time. That disease left her as if it were a bird and had wings. It has never come near her since. She has had other ailments of one kind and another, but that particular disease has gone away. We do not know that it will ever come back. We have no desire to see it again. Some wise men tell me that her time had not come, that she would have recovered without prayer. I will not say that this is not true, for I am not a prophet; I am a witness.

I know that there was no improvement before the confession and prayer. I know that there was a steady increase in unfavorable conditions. I know that, although she is a physician and is not given to special alarms, she felt afraid about herself. And I know that after I confessed my faults and prayed for her, God healed her and so far as that trouble is concerned, she has been well ever since.

Only a Testimony

I hesitated whether to narrate this story in the first person or not. On some accounts I should have preferred not to do so, but a witness has to say "I." No court cares to hear him say "you" or "them." He must say "I." So on reflection I have given my testimony as it lies in my mind, and it is a true testimony.

One may say to me, "Has death never entered your home?" Yes, it has. "Did you confess your faults and pray then?" Not in a faithful manner. If I had done so, I am free to say today that I believe I could have been spared the fierce trials that did come to me years before. I do not give the testimony because I think I am qualified to give instructions to other people, but I give my testimony as it occurred and largely because of my own previous failures.

If God would help some of my brethren to do thorough work in this manner, as on this particular occasion He enabled me, I believe they would find that when we confess our sins, God is faithful and just to forgive them; and that if we confess our faults one to another and pray one for another, healing will come into our homes.

I do not happen to have had in my personal experience knowledge of similar instances in the lives of others. I hope there are very few who need to make confessions before they pray for the sick, but evidently some do or James 5:16 would never have been written. The Holy Spirit says, "Confess your faults one to another, and pray one for another. . . ."

Of course some people need to do this or there would be no such injunction. I needed to do it. If I had done it earlier, it would have saved me much. But I am glad I learned the lesson at last and that God helped me on that particular occasion to triumph through His grace. If I have need, I hope to triumph again, and if these words are read by someone who has a like need, I pray that God will enable you to triumph.

Perhaps this will be as good a place as any for me to speak a little further respecting prayer for the sick, for I have, by God's grace, been enabled to see a number of cases where death seemed close at hand and where prayer to God drove it away.

Gifts of Healing

The Bible clearly intimates that God bestows upon certain persons what are called "gifts of healing," upon others "pastoral gifts," upon others "teaching gifts," etc.

I was made teacher, though certain other gifts in smaller measures have been bestowed upon me. I never had nor aspired to gifts of healing, but I have desired to be helpful to sick and burdened people, and I have at times prayed for them. No doubt many others did also, and I have seen most remarkable healings. For the encouragement of those who are called to pray for the sick, I would like to be helpful to them and I will mention another instance.

I came into my office one morning to begin my day's work. Just as I was about to take it up, a lady, very much excited, came in and said that I was desired to go and pray in a home where a child was dying. I said to her, "It is impossible for me to go at this time, but I will send a brother who can do so." I asked the Rev. Mr. Hall, at that time the assistant pastor of our church, a man of faith and of the Holy Spirit, to go in my stead. He did so, but returned after a time, saying that the family would be glad if I would come to the house. I went, stopping at our home on the way and taking Mrs. Blanchard with me.

A gentleman opened the door of the house. As he did so, I said to him, "Are you the father of this child who is so ill?"

"Yes."

"Well, are you a Christian man?"

"Mr. Blanchard, I am a traveling man. You know how hard it is for a traveling man to be a Christian, but I do believe in God, and I do believe in Jesus Christ, and I try to be a Christian."

I went on to the lounge where his wife was lying, herself just out of the hospital and very frail. She held my hand convulsively and sobbed bitterly as she said, "Mr. Blanchard, you know how hard it is to say, 'Thy will be done,' but I say, 'Thy will be done.'"

I went on into the next room. The little babe was lying on a pillow held in the lap of a neighbor. The doctor who had been attending him was sitting before him, his elbow on his knee, his chin resting in his hand, waiting to see the end. Already they had telephoned the nurse that it was unnecessary for her to come, that the baby was practically dead and she would be of no service.

It was impossible for me to see a sign of life in the child. There was not a trace of color. I could not see the slightest movement of the lungs. If the child had been in a coffin, no one would have objected to burial from anything which was obvious.

But we prayed for the little fellow, and as I went back I said to the mother, "I think God will give you back your baby."

At 5:00 o'clock that evening I telephoned the house to know how the little one was getting on. The person who answered the phone said, "Baby is sleeping quietly. The pink has come back into his cheeks. We think he is getting well."

Three days later, as I was about to leave town, I phoned the house and the mother answered the phone. "How is Baby?"

She said, "He is very well, getting on nicely." Then she added, "People used to tell me that God does not work miracles in these days, but I know He does. He has worked one in this house."

I have no doubt whatever that what she said was literally true. Of course God works miracles. The springtime is an uncounted host of miracles. We should be speechless with wonder were it not that we are so accustomed to it.

I am about to relate a most remarkable story. It came firsthand and it is an encouragement to men to pray. It does not belong more properly in this chapter than in several others, but as I am speaking of healing, though this particular case is not connected with the duty of confession, I will record it here.

A Railroad Engineer Testifies

I was a few weeks ago in the Eighth Avenue Mission in New York. On the platform by me sat a gentleman to whom I was introduced but whom I had never before seen.

When the meeting had progressed for an hour or so, Miss Wray, the superintendent, called upon him for a testimony. He said:

> Friends, about two and a half or three years ago I was in the hospital in Philadelphia. I was an engineer on the Pennsylvania Lines, and although I had a praying wife, I had all my life been a sinful man. At this time I was very ill. I became greatly wasted. I weighed less than one hundred pounds.
>
> Finally the doctor who was attending me said to my wife that I was dead. But she said, "No, he is not dead. He cannot be dead. I have prayed for him for twenty-seven years and God has promised me that he should be saved. Do you think God would let him die now, after I have prayed twenty-seven years and God has promised, and he is not saved?"
>
> "Well," the doctor replied, "I do not know anything about that, but I know that he is dead."
>
> And the screen was drawn around the cot, which in the hospital separates between the living and the dead.
>
> To satisfy my wife, other physicians were brought, one after another, until seven were about the cot, and each one of them as he came up and made the examination confirmed the testimony of all who had preceded. The seven doctors said that I was dead.
>
> Meanwhile, my wife was kneeling by the side of my cot, insisting that I was not dead—that if I were dead, God would bring me back, for He had promised her that I should be saved and I was not yet saved.
>
> By and by her knees began to pain her, kneeling on the hard hospital floor. She asked the nurse for a pillow and the nurse brought her a pillow upon which she kneeled. One hour, two hours, three hours passed. The screen still stood by the cot. I was lying there still, apparently dead. Four hours, five hours, six hours, seven hours, thirteen hours passed, and all this while my wife was kneeling by the cotside, and when people remonstrated and wished her to go away she said, "No, he has to be saved. God will bring him back if he is dead. He is not dead. He cannot die until he is saved."

At the end of thirteen hours I opened my eyes. She said, "What do you wish, my dear?"

I said, "I wish to go home."

She said, "You shall go home."

But when she proposed it, the doctors raised their hands in horror. "Why, it will kill him! It will be suicide!"

She said, "You have had your turn. You said he was dead already. I am going to take him home."

I weigh now 246 pounds. I still run a fast train on the Pennsylvania Lines. I have been out to Minneapolis on a little vacation, telling men what Jesus can do, and I am glad to tell you what Jesus can do.

I am absolutely certain that God is waiting to answer prayer—waiting to answer prayers for many. At times there are hindering things. Sometimes there are unconfessed faults. These are a deadly obstacle. Let us put them out of the way so that we may pray one for another and see men healed.

There never could have been the false faiths believed in and alleged healings which now prevail, if only men would act according to the Scriptures in the case of those who are sick. It is so easy for Satan to get people to say that there is no sickness, so much easier than the Holy Spirit finds it to get men to confess their faults one to another, and pray one for another that they may be healed.

(From *Getting Things From God*)

XVIII.

"Always to Pray, and Not to Faint"

CHARLES A. BLANCHARD

"And he spake a parable unto them to this end, that men ought always to pray, and not to faint."—Luke 18:1.

It is clear that we are dealing here with the duty of perseverance and it is well known to all those who have either thought or observed, that this is a point where many of us break down.

It is easy to be discouraged and God oftentimes delays answers to prayer because He wishes us to learn to trust Him in the dark, to believe when we cannot see.

Do not earthly parents do the same? Who is there who is wise with his children who has not at times waited to bestow some good gift which he had already willed, in order that his children might learn to confide? What difference can it make to the Almighty whether He bestows a good gift upon me at one time or another?

God's resources are infinite, so also is His wisdom and love. Why should He then delay? That He does we all know; that He intended to, the teaching of Jesus clearly evidences. "Men ought always to pray, and not to faint."

I have had friends who said, "I do not think we ought to ask God for the same thing repeatedly. He knows whether it is best for us to have it or not. He will surely do what is best. Why not, therefore, simply remind Him of our need and then wait?"

The objection to this teaching is that it is contrary to the word of Jesus Christ on the same subject.

In Luke, chapter 11, our Lord is giving particular instructions in regard to prayer. He deals with this very question of repetition in verses 5 to 13, and He clearly intimates that God will bestow good gifts upon men who persevere in prayer, which He will not bestow on people who do not persevere in prayer.

The man in the story came to his neighbor for bread. It was inconvenient to supply it, and the neighbor declined; but because of his importunity our Lord says he will rise and give him as many as he needs (Luke 11:8). Then He goes on to say, "Ask, and it shall be given you; seek, and ye shall find. . . ." And I think it is not by accident that He unites the prayer of importunity with the promise to prayer.

Seven Years, or Fifteen Years

In one of our church prayer meetings not long ago, a lady rose and said, "My father is a drunkard. I have prayed seven years that God would save him, and he is not saved. It seems as if God did not hear or did not care and I am discouraged. I do not know what to do."

She had only taken her seat when a lady rose and said, "My father was a drunkard fifteen years, and I prayed for him all through those fifteen years. Then he was saved, not alone from drink, but from all other sins. Now for fifteen years he has been a happy Christian. I think my sister ought not to be discouraged, but to pray on."

This is only one instance of many, but it was very impressive because of the two testimonies which came one after the other.

The case of Mr. Mueller's two friends is so often mentioned and so widely known, that I feel like apologizing for mentioning it here; but it was so remarkable an instance of this kind that I cannot well omit it.

I heard Mr. Mueller myself say in his address in Farwell Hall, Chicago, something like this: "I have prayed for two men by name every day for thirty-five years. On land or sea, sick or well, I have remembered them before God by name, requesting their salvation. They are both living. Neither is saved, but I shall continue to pray for them daily, by name, until they are saved, or die."

It is related by a friend who wrote of his life, after his death, that just about that time there were two persons for whom Mr. Mueller had prayed daily for sixty-two years, who were converted. I did not know the names in either case, so I cannot say that these two for whom he prayed sixty-two years were the two to whom he referred in the address which I mentioned. I have no doubt that they were. It would seem improbable that there should be more than one case of that kind.

Do not, however, lose the thought. Here was a man praying every day for sixty-two years for the salvation of two men before they were saved. At the end of that time they were saved. What a lesson for us! What a reproof for our lack of perseverance! What an encouragement to continue in prayer!

"Men ought always to pray, and not to faint."

Another Case

I do not wish to produce the impression that my own experiences are more numerous or more valuable than those of other persons, but it is natural that one should know his own life story better than that of other people. And further: one cannot testify directly to any experience except his own. It is one thing to say, "Somebody told me," and another thing to say, "This was my experience."

North of our college campus, some years ago there stood an old frame building. It was not particularly valuable in itself but the land upon which it stood was very valuable. One of our honored trustees purchased the house and the land and gave them to the college. This bit of land constituted about one-third of the block of which it was a part. Two-thirds remained. One portion of this two-thirds was owned in New York, the other in Nebraska. It was obvious to anyone who looked at the land situation that the possession of that strip would be very helpful to the college. It was adjacent and was much to be desired for a number of reasons.

I asked friends who owned it to give it to the college. They declined to do so. I repeated the request after an interval of years; still they felt it was more than they could do.

At last I began to pray that the Lord would give us the land. At times I left the walk and stood upon the ground, reminding myself that God had promised Israel what the soles of his feet trod upon. I reminded God of this same promise and as well as I could, claimed by faith this land for the institution. Still it did not come.

Years passed into other years. No one purchased the ground. It was good ground, beautifully located. It would have been a very pleasant place for residences, yet there it lay, unoccupied.

Finally the parties who owned the New York strip directed their agent to make sale. He put it on the market, intending to force the sale for what he could get. Special assessments were high and were to be increased.

I said to the owner, "What will you let us have the land for?" He said, "For so much." I went to a generous friend who had made us debtor many times and said to her, "For about two thousand dollars we can secure this property, which is admirably located, and which we really need." She at once said, "I think I can furnish the money within a few months." She did, and that portion of the land came into our possession.

Still there was the remaining one-third. It lay between the other two and it was for sale. The parties who owned it wished to sell it, and I desired it for the college. I thanked God many times for the two pieces which He had given and asked Him for the third piece. Nobody bought it.

There it lay—beautiful land, desirably located, to be purchased for a moderate price, yet it was held.

Finally the owner made us a proposition which, without the expenditure of any money on our part, would enable us to secure the land. We did secure it. It is now a part of the college possession. The legal transactions are not entirely complete, for one of the owners was not living and there were necessary proceedings in court, but the transaction is practically concluded, and the whole property is ours, not for our own uses but for the instruction of young people through all the years until the Lord comes and for a part in His work during the millennial years.

Answers Delayed

The most remarkable instance of delayed answers to prayer which has come under my own observation was suggested by Mr. Moody in a sermon which he preached many years ago. He called our attention to the fact that when Moses was praying for the privilege of going over Jordan into the Promised Land, the Lord did not tell him that he could not go over the river. He said to him when the request was pressed, "Speak no more to me of this matter."

That was not a refusal—that was a direction. Fifteen hundred years later Moses was in the Holy Land with Elijah, talking with our Lord about the work which He was to accomplish at Jerusalem. He did not cross over Jordan, as God told him he would not. He did go into the Holy Land, as he prayed that he might, but he went by way of Heaven.

Mr. Moody was speaking in this sermon of God's determination to answer prayer. I cannot remember the words which he said, but I remember very distinctly the impression which the facts produced. It was so wonderful to think that God should keep the prayer of Moses before Him all those 1500 years, and when He was to send down to the Mount of Transfiguration two redeemed ones to talk with His Son about the death which He was to die for their sins and for the sins of the whole world, He selected Moses and Elijah.

It is my firm conviction that the Lord's people, if they will inquire among their friends who are spiritually minded folk, will be astounded at the number of cases in which God has answered prayer after long delay. As I have said before, this has not *happened* so, and it is not the result of any inability on the part of God. He can work His own will at His own pleasure and in His own time.

I heard the president of a university once say that God could use foolish people to accomplish His purpose, but that He never did so voluntarily. I was startled as I thought of the words of the Bible:

*"God **hath chosen** the foolish things of the world to confound the wise; and God **hath chosen** the weak things of the world to confound the things which are mighty; And base things of the world, and things which are despised, **hath God chosen,** yea, and things which are not, to bring to nought things that are."*—I Cor. 1:27,28.

God does choose the instruments which He uses. He does not take them from necessity; He takes them because of His own choice. And God does not answer prayer after fifteen hundred years or after seven years or after fifteen years or after sixty-two years because He could not answer in as many months if it pleased Him. There is a reason.

The Reason

It is safe to say that in a majority of instances of long delay, God has a number of purposes to accomplish. In the first place, it is a test of our own faith and obedience. He tells us always to pray and not to faint. Delays in answers to prayer are one means of testing us to know whether we can do this or not. It is also a wonderful confirmation of faith when the answer does come.

If I receive a gift after praying for it for ten years, my mind is impressed very differently from what it would be if I received the same gift after praying only ten minutes.

We shall never understand God's dealings with us here unless we remember that we came into the kingdom of God as babes and that He has to educate us, train us, raise us (if you allow the expression) precisely as parents have to train, educate, raise children. We are children and He is our Father. He is the Creator of our bodies, but He is the Father of our souls and He wishes us to be strong and pure and holy and useful, just as any good father wishes his children to be. To this end He disciplines. And one of the ways in which He disciplines is by delaying answer to prayer.

I was in New York some years ago, calling upon an old friend, a graduate of Knox College during my father's presidency there. In an adjoining room lay the daughter, long sick, at that time supposed to be near to death. I had prayer with her and was glad that God seemed to show mercies to her in her poor, wrecked and tormented body.

For some little time it looked as if she might recover, though I do not believe this was the plan of God.

The next year when I was in New York I found that she had died. A friend who was intimate with the family said to me something that was very terrible about her dying—that a friend came to the room, prayed for her and said: "God, You have promised to answer prayer, and we have complied with all the conditions; we command You to heal this sick one."

I did not wonder that she died; I wondered that the person who offered the prayer did not die. Except that she was ignorant and God could pardon her, it seemed to me that He would certainly have struck her dead then and there.

God Takes No Instructions From Men

God does not permit men to give Him orders. "He sits on no precarious throne, nor borrows leave to be," and He does not wish to have people say that they command Him. I do not think that He cares to hear us say that we have complied with all the conditions of successful prayer. I am certain He wishes us to do this, and I am certain that when we do it, He knows it and is satisfied, and I am quite sure He does not require us to tell Him that since we have complied with the conditions, it is time for Him to fulfill His Word. This seems a frightful blasphemy, and I hope that none of the Lord's children who read these words will ever be guilty of so offending against the Majesty of Heaven.

A sensible person proferring a request to an earthly monarch would never think of doing so in such insulting and outrageous terms. Is it not strange that our brothers and sisters can sometimes insult God by addressing Him as they would never dare to speak to a human being?

George Mueller Again

I remember hearing George Mueller say, when he was telling us about praying for those two men thirty-five years, that it happened in the providence of God that the first persons he spoke with in the name of Jesus after his own conversion were very quickly saved.

On one occasion two young men laughed when he spoke to them on the subject. He went into his bedroom adjacent, fell on his knees and with tears begged God to save those two young men. When he came out, they were both of them ready to submit to God.

He said he received the impression that everybody he spoke to or prayed for would be immediately converted, and that when he began to pray one year, two years, three years, four years, five years, for the same person with no apparent result, he was surprised and a bit disheartened. But he reflected that God's promise was not to answer in five minutes or five years or fifty years, but to answer—that it was his part to believe and to continue making request and that, if he did this, God would certainly fulfill His part of the contract. So he said, "I lost the feeling of disappointment which I had had and was encouraged to lay hold on God patiently, perseveringly every day until the answer came."

The Garden Prayers

In this connection I think it is helpful to remember about our Lord's praying in Gethsemane. He prayed once, He prayed twice, He prayed the third time. And it is interesting to note that the Word says, in speaking of these repeated petitions, "saying the same words" (Matt. 26:44).

How can one reconcile this fact with the teaching of some who say that when we have once proffered a petition, it is an exhibition of distrust or a rebellious spirit if we make the same request again? I do not believe this is true. Had it been, certainly our Lord Jesus Christ would never have prayed three times, saying the same words each time.

The fact is, we must be taught by the Spirit how to pray. Sometimes He will teach us to pray once and to look upon the transaction as completed. Sometimes He will bid us pray more than once, and when He does so, we must persevere in prayer.

"Men ought always to pray, and not to faint."

I remember my father once visited a dying man in the city of Cincinnati, where he was pastor of the Sixth Presbyterian Church. The dying man had great difficulty in speaking—in fact, could scarcely speak at all. When my father asked him if he would like him to pray, he nodded his head affirmatively. My father said to him, "Shall I pray for your wife and children?" He shook his head negatively. Then, gathering up what strength he had, he said, "Yesterday I prayed for them."

Yesterday. In other words, he had closed that transaction with God, and he did not wish to re-open it. He had prayed for those dear people once; he knew God had heard him and would answer in due time. In his bodily frailty his faith was strong, and he did not care to pray twice when he believed he had already the answer of God.

When I Prayed for a Friend

I have had that same experience, not as a dying experience, but as a living one.

I was years ago very much burdened for a friend. I prayed repeatedly that the Lord would do a certain thing for that friend. At last it seemed to me that God said to me by His Spirit, "You leave that matter with Me, and I will take care of it." I did so.

I have never prayed that prayer since so far as I know. Sometimes I have thought of doing so and almost began to pray. Then it has come to me that that is a completed transaction between God and me, so I have stopped and thanked Him that He has accepted my petition, that He would answer my prayer, and I have left that matter definitely in His hands.

It is blessed to do so and from time to time remind Him that He has promised and that I know He will fulfill my petition in His own time.

I have had that same experience about erecting buildings. I have thanked God for them. I have seen them in my mind fully completed, standing fair and beautiful on the ground, when not a shovelful of earth had been turned, when not a brick or stone had been laid.

If I am speaking to those who have been burdened because of unanswered prayer—and I do not doubt there are some such among those who will read these pages—let me encourage you. There is no such thing as proper prayer in God's will unanswered in this world, but there are prayers, the answers to which are long delayed. It is well that it is so. It would harm us if it were otherwise. If you will be victoriously patient, you will be victoriously successful in your praying.

(From *Getting Things From God*)

SAMUEL DICKEY GORDON
1860-1936

ABOUT THE MAN:

S. D. Gordon was never given a degree of doctor, and he always preferred to be called simply Mr. S. D. Gordon. His full name was Samuel Dickey Gordon and he was born in 1860. He served as assistant secretary of the Y.M.C.A. in Philadelphia for two years, then was made secretary of the Y.M.C.A. in Ohio, where he served nine years.

Since that time he devoted himself to public speaking in this country, Europe and even in the Orient. In 1895 he was invited to the Moody Bible Institute where he delivered a course of lectures, and his first *Quiet Talks* volume was published at that time.

A world tour was undertaken by Mr. Gordon during which time he spent eighteen months in this country and a year in the Far East. A warm supporter of Keswick, Mr. Gordon spoke at the convention in 1909, then again at his last visit to Britain in 1932.

He died at his home in Winston-Salem, North Carolina, June 26, 1936.

XIX.

The Finnish Gold Story

How God Miraculously Increased the Money for His Chapel Till It Was Enough, in Answer to a Woman's Prayer

S. D. GORDON

"If True"

God never disappoints anyone. "Thou, Lord, hast not forsaken them that seek thee" (Ps. 9:10). He never has. He never does. He never will. He cannot. That does not mean that there are no disappointments. We all know too much of life to believe that. But it does mean that they are never due to God; on the other hand they come in spite of God. And they mean as much pain to Him as to us—maybe more.

God never breaks His Word. He is very jealous about that. No banker's word given in solemn promise is half as dependable, for banks may break, but God cannot. The Scripture cannot be broken (John 10:35). It never has been broken yet. God is watching jealously over His Word to see that it shall never be allowed to fail by so much as the dotting of an *i* or the crossing of a *t* (Jer. 1:12; Matt. 5:18; 24:35).

True prayer never fails. It cannot because it depends on God and on His pledged Word. I say "*true* prayer," because the word *prayer* is used in a slipshod way for much that the earnest heart knows within itself to be not true prayer.

Prayer itself is a very simple thing. It is the pleading or claiming by a sincere heart for some needed thing, based on some promise of God's Word and pleaded on the ground of the blood of Jesus (Rev. 12:11). Such prayer is very simple. Its strength, so far as the man praying is concerned, is in its simplicity. Such praying never fails. It never has;

it never does; it never will; it cannot. Heaven and earth will pass away before such prayer can fail.

It is barely conceivable that under certain extraordinary circumstances of the unlikeliest sort, the Bank of England might possibly be obliged to close its doors or the government at Washington fail to meet the interest on its bonds. Such things have happened. But God will not permit any trusting child of His to be disappointed, so far as He is concerned. Bonds reckoned as "gilt-edged" and negotiable paper as "A-1," do not rate high on the Exchange of God nor on the Exchange of His trusting follower, as His own pledged word.

Not a word He has spoken
Can ever be broken.

When those earthquakes of the book of Revelation come along, well-secured first mortgages, "gilt-edged" bank stock, and "fancy" securities will not be worth the beautifully engraved paper on which they are written. But not a letter of this old Book of God will be affected; not a scrap of God's power shall be touched. There will be no shrinking in those securities. They will rate higher than ever before.

There are living illustrations of this in every part of the world. There are as striking stories in present-day life as that of the nameless widow's bottomless barrel up on the east coast of the Mediterranean (I Kings 17:8-16). In many a shut-away corner of the earth God is proving Himself unfailing to those simple and strong enough to trust Him and to walk the difficult, despised path of faith in Him.

I ran across such a story recently. And I want to tell it as simply as it came to me. Yet I do not tell it as an exception, but rather as the rule of what God is doing for His trusting and trusted ones (Gen. 22:16-18; John 2:24, 25).

The trailing arbutus modestly hides its beauty and its sweet fragrance under the friendly green, out of sight. The lily of the valley seeks the shaded, retired nook. The sweetest flowers are not found in the shop window. They are known only by those who seek them out in the quiet seclusion of the valley or hillside.

There is a wondrous modesty about truth. Shall I say, with awe-touched words, that there is a sweet modesty about God. He speaks to all in the unfailing sun, the noiseless moon, the life-giving rain and dew. But His best is reserved for those who come away into the inner circle. He opens His inner heart to all who will come into heart touch, but only to these (Ps. 25:14, margin; John 15:15).

This story is of a humble, quiet woman in one of the shut-away corners of the earth; of the sad spiritual need of her neighborhood; of her simple bravery in trying to do something to meet that need; of an hour of great distress when the enemy pressed hard and her soul was in sore straits; and of God's unfailing faithfulness. This is the whole point of the simple recital—God is faithful (I Cor. 10:13). His Word cannot be broken. Prayer never fails.

I think I will tell the story as it worked itself out to me, for there is to me, and ever will be, a distinct touch of awe—a touch of God's own hand—in the way in which I came to know the story personally. There is a story of guidance, guidance of an exquisite sort, as a prelude to the story itself.

It was a winter's night up in Stockholm. The evening meeting was over, and a number of Christian friends were gathered about the supper table. We were talking, as we ate, of our experiences of God's goodness. One lady present was induced to tell, through interpretation, a story of the unusual experience of a friend of hers in Finland.

It was about a woman who had to pay an unjust bill for lumber used in building a little chapel. She hadn't enough money; all efforts to get more failed; legal action threatened; then during prayer the money in her little treasure-box increased in amount until there was enough to pay the claim. There are the bones of the story.

It quite startled everyone who heard it. Such a thing was unheard of in modern times. And doubt was freely expressed by some of the most earnest and thoughtful ones present. The doubt was not of God's power to do such a thing, but of the accuracy of the story. The woman in her excitement must have made a mistake. Some friend was secretly helping, it was thought. Was she used to counting money? Was the box locked up so that no one else could get access to it? She was probably a good woman, but rather excitable. So question and comment ran on.

As I listened to the story, then to the comments, I thought that if it were true—and our friend who told it to us and who personally knew the woman in it, seemed quite assured herself of its being so—it should not be told until it could be thoroughly verified, but that if it could indeed be verified, it should be told and told widely. So my wife and I began to slip in a daily petition at praying time that if it were true as told, we might be led up to the little remote village—somewhere in Finland, I knew not just where—to learn the story at firsthand; and that I might be privileged to speak in the little chapel.

"Step by Step"

(Proverbs 4:12: "As thou goest, step by step, the way shall open up before thee."—*Free Translation.*)

Several months went by. A request came late that winter from Finland, but I was unable to accept because of other work at the time named. Then came another urgent request for a summer appointment in Finland, which I was glad to be able to accept. But it was on the southern coast of Finland, and this was a long distance—a full twelve hours' journey— from the village of the story. Still the daily prayer went up that the Father's own plan in this would work out.

A little while later, while speaking in Christiania, a letter came requesting attendance at the annual meeting of the Free Church of Finland. I had never heard the name of the place of meeting before and hadn't the remotest idea just where it was. So it was with intensest interest that we hastened downtown to a tourist office to see a map and find out just where this place was.

A touch of awe was felt as we saw that it was in the far northern part of Finland and that we must pass straight through the village of the story to get there. The date of this second appointment came immediately upon the heels of the first. It began to seem very plain that we were "being taken" to the scene of the story. And that made it look as though it were indeed true and that there was a purpose of God in its being known and told. But I determined to sift it most rigidly.

Then there came a letter from the woman herself who had the experience and with whom I had corresponded in the winter, saying that she was to be a delegate at this Free Church meeting and asking me to speak at a district meeting of ministers and others appointed to meet in her village a week later. Then came a request from the summer school of Finnish University students at a place within two hours of this village I was thinking about.

Both places and dates of these gatherings fitted together as though it had been so arranged for convenience in travel. The quiet sense of awe deepened. I felt that it *had* been arranged. There was a plan of action being worked out. The feeling that I was being led on by an unseen hand grew and stilled me. I was being led to where I would meet this person, then straight into her village and into her own home, and to speak in the little chapel, which was itself the standing witness in wood and brick of the wondrous experience.

I had been praying that if that journey to Norway and Finland were indeed God's own plan, the dates and places might dovetail. And no itinerary carefully studied out for months before had ever dovetailed more beautifully than this was doing. I was enabled to attend five annual national gatherings, each of which touched the whole of Finland and each a different circle; and one less representative in attendance—all within three weeks.

I learned afterwards that our friend of the story had been praying that her unusual experience might in some way become widely known, so that God's great faithfulness might be more known and appreciated. Then when first she learned that I was coming to Finland she began praying that the doors might open very wide to me, but was careful to do nothing toward that end herself, so that God's own purpose and power might be more evident. It is seen now how fully both these prayers were answered.

Then our prayer had begun to include another very important item; namely, a good interpreter for the story. I would need one who was perfectly free in English as well as Swedish if I were to get a clear, intelligent understanding of the story. My experience in listening to broken English made me feel keenly how absolutely essential this was. Yet I knew that, humanly, it might be very difficult. For good interpreters are rare.

As it turned out it was even more difficult than I knew. For the people of this inland country district of Finland spoke and understood, for the most part, only Finnish, the language used by about seven-eighths of the Finnish people. And so the interpreter who would have done for me ordinarily would not answer the purpose now unless he could speak freely three languages—namely, Finnish and English for the meetings, and Swedish also for the story, for that was the native speech of the woman of the story.

And as it all turned out the answer could not have been better. One of my interpreters at the Free Church meeting—the Finnish interpreter— was an acquaintance of the woman of the story. She is a schoolteacher in the Finnish capital and combines in rare degree the intellectual and spiritual qualities that must combine in good interpretation. Finnish is her native speech; she has known Swedish also from early girlhood, and she spoke English as freely as I could wish.

I heard afterwards that she is widely known as a schoolteacher, as an expert interpreter and as a very earnest Christian. I have had no one in all my experience with interpreters who combined spiritual grasp and insight and spiritual sensitiveness with the keen, accurate intellectual equipment to a fuller degree. And I have been unusually blessed in the rarely qualified interpreters whom God has graciously sent to me. This lady was on her vacation, and her arrangements were such that she could come. She graciously offered to make her plans suit our need and came for whatever days I would say. I have anticipated a little in order to group together the items in the rare guidance that surrounds the story.

The Background of the Picture

It was with an unusual sense of awe and of God's gracious presence, ever increasing, that we went on to Finland and began the round of appointments there. I shall never forget those three weeks in Finland. If ever I was moving in the current of the stream of God's will, surely it was then, as constantly revealed by the quiet, irresistible power felt and seen in the meetings. I had only to think of steering—steering to keep in the current; the power was in the current.

So we came to meet our friend of the story, and so we came to her village—two hours by rail inland from the Baltic coast of Finland. At last we came into her own simple home and then into the plain little wooden chapel with its wondrous story of God's faithfulness.

We had nearly two days to get acquainted with our new friend and to learn her story, before the meetings began. We found that she is the postmistress. There really is not a village—only a railroad junction, whose importance is made the greater by the extensive railroad operations being carried on here by the Russian Government.

We found a very quiet woman in middle life, whose gentle, patient face told plainly her life story of careful planning, hard work and thinking of others. Her father had been a clergyman of the old conservative State Church in Abo, the ancient cathedral center of Finland, where her early life had been spent; her mother's father was a physician.

She has been postmistress here for more than twenty years, a position which can be held only by one passing the rigid government examination. That means more than it would in the United States or in England, for the post office in the country districts of Finland is practically the national or government bank. In the absence of banks, most money changes hands by registered mail instead of by bank check. The extensive railroad operations have much increased the volume of post office business at this point—the work requiring usually three, sometimes four or five assistants.

I found that during one quarter recently the registered mail passing through her hands, whose contents were known, contained almost one million Finnish marks (a German mark is about twenty-five cents or one shilling; a Finnish mark about twenty cents, or tenpence), that is about $200,000 or 40,000 pounds. That would make the annual sum passing through her hands that year, roughly, $800,000 (160,000 pounds); though I got the impression that that was a rather heavier quarter than usual. Besides this was registered mail whose money contents were not declared. This at once showed the great importance of her post and the responsibility with which she was entrusted by the government.

Her books were as carefully kept as any bank account books I have ever examined in my earlier banking days; not only with the painstaking accuracy, but with the neatness of a skilled accountant. This seems a sufficient answer to the comments I heard when the story was told in Stockholm. She was accustomed through the years to the careful counting of, and accounting for, large funds. Painstaking accuracy in money matters had become a life habit deeply grained in.

Then a few questions brought a picture of the sore need out of which the experience had grown. Finland, of course, has a State Church—the Lutheran—which is practically the only church in the country, the Free Church movement being of comparatively recent origin and not yet legally organized as a church. The whole country is divided into parishes, many quite large. The parish here, I found, was a large one with one church building in a population of some four thousand people and in a territory eighteen English miles across. This church was about two and a half English miles away; the nearest others being four, ten and twelve miles away. Meetings had been held in the houses and schoolhouses; many had been converted, and many others greatly blessed. But the need of a little chapel was sorely felt. Our quiet friend was the leader in all this, as well as in the building of the chapel.

The story of the building of the chapel was a most fascinating one, but I think I must come at once to the story of the money.

The Sore Need

While the building was going up, there came in a bill for lumber which had been bought and received. But the amount was larger than it should have been. With the bill came a peremptory letter demanding immediate payment and threatening legal action. The bill was for seven hundred and fifty-one Finnish marks (about $150, or 30 pounds), being twenty-seven dollars (5.8 pounds) more than the right amount. The common commercial custom of the country provides for long credit. The amount was unjust, the usual time of payment was not given and legal proceedings threatened. This was a wholly unexpected and distressing complication.

She was troubled to know what to do about the unjust increase in the bill. The difference of over one hundred and thirty marks was a serious one, in view of the condition of the chapel funds and the great difficulty experienced in getting funds. She could refuse to pay and go to law, but that meant endless trouble and additional expense; and, further, she could not feel free in her heart about engaging in a lawsuit over the Lord's work.

The words of Matthew 5:40 came repeatedly to mind. Finally she decided to pay the full amount if she must, but only under strong protest against the injustice. It greatly strengthened her afterwards in praying for the money that she was acting in the spirit of the Master's teaching.

The chapel funds were made up wholly of freewill offerings by the people attending the services. The people are very poor; the funds were very low. Our friend stood quite alone in the responsibility. There had been much opposition among the church people to the chapel being built. It was a time of sore stress of soul. She cried to God, and there came to her a great quiet peace that seemed to brood over her. Then she commenced praying for the money. This was in May of 1908. The legal action, if taken, would give her until October.

Then followed a never-to-be-forgotten time of tireless effort, constant disappointment, unceasing prayer, sore stress of spirit and yet a strangely quiet peace—all intermingled. Every effort to get the money, either by gift or by borrowing, was entirely fruitless. There seemed only a stone wall at every turn. There were criticism, reproach and even sneers, but very little money. Her difficulty became known in the little community and was freely discussed, especially by those opposed to the chapel, who said that now it must be sold to pay this debt.

Still she prayed. In her words, "The prayer lamp burned day and night." It was a time of great searching of heart and sore strain in her spirit. The final time of payment drew near. Now something must be done. The law officer or sheriff was a friendly man, but of course must do his duty. A last effort, involving a journey to a nearby town, proved unavailing. The man she hoped to see was abroad; his wife thought she ought not to have begun building till she had the money. As she returned on the train her spirit was in deepest concern, and yet there was that strange sense of peace that would not leave.

The telling of it to us brought back the experiences so vividly that she had to pause at times to get better control of herself inwardly, though outwardly she was always very quiet and controlled. And we waited with a deep and deepening sense of awe as we were allowed to look into the secret recesses of a human soul and witness a little of the intensity of its struggles.

That was a wondrous time on the train. The brooding presence of Jesus seemed so near as she quietly sat thinking, while the train noisily hurried on. Her soul was drawn out in prayer to an unusual extent. In her dire extremity she cast herself upon God. Then there came into her mind something she had thought of all during the building of the chapel. But now it seemed to have a new meaning. Her mind was turned to the time in the desert when the loaves and fishes were multiplied. Then this prayer seemed given to her, that God would touch her slender chapel funds and do as in the desert—make them sufficient for the need.

On her return home, as soon as she could get time from her work, she went to the drawer to get the little box where the chapel funds were kept. She had counted the money before that last journey and found she had just three hundred and fifty marks ($70, or 14 pounds). Now she took the box out to the sitting room. She had on hand ninety marks ($18, or 3.12 pounds) of her own personal money. This she added to the Lord's money and poured all out upon the table. It was at the noon hour. The post office, which was in one part of the dwelling, was closed. She was quite alone.

She bowed in prayer over the table, spreading her hands out over the little heap of money, and prayed that God would indeed do as she believed He was leading her to ask. In simple childlike language she said, "Lord Jesus, bless *Thy* money as Thou didst bless the loaves in the wilderness. I will put my loaves, too, in Thy hands, and do Thou let them with Thine meet this need; let this money cover the amount of this bill." So she remained a little in prayer.

Then she counted one hundred marks ($20, or 4 pounds), and put it in a little heap by itself, then a second hundred, and a third, and so on, until there were seven such heaps of one hundred each and a smaller heap of fifty-one marks. And she noticed that there was now much gold, though there had not been much gold in the box. This brought to her mind the words of Isaiah 60:17.

With a great awe filling her being, she fell upon her knees thanking the Lord Jesus; then she rose and carefully counted again. Again she placed her hands upon the money, praising Jesus whose presence seemed very real, and again she prayed that the money might remain until she could pay the law officer.

We went with her as she unlocked the drawer in which she always kept the Lord's treasure-box, and reverently handled the plain little wooden box. No one looking at the big businesslike bunch of keys which she always carried in her pocket and watching her unlocking the various drawers for papers and record books and carefully locking each again, could have any doubt about that box being locked securely where no hand but hers could get at it.

Then she saw the sheriff, or law officer, and told him that now he could come for she had the money. He couldn't believe her, knowing well her struggles, and asked where she got it. In her simple quiet way she said the Lord had sent it. Two days later he said he would call on the morrow to collect the amount of the bill.

That day, when free from the post office duties and quite alone, she took the box and spread the money out again. Now she felt an impulse to put her own ninety marks in a little heap by itself before counting the rest. She obeyed this impulse. Again she spread her hands over the money and prayed and praised; again she counted, and now an additional touch of God's power was revealed—there was the full sum of seven hundred and fifty-one marks without her own scant, hard-earned and hard-saved money.

With heart too full for words she fell upon her knees praising the Lord again and again. She understood better now what the Master was doing; she had freely given all her own reserve, but He would make the funds enough without her own slender store. Again she prayed that the money might remain until the collector came.

The next day he came. She had him sit at the opposite side of the table while she told him her story. He was much moved. Then she did as before, poured the money out of the box, quietly prayed and praised over it, then counted it out to the man. Now some few silver coins were left over after the bill was paid, though she had put her own money aside. She had often prayed that the Lord's little treasury box might never be quite empty, and that prayer was now being remembered. The collector was greatly moved and drew five marks from his pocket, saying, "I want to put a little to this wonderful money."

So the money was paid, and the legal receipt duly made out.. Then our friend wrote a note to be sent with the money to the lumber dealer. It said that the amount of the bill was unjust as he knew and was now being paid under strong protest, but in accordance with the spirit of love in the words of the Saviour in Matthew 5:40. So the bit of witnessing went with the gold.

That is the story. She had three hundred and fifty Finnish marks in a little box under lock ($70, or 14 pounds). To this she added ninety marks of her own, making four hundred and forty marks in all. This sum increased to seven hundred and fifty-one marks, an increase of three hundred and eleven marks (slightly over $62, or 12.8 pounds). Then a second time it increased to seven hundred and fifty-one marks, without her own ninety marks, a total increase of four hundred and one marks (slightly over $80, 16 pounds); then it still further increased a slight sum, which remained in the box after this bill was paid.

This increase came through prayer alone, without human means being used, though the utmost effort had been made to get human help. The prayer was offered only because she felt moved to do so. The increase came only after five months of tireless yet wearying effort, continual prayer, sore strain of spirit, very much suffering of mind and spirit, and after real sacrifice that cut deep down into her own life. And that sacrifice was, as I incidentally learned, only a part of the sacrifice she had been yielding to in her own home and life, at every step, since the building of the chapel had commenced.

This was the same sort of thing that took place daily for many months with the widow of Zarephath (I Kings 17:8-16). It is identically the same as occurred with that prophet's widow, whose two sons were about to be sold into slavery to pay her debt (II Kings 4:1-7), and again, with the multiplying of the loaves to feed the hungry in a time of sore famine (II Kings 4:42-44). It is not different in kind, only in degree, from the feeding of the great multitudes twice, by our Lord, with a few loaves and fishes and enough pieces left over and carefully gathered to feed still other hungry souls (Matt. 14:15-21; 15:32-39, with parallels). It belongs in the same group with the two great catches of fish in the Gospels, where the Master's presence increased the supplies required for the need (Luke 5:1-11; John 21:1-14).

I must confess that we had rather a wet time—the interpreter, my wife and I—as we sat with our friend, listening to her story, looking at her neatly kept diary of those wondrous days, watching reverently as she lived over again the stress and then the joy of those days; pausing with her as the sudden flush of feeling was quietly gotten under control, then listening again and questioning and in our hearts trying to praise such a faithful Saviour and Friend and Master.

What It Means

The teaching of this simple, startling story is very plain. And most earnestly do I ask that no editorial shears shall ever part this paragraph and what follows from the story itself. The teaching is *not* that we are to ask God to multiply our money in this way. Or even that we *may* do so. If ever again He leads some trusting child of His to do something of this same sort, that one will recognize His leading without needing to depend on such an incident as this and will recognize it better yet as the results come.

This same thing may not occur again in a generation or in many generations. I have never before heard of such a case, though for years I have kept a sharp lookout for striking actual experiences of God's dealings. This came in a sore emergency; it was an emergency transaction.

The simple teaching of the experience for us is this: God never fails anyone who depends upon Him; He never disappoints; His Word never fails. True prayer, guided by the Holy Spirit, bathed in the spirit of sacrifice, never fails and cannot. Should an emergency arise where men have wholly refused to let Him use them in sending help and everything else fails, He will do an act of creation before He will let His Word fail or let any trusting child of His be disappointed in his dependence upon

Him. God Himself is the only One who knows when such an emergency arises. *His Spirit guides the prayer.* This is the one touchstone of all true prayer.

Some might think, without thinking much, that here is an easy way out of money difficulties—if we can go to God and have our money increased in this way. Yet such a thing may not occur even in sore need. For notice, this little chapel is not yet wholly paid for. This is one of the burdens of service which our Finnish friend, at her country post office up yonder, is carrying just now and constantly praying over. There yet remains over eight hundred dollars (160 pounds) unpaid. (The title to the property is vested in a holding board of trustees which has been formed to hold title to all Free Church property in Finland, so best meeting the legal situation.) That is a large sum to these people to whom the chapel has become a spiritual home; much more than it sounds to American or British ears. They are poor country folk. The money being given constantly comes out of hard-earned, carefully counted and frugally eked-out funds. Our friend has no thought of praying that this debt shall be met in like manner. That prayer has not been put into her heart. Where it is all to come from she often wonders, as she prays and plans and nurses the funds, and prays some more.

The School of Prayer

There is a further bit of a living sermon here. It is this: True prayer is put into our hearts by the Holy Spirit. The yearnings of our hearts after God, for loved ones, for special needs, are simply echoed yearnings. They are in God's heart. They are there first and most. They are simply echoed in our hearts from His. His great yearning is that we shall be in such simple touch with Himself that He can echo His own heart's longings in our hearts.

In our quiet brooding time, alone with Him over His inspired Word, day after day, He draws near to us. He trains our judgment; He schools our understanding; He disciplines our inner spirit; He opens the ears of our hearts (Eph. 1:18); He teaches us what to pray for and how to pray and—even more—how to pray persistently.

There was a special session of five months in that schoolroom of prayer before He put into our Finnish friend's heart the prayer which from the first He planned that she should offer. She wasn't ready to offer it till it was put into her heart. If she had offered it sooner of her own accord, it would have brought nothing.

True prayer is not a matter of logical conclusion mentally arrived at from examining some promise of God's Word. It is far deeper than that, while still very simple. True prayer is hammered into shape upon the anvil of the knees, while the fire burns hot and every strike of the hammer is keenly felt.

It is difficult to tell the sense of awe mingled with intense interest with which we went down the very dusty country road to look at the little chapel. It was a very unpretending structure, thoroughly built and practically arranged. There was a smaller room opening out of the larger, with a little combination kitchen and sleeping room at one side. Upstairs was the "prophet's chamber," combining sleeping and study room for the preachers when they were so blessed as to have someone come.

But Sunday is a busy day regardless of the presence of a "proper preacher." At ten is a Sunday school in Finnish, at noon a preaching service which our friend takes when no one else can be gotten, at four a Swedish Sunday school. The caretaker is a woman of practical versatility, keeping the place in order, opening it for services, sleeping in the combination kitchen and, being a converted woman, teaching the Finnish Sunday school. About two hundred can be crowded in when all available space is thrown together.

But there were many more than that during the few days of meetings. The inner space was crowded almost to discomfort, speaker and interpreter having no extra elbow space on the platform. And each window brought to view a group of eager listeners standing without. Was it any wonder that in such a building the Spirit of God moved so mightily, though gently, upon human hearts! It seemed as though the heavens opened and the upper gales blew softly down and swept over the people. Heart doors that had been tight shut opened up at that touch and some only partly open swung wide.

As we walked over the little chapel with our quiet friend, questioning, listening, thinking, it became clear and then clearer that this story we had come for was only one chapter in a story. It was a sort of climax chapter; those going before were of the same sort, all leading up to this climax. It was a long story running through a number of years—a story of longing, of struggle, of steady, patient fight against difficulties of every imaginable sort, of most stubborn resistance to all her plannings, as though some unseen spirit force were pitted against her, of persistence in effort and prayer always *just a bit more* persistent than the resistance and of an unfailing, unseen Friend by her side. Here seemed to be one secret of the final victory. This was the decisive factor. It was persistence that had won and won only because it was more persistent and would still hold on just a bit longer.

The Master's Word in that prayer parable of Luke 18 (Luke 18:1-8) came to mind, "always to pray, and not to faint." The chief thing in the conflict of life and of service is prayer. The chief temptation in such fighting and prayer is to tire out and give up. It seems as though some invisible power were trying to wear us out, to exhaust our bodily strength and so our persistence. The chief factor in prayer, on the human side, is persistence—a gentle, cheery, undiscourageable persistence, but without the common element of stubbornness.

That word *stubborn* really stands for a sort of blind animal doggedness, from which the elements of intelligence and reasonableness are absent (Ps. 32:9). There is a strength that is strong enough to hold on, but not strong enough to do it graciously and to yield on nonessentials. The persistence that the Holy Spirit gives and strengthens, sees, feels, listens, shifts the position slightly here and there to meet the opposition more intelligently, but never yields on the main issue. Yet there is a quietness, a cheeriness, a gentleness of spirit, a sweet reasonableness wholly absent from persistence of the stubborn sort. This has enormous influence in breaking down the opposition.

Only the Holy Spirit can give such persistence. And He can give it only to him who goes to school daily, steadily and tries faithfully to learn his lessons. That is what the Master means by "not to faint." This cheery undiscourageable persistence (Luke 11:8,9) is one of the great traits of the prayer that changes things; the other is definiteness (Matt. 18:19; Mark 11:24).

Merely a Climax

Our friend's experience brought this all up to mind afresh. In the beginning it seemed wholly impossible to get a lot on which to build. Slowly, bit by bit, things changed. The foreign owner of the land wanted came unexpectedly on a visit to his property. The direct appeal was favorably received at last. In the change of ownership of a large tract a free grant was made for the chapel, then a bit of cunning, underhanded red tape threatened to affect the clear title. Finally the bit of land was secured with a clear title in perpetuity.

But it was fighting and keen work, one ditch after another, every step of the long, slow way; persistent opposition, yet more persistent hanging on, with the wondrous, unseen Friend never failing in suggestion and in strength.

Then when building could be begun, it seemed impossible to get lumber. None was to be gotten anywhere. The season's supply was all bought up. But the faithful, inner Friend kept her hopefully hoping in the midst of most hopeless circumstances (Rom. 4:17-21). Then an unexpected raft of logs came floating down the river. So, step by step she plodded on. Prices were lowered; unconverted men offered their labor; the best builder was secured; difficulties rose and were downed.

It was one long story of opposition, reproach, criticism, prayer and the unfailing faithfulness of God. The bit that came at the end was simply a climax. It fitted perfectly as a capstone to the whole structure of faith going up with the going up of the chapel. That capstone was brought forth with glad shoutings of praise to our wondrous, faithful God (Zech. 4:6-10).

And to the praise of His grace it is put down here that men may trust Him more, and more simply.

For a complete list of books available from the Sword of the Lord, write to Sword of the Lord Publishers, P. O. Box 1099, Murfreesboro, Tennessee 37133.